JOHANN WOLFGANG VON GOETHE

FAUST
Part One and Part Two

A New Translation by
Carl R. Mueller

GREAT TRANSLATIONS SERIES

A SMITH AND KRAUS BOOK

Published by Smith and Kraus, Inc.
177 Lyme Road, Hanover, NH 03755
www.smithkraus.com

First Edition: December 2004,
10 9 8 7 6 5 4 3 2 1
Manufactured in the United States of America

Cover and Text Design by Julia Hill Gignoux, Freedom Hill Design

The Library of Congress Cataloging-In-Publication Data
Goethe, Johann Wolfgang von, 1749-1832.
[Faust. English]
Faust / Johann Wolfgang von Goethe ; a new translation by Carl R. Mueller.--
1st ed.
p. cm. -- (Great translations series)
ISBN 1-57525-345-3 (cloth) -- ISBN 1-57525-360-7 (pbk.) --
ISBN 1-57525-381-X (Part I)
I. Mueller, Carl Richard. II. Title. III. Great translations for actors series.
PT2026.F2M84 2004
832'.6--dc22
2004045378

To
Ron Sossi
and
The Odyssey Theatre Ensemble

CONTENTS

PART TWO

ACT I

INTRODUCTION

I

Goethe's *Faust* is the most audacious literary work in Western civilization. It has been said that it makes Joyce's *Ulysses* and *Finnegan's Wake* appear traditional. Well, perhaps not, but it is nonetheless a work of tremendous scope that encompasses virtually every form of writing in every format, from the four-foot *Knittelvers* to classical hexameter, blank verse, and many additional free forms. Having been written over a long period of time, from the 1770s to 1832, the year of Goethe's death, *Faust* is also a compendium of interests reflecting its author's universal mind, for Goethe was nothing if not *the* Renaissance man of the European Age of Enlightenment, those interests being mythology, culture, art, statesmanship, war, courtly life, economics, natural science, and religion. In effect, *Faust* is the crowning literary work of German Romanticism, a movement whose dates can roughly be said to lie between 1770 and 1850.

This was a period of great ferment in Germany, especially in its early days in the period of Storm and Stress, when German artists revolted against the courtly use of French and insisted that their own language be permitted to flower. German Romanticism was a revolution in every sense—social, political, literary. Rigid French rules regarding form were overthrown for more natural means of expression. The false face of French manners was rejected, the façade stripped away in order that nature could show and express itself freely; unreasonable decorum and social rules were relaxed. The fixed forms of art, literature, and politics, of behavior and morals were loosened and superceded. In theater the classical unities of time, place, and action were rejected. The conventional subject of art was no longer limited to the aristocracy and court life, but encompassed the whole spectrum of experience. And in the realm of aesthetics, beauty was no longer viewed as a constant. Romanticism, then, was not a flight into an ideal dream world as is so often claimed, but an attempt to embrace *all* the real world.

Romanticism rejected "poetic" diction in favor of all words; it widened the body of accepted mythology from the Greco-Roman to include Germanic and Celtic myth as well; uniform stage settings gave way to multiple stage settings; courtly stage settings gave way to local-color settings: forests, huts, seashore, mountains, to mention only a few possibilities. The high seriousness of classical French tragedy was leavened now by a mixture of genres. In painting academic rules were expanded to allow for other than antique subjects and classically posed bodies; any subject was now permitted, the whole world as subject. In music there were no more forbidden chords, modulations, tonalities, but, rather, the whole range of combination of sounds. History that once taught that there was no civilization since the fall of Rome turned back to discover the Middle Ages and the Renaissance. Cosmopolitan sophistication as the only acceptable mode was opened up to include the folk in many of its manifestations, from fairy tale to the music and dance of the people. The materialist view that only what is seen is valid gave way to a new definition of reality, namely that life constituted the unseen as well as the seen: dreams, spirit world, and the supernatural. In politics the movement was from monarchy to democracy, to freedom for the people, an attitude fanned by the French Revolution of 1789 as well as the revolutions of 1830 and 1848.

In summary, these revolutions allowed for certain characteristics in the arts that were new (or newly introduced), such as the juxtaposition of the grotesque and the sublime (a style borrowed from the medieval Gothic tradition). Individualism became the order of the romantic stage (Goethe's Götz, Egmont, Faust, Schiller's William Tell, Don Carlos, Mary Stuart), as did freedom. Nature took its place in poetry and theater as a vital and salutary force; pantheism ruled; Goethe, it must be said, found infinity in every breath of the finite, and it is this expansiveness that permeates every page of his *Faust* and makes it the revolutionary work that it is.

II

This introduction will not presume to offer a thoroughgoing interpretation of Goethe's *Faust*. That would be presumptuous. So various is this epochal work that it may well not permit interpretation; or, better yet, that interpretations are as numerous as its readers. But not even that does justice to the work's range of possibilities. Perhaps it is best to say that the meaning of *Faust* changes with every reading. Read it first as an adolescent, then again at middle age, and finally at full maturity—not to mention many times in between—and it conveys something different each time. The work grows as its reader grows, and that is the only "meaning" of great literature that means anything.

Rather than attempt to critique *Faust* this introduction will lay out some developments that appear deliberate in Goethe's design, issues that the reader can then accept or reject as seems best. And the best place to begin is at the most basic, indeed abstract, of levels. *Faust* is concerned with four main issues: Being and Becoming, Formation and Transformation, the Union of Opposites, and Individuation, as each of these dualities relates to the human organism.

The static nature of Being is as anathema to Goethe as it is to Faust. Faust's early stated ethic is never to become so enamored of any given moment that he would choose to remain and in doing so resign the search for the next highest level of development. In making his binding contract with Mephistopheles Faust enunciates his credo: "If ever I say to the moment: 'Linger awhile, you are so fair!' then cast me in chains, for I'll be glad to die! Let the bell toll for me then; then you'll be freed of your service; let the clock stop, let its hands fall, and time for me will be at an end!" What motivates the action not only of Faust but of everything in the work is Becoming, that which is in a state of constant flux and development. In effect it is the principal of Yin/Yang, another way of expressing the concept of Formation and Transformation. In the last analysis it is the Union of Opposites that gives Individuation, and with Individuation comes a transcendence to be constantly Becoming.

Every transformation in *Faust* leads to a Union of Opposites, and Goethe uses male and female as his paradigm. The Prologue in Heaven begins in an all male Heaven, God the Father and Angels; the play ends in an androgynous Heaven in which the Female is the instrument that leads to Salvation/Individuation. The female, however, goes through a series of evolutionary developments in the course of the play. She begins at the lowest level, in the Witch's Kitchen scene, as a monkey, then as a negative aspect of the feminine, the Witch, then as the human Gretchen, the human-mythic Helen, as Manto the divine prophetess, as Venus in the form of the divine-mythic Galatea, next as the Blessed Virgin, the Mater Glorioso, and finally the feminine as pure Idea, the Eternal Feminine.

Faust, too, goes through major transformations, from the despairing, suicidal man of his opening scene to his final of many transformations, as Doctor Marianus, a wise man of the Middle Ages whose name, not incidentally, represents an androgyny— a masculine ending on a feminine name.

Even Mephistopheles has a transformation: from dog to devil. Whether Goethe was playing with an ancient concept of dog as man's best friend is not unlikely, for a dog frequently accompanies the classical hero on dangerous missions. As man's best friend he serves as guide, and that is precisely how he tends Faust. This is no garden-variety Christian Devil that Goethe has given us, but one who represents Faust's alter ego, intimately knowledgeable regarding his carrier, a factor whose aim is to lead Faust into a state that is decidedly antimedieval in its insistence on individuation. He is forever telling Faust in one way or another (in one dream scene after another where in fact they take on a host of different personas), to "dig his own gold." That advice is the through line of the work as a whole. But Mephistopheles as alter-ego is the shadow side of Faust and as such is the bearer of all that Faust fears (or has been taught to fear by medieval social conditioning), and so he is always on the defensive, always rejecting potentially good advice.

Faust laments early in the play that he has two souls abiding in his breast, a double bind we might call it today, precisely what is described above, the Faust/Mephistopheles syndrome, and it tears him apart from the moment of their meeting to their final parting. In classical terms Mephistopheles serves as the Psychopompus, the spiritual guide to Faust's questing but frightened soul. If in the end that spiritual guide turns sour, negative in his leadership, it is because he has suffered degrading rejection once too often and is finally out to bring down the very one he came originally to lead to transcendence. The glory of that transcendence, that Union of Opposites, is foreseen in the grand culminating dream scene in act two of Part Two when, on the shores of the Aegean, fire and water are miraculously joined in the archetypal image of a flaming ocean, as Homunculus, that inspired image of Faust as eternal striver, breaks the phial of his flaming self on the waves of the open sea in order to "become."

Faust, however, goes terribly wrong; he succeeds in material terms, not in spiritual, becoming a tyrant who uses human labor to create a kingdom for his egocentric self in isolation from society. He reclaims the tideland of a vast shoreline with a vast landfill project. In doing so he pushes back, virtually out of sight, the sea, that element of life and productivity which Goethe spends most of act two exalting to a supreme position, an archetypal image of the feminine. This "repression" of the sea/feminine (not the first in Faust's odyssey) leads him to his male position of power to the exclusion of the tempering and creative feminine factor. In act four Faust takes up with Three Violent Giants as accomplices, a sign of the direction in which he is heading. In the opening of act five we see an emanation of Faust as the Wanderer while the real Faust sits in his castle fortress on the land reclaimed from the ocean. This Wanderer is the former Faust as man of conscience. The old peasant couple Philemon and Baucis once saved him from the waves. He revisits them now in memory and learns from them of the Faust in his castle and the inhumanity of his egocentric enterprise. Baucis as wise old woman warns against trusting what was once the ocean's bottom, one way of saying that Faust's action in the land reclamation was ill advised.

In the next scene the centenarian Faust in his castle complains about the old couple and their peasant cottage. It spoils for him an unrestricted view of his vast possessions. He wants them gone and orders Mephistopheles and the Three Violent Giants to relocate them to the pleasant little property he has chosen for them. They do so, but use totalitarian tactics and the couple are burned along with their cottage. With them, however, the Wanderer/Faust is also destroyed when he tries to lend aid to the old couple. When Mephistopheles tells Faust of the "accident," Faust curses them for violating his command: death was not his order. It is the right hand denying complicity with what the left hand has done, and yet we know that that "pleasant little property" was merely a euphemism for the grave. Just as Banquo serves as the conscience of Macbeth and must be got rid of, the old couple, the Wanderer, the lindens, the chapel and the church bells, are a reminder of earlier, less drastic times for Faust and must be eliminated at any cost to assure his peace of mind. That cost, as it turns out, is to have Care (*Sorge* in German) breathe on him and make him blind.

III

One question that is always asked is why Goethe causes his Faust (despite his manifest and grievous errors) to be saved. The answer may not please the questioner, but it was good enough for Goethe. Faust is saved, his "immortal part" carried by a chorus of Blessèd Boys into the empyrean, transformed into Doctor Marianus as an image of what he will become when the impurities of his earthly ways are washed clean, led on by the Eternal Feminine— Faust is saved because he never wavered in his striving, never said to any passing moment: "Linger awhile, you are so fair!" but remained true to his driving spirit to become, to transform, to individuate. Action is all in Goethe's universe, an ethic Faust manifests early in Part One when he begins to translate into his native German the Gospel of Saint John. Having translated the opening as "In the beginning was the Word," he halts and questions whether the word can be so important. He then tries "In the beginning was the Mind," and then "Force." It is only when he translates the Greek *Logos* as "Deed" that he knows he has it right—a primal lesson for any translator worth her or his salt.

Carl R. Mueller
Department of Theater
School of Theater, Film and Television
University of California, Los Angeles

A NOTE ON THE TRANSLATION

This translation of Goethe's *Faust* is fairly straightforward. It would be foolish to say that other translations of the work have not been consulted. A score of them, in fact, in several languages. Translation is— must always be—a process of trying to do better than anyone before you, otherwise why make the attempt in the first place? And yet, even a competitor is capable of doing something right as well as something wrong. It is for both of those reasons that the new translator consults his competition. We borrow here and there just the right word, perhaps even just the right phrase, because we feel it serves the work as well as possible and not to use it is to serve the work badly. We also learn from our competition what not to do, how not to say it. And finally, we look for guidance in passages that have even the critics arguing. How does so-and-so interpret this or that difficult passage? Sometimes we find an answer that suits us, sometimes not, and we are forced to come to our own conclusions, as have so many before us.

As for completeness, this translation is essentially complete. In Part One very few lines have been omitted, lines, expressions, sentiments that don't sit well in the new language. One example is Faust's sentimentalizing over Gretchen's bed. All but a line or two of that speech is intact. What is stricken is a sentiment that in English becomes maudlin. The only substantial cut in Part One is the Walpurgis Night's Dream scene, which has no relationship whatsoever to the play and has been described by one Goethe scholar as not being "woven organically into the texture of the play as a whole and [that] Goethe made a regrettable blunder in embedding the scene in his *Faust*." In Part Two there is only one major omission, the so-called Helen scene that opens act three. It is a scene that has its critical defenders as well as its detractors. Is it or is it not dramatically relevant? It is this translator's feeling that it is not sufficiently relevant to the main thrust of the play as a whole to justify inclusion. It is, quite simply, static and an attempt by Goethe to prove that he could write a Greek tragedy in German following the stringent metrical demands of classical Athenian tragedy. Unfortunately, it doesn't succeed.

FAUST

❧ PART ONE ☙

I ↝ DEDICATION

You come, hovering forms, as in youth's day
You once appeared to my so muddled gaze.
Shall I now hold you fast, shall I essay
To turn again to that so-muddied daze?
You throng around me! Good! Rule as you may,
As from the mists you rise out of that haze;
The magic air about you stirs my breast
With youthful tumult and divine unrest.

You bring with you visions of happy days,
And many a dear loved shadow ascends to view;
Like some faint haunting old forgotten lays,
Love, first love, friendship come back with you;
My heart looks back at life's bewildered maze,
And pains long laid to rest arise anew
And name those loved ones lost before their day,
Swept, while life was beautiful, away.

It saddens me to think they will not hear
These songs to whom my earliest songs I sang;
They are all gone, those gathered friends so dear,
Echoes hushed that once responsive rang;
My sorrows now fall only on the stranger's ear,
Whose praises to my heart are a bitter pang,
And all who once heard my song, and flattered,
If still alive, around the world are scattered.

A yearning fills my soul, unknown so long,
To that sad spirit world again to go;
Like an Aeolian harp, my whispered song
Now trembles in the air in accents low;
A shudder thrills me as old memories throng,
The stern heart melts, tears fast on teardrops flow;
What I possess seems far, far off to me,
And what once was becomes reality.

II ❧ PRELUDE IN THE THEATER

The DIRECTOR.
The THEATER POET.
The JESTER.

DIRECTOR:
Very well now, friends, I want the truth.
It's the least I can expect. After all,
this isn't the first storm we've weathered together.

Tell me now,
what can we expect of this German tour?
I admit,
what I want most is to please the masses,
because as far as they're concerned
it's live and let live.

The tent's up, the floorboards laid,
and now it's for us to show them a good time.
They're sitting out there now,
wide-eyed, eyebrows raised,
patiently waiting to be wonder struck.

I know what the public wants,
and I know how to give it to them,
but I've never been so embarrassed
as I am at this moment.
It's true,
what they're served up on our stages
is pretty awful stuff, but, by God,
they've devoured whole hordes of books.

So how do we concoct something fresh and new?
Perhaps even something important
that will also amuse them.
I admit, there's nothing I like better
than a crowd bumping and jostling its way
in a mighty surge through our narrow gate to Paradise,

up to the box office,
even before four, and like starving
men rushing the baker's door,
all but breaking their necks to get a ticket.
Who but the poet can tame such a crowd
and work such a miracle?
And so, dear friend, I leave it to you!

POET:

Don't talk to me of that vulgar herd!
One sight offends the spirit!
Protect me from the mob
that drags us unwillingly into the abyss!

No, lead me to some peaceful retreat
where pure joy blossoms for the poet,
where Love and Friendship,
with God's own hand,
create and nurture the poet's inspiration.

Ah!
The blessing that makes its way from deep inside us,
syllables that lips have stammered timidly into scenes
(successful now, another time not)
are swallowed in a single violent moment.
Only years will tell, years of ripening,
till it blossoms into perfection.
What glitters and flashes lives for a day.
The true is never lost to posterity.

JESTER:

Posterity!
Spare me the word! I hate it, hate it!
Laughter is what we need.
Here! Now! Fun!
It's what they've come for.
Let's give it to them.
One stout and sturdy clown who knows his business
is nothing to be sneezed at.

He knows what it takes to please the masses,
and the bigger the crowd
the easier it is to work them.

So much for that.
Now, show us your best, my boy.
Let imagination sing with all its choirs—
reason, common sense, feeling and passion, too.
Just don't forget to throw in a little folly.

DIRECTOR:
Not to mention plenty of action.
It's what they've come for,
to see,
to see things happen,
it's what they like.
Unreel a string of actions before their eyes,
make them gape in wonder,
and you've got them where you want them,
in the palm of your hand.

Mass is what it takes to please the masses,
mass and variety.
In the end,
everyone chooses what he most likes,
and goes home happy.
But whatever work you manage to put on,
give it in pieces,
serve it up like a ragout,
and you'll have a success.
It's easy,
as soon as it simmers you dish it out.
Why give it to them whole
when they'll pick it apart in any case?

POET:
How can you?
How can you ask me this?
I'm an artist,

I don't stoop to such things.
Is this what you've come down to?
Lowered your standards to the level of hackwork?
A butcher's trade?

DIRECTOR:
Complain all you like,
it makes no difference.
What matters most in doing a job right
is having the proper tools.
Know the people you're writing for:
it's soft wood you have to split, not hard.

One of them comes bored out of his wits,
another with a belly about to burst,
and worst of all,
many come straight from reading the newspapers.
They come to us distracted,
absentmindedly,
as though they were off to a masquerade,
only curiosity leading them on.

And the ladies,
ah, the ladies, they appear
decked out in all their finery,
mounting their own little play,
and what's more, without pay.

What are you dreaming up there in your ivory tower?
Why should a full house make *you* happy?
Take a closer look at your customers.
Half are cold and the other half coarse.
One looks forward after the show
to a game of cards, another
to a wild romp with a whore.
Is it for that you torture the Muses?

Ah, poor fools!
My advice is pile it high as it will go,

and then a little higher.
Confuse them with mystification is best;
it's easier than trying to satisfy them.

But what's got you now?
Are you in pain or rapture?

POET:

Go on, go, go find yourself another slave!
Do you know what you're asking?
You expect a poet frivolously to squander
the greatest gift that Nature offers him!
The right to be a man!
For *you!*

No!

What is it allows him to stir men's hearts?
What is it allows him to conquer Nature's elements?
One thing only:
the harmony that flows from the poet's breast,
that gathers in its embrace the multiplicity
of Nature's discrepancies,
and draws them back into his heart
as a harmonious whole.

When Nature winds life's endless thread
indifferently on her spindle, and all
life's fractured sounds roar in discord,
who harmonizes the monotonous, meaningless drone
and makes it sing in orderly choir?
Who invites the tempest to rage in passion?
And the sunset to glow in the earnest soul?
Who scatters springtime's sweetest blossoms
on paths for young lovers to walk on?
Who twines from insignificant leaves
crowns to honor the brows of the deserving?
Who assures us of Olympus and unites the gods?
The power of Man made manifest in the poet.

JESTER:
>All right, then, do it.
>Use these marvelous powers of yours.
>Conduct this business of forging verses
>the way you'd manage a love affair.
>
>You meet by chance,
>feel a tingle,
>stick around,
>and bit by bit you get involved.
>Happiness thrives,
>then it's endangered.
>First you're enraptured,
>then writhing in anguish.
>And before you know it,
>you've got a whole novel.
>And that's how it's done.
>
>So let's do it.
>Let's give the play that way!
>Plunge your hand into the fullness of life.
>We all of us live it,
>few of us know it;
>but it's interesting wherever you grab it.
>Variety, color, confusion, error,
>and then a tantalizing soupçon of truth.
>That's how the best beers are brewed,
>a brew that refreshes and makes you think, too.
>
>Ah, the best of youth will flock to your play,
>eager for any revelation.
>The sentimental will suck melancholy strength,
>and this and that and everyone
>will take from it what each has felt in his heart.
>Being young they're as ready to weep as to laugh;
>they still have ideals and delight in illusion.
>Adults you can never please,
>they've stopped growing,
>but youth will always be grateful for what you offer.

POET:

    Then give me back those days again
    when I myself was still unfinished,
    when an endless fountain of songs
    welled from my soul, when the world to me
    was veiled in mystery, when each bud
    was a miracle of promise
    as I went out to pick the thousand flowers
    that thronged the valley.
    I had nothing then,
    but it was enough—
    the yearning for truth and the joy of illusion.
    Give back to me each reckless longing,
    the deep and anguished happiness,
    the strength of hate,
    the power of love!
    Oh, give me back my youth again!

JESTER:

    Youth, old friend, is what you'll need
    when enemies threaten in the heat of battle,
    when pretty girls throw their arms around you
    and squeeze for all they're worth,
    when in the distance the victory wreath beckons
    from the hard-won goal, when after the whirl
    of the frenzied dance you drink away the night.
    But to strike the familiar strings boldly yet gracefully,
    to wander leisurely life's sweet digressions
    to a self-set goal, that, old friend,
    is *your* duty,
    and we honor you no less for it.
    Age doesn't make us childish, as they say,
    it only finds the child that's with us still.

DIRECTOR:

    Enough talk!
    Let's get down to business.
    Action!
    While you two trade compliments,

you could be doing something useful.
And don't complain you're not in the mood.
Wait for it and it never arrives.

And you, you call yourself a poet?
Then let's see some poetry!
What we want here is strong drink,
so let's get it brewing.

What you put off today is put off tomorrow,
and we haven't a day to lose.
What we need here is a man of resolution,
one who seizes the Possible by the forelock
and won't let go, a man who refuses
to stop because he's committed.

You know what the German theater is like,
we can experiment all we please.
So don't spare on scenery and stage effects.
Stars and suns and moons are had for the asking.
There's fire, and water enough for a flood,
and plenty of cliffs to jump off of,
not to mention an assortment of birds and beasts.

Show us on this petty stage of ours
the full scope of creation,
and travel with the speed of imagination
the course from Heaven through the world
to the bowels of Hell!

III ↝ PROLOGUE IN HEAVEN

The LORD.
The HEAVENLY HOST.
The three ARCHANGELS step forward.

RAPHAEL:

> The sun sings grandly, as of old,
> Joining with his brother spheres,
> Marching in his destined course,
> His thunders clap about their ears.
> The angels at his gaze grow strong,
> Though fathom it they never may;
> These works sublime survive forever
> As bright as on the primal day.

GABRIEL:

> Swift, ah, swift, past understanding,
> The earth whirls ever onward! Mark!
> The radiance of that primal day
> Alternates with deepest dark.
> Behold, the sea's broad billows surge
> From out its depths with primal force,
> Lashing rocks and crashing shore,
> With sun and stars in endless course.

MICHAEL:

> Tempests rage in rivalry
> From sea to land, from land to sea,
> Forging from their raging furies
> A chain of mightiest energy.
> Lightning flashes its desolation
> With thunderous strokes along the way,
> But we, Lord, your angels, honor
> The gentle progress of your day.

ALL THREE:

> The angels at your gaze grow strong,
> Though fathom you they never may;

Your works sublime survive forever
As bright as on the primal day.

MEPHISTOPHELES: *(Entering.)*
Lord, since you approach us once again,
and ask how we're getting on;
and since in the past
I've never been made feel unwelcome,
I present myself once more among your servants.

You'll forgive me, I know,
if I make no pretty speeches,
but, you see, I'm just not very good at it,
not even if I'm scoffed at and scorned.
I'd make you laugh, I know, with my sorry pathos—
except that you gave up laughter eons ago.
I mean, really,
what can I say about your sun and your worlds?
Nothing; nothing at all.
All I see is how men torment themselves.
And as for that little lord of creation,
he's no less "wondrous" than on the day you made him.
And yet, I'd say, he might be better off
if you hadn't blessed him with that glimpse of heavenly light
that he calls Reason, and which he uses
to make himself more beastly than any beast.

You'll pardon my saying so,
but to me he resembles more the long-legged cricket
that does nothing but leap about,
higher and higher,
only to end up back where he began,
deep in the grass singing the same old song.
If only he'd stay in the grass!
But he pokes his nose into every kind of filth.

THE LORD:
Is that all you've come to say?
Do you always come here only to accuse me?
Is there nothing on earth that ever pleases you?

MEPHISTOPHELES:

　No, Lord!
It was a mess to start with,
and it's a mess still.
How I pity those poor people!
They're so miserable.
I haven't the heart to plague them, poor things.

THE LORD:

Do you know Faust?

MEPHISTOPHELES:

The doctor?

THE LORD:

He's my servant.

MEPHISTOPHELES:

Servant! Well!
He certainly has an odd way of serving!
No earthly food or drink for *that* fool!
The ferment in him has driven him so far
that he almost half knows his folly.
He demands of heaven its fairest star,
and of earth its wildest abandon.
Nothing, near or far, ever satisfies him.

THE LORD:

He may be confused at present,
but I'll soon lead him into the light.
The gardener knows that when the tree turns green
blossoms and fruit can't be far behind.

MEPHISTOPHELES:

What will you wager?
You'll lose him yet, you will, if you allow me
to lead him gently down my primrose path.

THE LORD:

As long as he walks the earth I forbid you nothing.
Striving and straying are a well-known couple.

MEPHISTOPHELES:

For which much thanks.
I've never been fond of the dead.
It's fresh, plump rosy cheeks I take a liking to.
No, I've never favored corpses.
Cat and mouse is more my style.

THE LORD:

Good, then, I leave it to you.
Divert this spirit from its primal source.
Lure him, if you can lay hold of him,
down your wayward path to perdition.
But have the courtesy, like it or not,
to admit to your shame when you've failed.
A good man, no matter how off course,
always knows the right path from the wrong.

MEPHISTOPHELES:

Good enough.
And I assure you it won't be long.
I'd say it's a pretty safe bet.
But promise me, if I succeed,
you'll let me triumph from the bottom of my being.
I'll see him eat dust,
and with a passion, too,
like my distant cousin the celebrated serpent.

THE LORD:

There, too, you're free to do as you please.
I've never hated the likes of you.
Of all the spirits of negation, rogues like you
are the least of my troubles.
Man's will to action nods off all too easily
and leads him into unproductive repose.

It's why I approve your method:
tagging along to prod and prick him on,
as any self-respecting devil must.

(To the ARCHANGELS.)

As for you, God's true and faithful sons,
rejoice in the world's endless living beauty!
May the power of Becoming
that lives and works eternally,
encompass you in the gracious bonds of love,
and give to the unstable world of seeming
permanence by fixing it in eternal thought.

(The heavens close, the ARCHANGELS disperse.)

MEPHISTOPHELES:
I enjoy seeing the old boy now and again,
taking good care to stay on friendly terms.
It's really quite decent of so grand a lord
to chat with the Devil in such a human fashion.

IV ↜ NIGHT

A narrow, high-vaulted Gothic Chamber.
FAUST sits restlessly at the desk in his armchair.

FAUST:
Here I stand!

A fool!

I who have studied and crammed Philosophy,
Law, and Medicine, and even, oh, God! Theology,
from end to bitter end!
And what has it got me?

Nothing.

Not one jot wiser than before.

Oh, I have my degrees,
they call me Master of Arts, and Doctor!
And for these ten years now
I've led my students around by the nose,
upstairs, downstairs, backwards, forwards—
and learned?
That there's nothing to be learned.
Nothing!
And that is the dread that eats at my heart's core.

Oh, but I'm no dunce.
I'm better than all these "doctors," these "masters,"
these "clerks" and "priests,"
and not even fear of Hell or the Devil
can make me tremble with scruples or doubts.

And what is my reward for all that?

The loss of all joy in life.

Why pretend?
Why assume I know anything worth knowing?
Why delude myself I can teach anything
to improve or convert mankind?

And what has it got me?

Just this!
I'm a pauper.
Or nearly so.
I have neither property nor wealth,
nor worldly honor.

No glory.

Show me a dog who would lead such a life!

And that's why I've turned my mind to magic,
to see if the spirit's power
can help me wrest secrets from the spirit world and
save me the dreary sour sweat of saying
what I know nothing about!
To see what holds the world together
at its innermost core,
and seeing its working and germinal forces,
end this endless traffic in words.

Ah, full moon!
If only you saw my agony for the last time.
You that I have watched at my desk
as I've sat here awake.
You that I have seen climbing the sky
through many a long night,
shining across my books and papers!

Melancholy friend!
If only we could walk together
in the high mountains,
bathe in your beloved radiance,
float at the mouths of caverns with spirits,
weave across meadows in your twilight glow, and,
freed of all this mystification of learning,
bathe myself to health in your dew!

Ah!

But here I am!

Still!

Stuck in this God-damned hole in the wall,
where even the blessèd light of Heaven
forces its way through filthy, painted panes;
confined by piles, by heaps, of ancient books,
worm-gnawed and covered with dust;
sooty papers crammed high as the ceiling;

retorts and canisters thrown helter-skelter,
old instruments crammed everywhere!

And on top of it all?

The rubbish of ancestral memory!

Ha!
That's your world, Faustus!
At least that's what they call it!

How can you still wonder
what makes you tremble with fear?
What else but the pain of that fear
that smothers the very urge to live!
God created man
in the bosom of nature's fullness,
not circled round by skeletons and animal bones
and grime and mold!

Out of here!
Out!
Out into the world!
Out into nature!

And this book, this strange, this marvelous book
by Nostradamus is all the guide you will need!
With it you will read the course of the stars
like an open book. Nature will teach you
how spirits converse with spirits.
What a waste to brood in arid speculation
over magic symbols!

Spirits, I feel you hovering near.
Answer me, if you hear!

(He opens the book and perceives the sign of the Macrocosm.)

Ah!

What is this vision that suddenly seizes my senses!
I feel the holy fire of youth
coursing through every vein and nerve!
What god was it wrote these symbols
that calm the storm of torment inside me;
that fill my wretched heart with joy;
that with some mysterious force
reveals the forces of Nature around me?

Am I a god?

I?

Oh, suddenly it's all so clear, so clear!

I see in the pure lines of this symbol
all of Creative Nature at work.
I understand the philosopher for the first time.

"The spirit world is open, not barred.
Your mind is closed, your heart is dead!
Rise up, young man, and bathe your breast
in the rosy flush of dawn!"

(He contemplates the symbol.)

Ah!

How all things weave into a unity!
Each living and working in the other!
Heavenly forces ascending, descending,
passing golden vessels from hand to hand!
Flying on fragrant wings between heaven and earth
till all creation sounds with one grand harmony!
What a brilliant show!

Ah!
But only a show.

Infinite Nature, where do I take hold?
Where are your breasts?
Those fountains that nurture all life that I so long for?
Why, when they are offered to all,
must I thirst in vain?

(He turns the pages impatiently and sees the symbol of the Earth Spirit.)

How differently this symbol affects me!

Earth Spirit, you are closer to me.
I already feel the surge of new energy
warm me like wine. I'm emboldened
to venture out into life, to endure the joy
and pain of earth, wrestle with its storms,
and never in the face of grinding shipwreck
know despair.

Clouds are gathering above me!
The moon hiding its light!
The lamp goes out!
Vapors rise!
Red beams dart about my head!
Terror breathes down upon me from the ancient vault
and seizes me!

Spirit that I have sought,
I feel you hovering near!
Reveal yourself!

Ah!

It tears at my heart!

All that I am
struggles and gropes toward new sensations!
My heart is all yours!

Reveal yourself!

You must, you must!
Even if it costs me my life!

(He seizes the book and soundlessly pronounces the symbol of the
Earth Spirit. The EARTH SPIRIT appears in a flash of red flame.)

SPIRIT:
   Who calls me?

FAUST: *(With face averted.)*
   Appalling vision!

SPIRIT:
   You have used mighty means to draw me,
   and have long sucked at my sphere,
   and now—

FAUST:
   Ah! No! I can't bear to see you!

SPIRIT:
   You pleaded breathlessly to see me,
   to see my face, hear my voice.
   I yield now to your soul's mighty urging,
   and here I am!

   But look at you now,
   you would-be superman!
   Cowering like some pitiable creature!
   Where is your soul's call now?
   Your promptings?
   Your urgings?
   Where is the heart that expanded to hold a world
   of its own making in itself;
   that sustained and cherished it;
   that trembled with rapture
   at the thought of equaling the spirit world?
   Where are you, Faust,
   whose voice rang out to me with such passionate urgency?

Are you that "thing" that trembles at its very core
at the sound of my voice,
a terrified, fleeing, writhing worm?

FAUST:

Am I to yield to you, you flaming form?
Here I am!
Faust!
Your equal!

SPIRIT:

In floods of life,
In storms of action,
In ebb and flow,
In warp and weft,
Birth and death,
An eternal sea,
A changing pattern,
A glowing life:
I weave at the whirring loom of Time
The living clothes of the Deity.

FAUST:

Busy Spirit circling the wide world,
how near I feel to you!

SPIRIT:

You are like the spirit your mind can grasp,
not me.

(The SPIRIT vanishes. FAUST collapses.)

FAUST:

Not you?
Who then?
I?
Created in God's image?
Not equal even to you?

(A knock at the door.)

O death! I know that knock.
My assistant.
My life's supreme moment destroyed.
My wealth of vision interrupted
by that plodding pedant!

*(WAGNER, in dressing gown and nightcap, enters carrying a lamp.
FAUST turns away in annoyance.)*

WAGNER:
> Forgive me, I heard you declaiming.
> A passage, surely, from an old Greek tragedy?
> An art form I'd gladly turn to a profit,
> for nowadays, they say, it has its advantages.
> And I've often heard said
> a preacher could learn from an actor.

FAUST:
> Yes, if the preacher himself is an actor—
> which happens from time to time.

WAGNER:
> Yes, well.
> But when a man is confined to his study,
> and never sees the world except on holidays,
> and then only at a distance,
> through a telescope,
> how is he to guide it by persuasion—
> the world?

FAUST:
> If you don't *feel* it, it's a lost cause.
> It must well up from deep in your soul
> and win the hearts of your hearers with its primal energy.
>
> But, no,
> better you go on sitting there with scissors and paste,

concocting a ragout from other men's feasts,
blowing paltry flames from your pile of ashes.
It will win you the applause of children and fools,
if that's to your taste.
But you'll never move men's hearts or unite them
unless it comes straight from your own heart.

WAGNER:
Yes, but it's the delivery that counts;
and believe me, I know how much I've still to learn.

FAUST:
Make an honest living.
Don't go around a fool with bells tinkling.
Good sense and an honest message speak for themselves
without much art. If you're really serious,
and have something to say,
what need is there to hunt for words?
You and those dazzling speeches of yours,
crammed with bits and pieces from everywhere,
are about as refreshing as the foggy autumn wind
rustling dry leaves.

WAGNER:
O God!
Art is so long and life so short!
There are times in my studies
when my heart sinks with any confidence
I once had. So much to master
to work your way up to the sources!
And before we're even halfway there
we're dead, poor devils.

FAUST:
Your manuscript!
Is that the holy fountain
that will quench your thirst forever?
You'll never know refreshment
till it flows from deep within you.

WAGNER:

You'll forgive me, but it's a great delight
to enter into the spirit of times past;
to know what wise men before us thought,
and then measure how far we've come in the meanwhile.

FAUST:

As far as the stars! Yes!
Times past, my friend, are a book with seven seals.
And what you call the spirit of the times
is nothing more than the spirit of you gentlemen
in which the past is reflected.
And a sad affair that reflection is, too!
One glance and you run for your lives.
A trash barrel!
A junk room!
At best, a blood-and-thunder play
with excellent pragmatical maxims
suitable for the mouths of puppets.

WAGNER:

But what of the world?
What of the hearts and minds of men?
Surely we all want knowledge of such things.

FAUST:

Knowledge!
Yes, what's *known* as "knowledge."
That's what you mean, isn't it?
But who'll call the child by its right name?
Who would dare?
The few who really knew—the few who were
foolish enough not to keep it to themselves,
who spilled their full hearts to the rabble,
their feelings, their visions,
have from the beginning of time been crucified
and burned at the stake.

But you must excuse me, my friend.
It's very late; we really must stop for now.

WAGNER:

I'd have happily sat up all night
talking so learnedly with you.
But tomorrow is Easter Sunday.
You must allow me another question or two.
I've studied like a dog, and know a lot,
but I want to know everything.

(Exit.)

FAUST:

How is it that they never give up hope?
Here is a man who clings for his very life
to everything that is shallow, digging greedily
in the earth for treasures, and rejoices
when he finds an earthworm in the earth!

What right has a human voice to speak here?
And especially the voice of such a dreary pedant?
Here where the air around me teemed with spirits!

Still, I thank you this once,
you sorriest of all earth's creatures.
You wrenched me from a despair
that was close to destroying me.
An apparition so vast it dwarfed me!
A nothing!

I, image of the Godhead!
I, so certain I would look into the mirror
of eternal truth! Already basking
in the pristine light of heaven's glory,
trailing mortality behind me!

What a fool!

Thinking myself greater than angelic cherubim,
able unhindered to flow through Nature's veins
and revel in the act of creation like the gods!

Ah, but the punishment!
One thundering word has brought me to my knees.

Equal to you?
No.
The power to summon you here?
Yes.
Yes, that I had.

But not the power to hold you.

O that moment!
That supreme moment
when at once I felt so great and so small!
And then to be thrust back, ruthlessly, into uncertainty,
the fated lot of man.

Who will teach me?
What must I shun?
Do I deny my urge,
my quest to seek the source of all life?

Ah, not only the deeds we *do*,
but those done *to* us,
turn us from our goal.

Our mind's most glorious thoughts are
forever violated by the vulgar dross of matter.
Once we achieve the good of this world,
ideals are despised and deemed illusion,
and only comfort serves.
Noble sentiments that once were life's breath
are drowned in earthly chaos.

There was a time when the winged and hopeful flight
of imagination soared out into infinity;
but now, when misfortunes come,
one after another,
a tiny space is all it needs.

Care nestles itself in the heart's depths,
where it brings unease and mysterious pains,
destroying all life's joy,
always hiding behind new disguises,
unknown masks.
She may come as house and home,
as wife and child, as fire, water,
dagger and poison, making you quake
at the thought of what never happens,
and weep over things you never lose.

I'm not like the gods.
How well I know that.
I'm a worm in the dust crushed by a passing foot.

And what is this but dust?
This prison I'm in with its hundred compartments?

Rubbish!
All of it!
Trifles!
Nothing!
A moth-eaten world!

Is this where I'm to find happiness?
And after a thousand books discover that men
have tormented themselves eternally
and only a few have found happiness?

(He looks at a skull.)

What are you looking at?
You grin, and your skull is hollow, and you
whisper to me that, just like me, you once groped
blindly for enlightenment and truth,
and, like me, went hopelessly astray.

Even my instruments mock me.
Wheels and cogs, cylinders and bridles.

Useless!

What do you open?
You were my keys.
I stood at the gates panting with expectation,
but you unlocked nothing.
Even in the sun's uncompromising light
Nature remains a mystery.
Demure, chaste, she lifts no veil.

Nothing.

And you, Faustus, with your levers and screws,
are impotent in the face of Nature;
as impotent as these ancient instruments
I've never used:
my father's tools, grimy,
gathering soot from my smoking lamp.

What a fool.

I should have squandered the little I had,
rather than waste my life under the weight of *this!*
To own what the past has left, you must use it.
Not to is a terrible burden.
Only what the moment creates can serve the moment.

(He sees a flask on a shelf.)

That flask—
why does it draw my eye like a magnet?
It clears my mind like moonlight
suddenly flooding a dark forest.

Come,
come down, you rarest, you holiest of vials!
I praise the human cunning that made you,
you distillation of sleep-inducing herbs,
quintessence of subtle poisons!

Show your master how you can save him from this.
I look at you and my pain is eased.
I grasp you and my striving lessens.
The flood tide of my spirit slowly ebbs,
and I am carried out onto the open sea
where the great waters glisten below me
and a new day lures me to new shores.

A fiery chariot sweeps down for me!
I'm ready now for the journey,
a new course, new spheres of pure activity!

How exalted!
The divine joy of it!

And yet, just now you were a miserable worm.

How do you dare to deserve this, Faust?

I'll turn my back to the sweet light of the sun,
tear open the gates that
frightened men pass by in silence!
The time has come to prove by deeds that man
will not be intimidated by the gods,
but be their equal, bold enough to face
that dark cavern where imagination condemns itself
to torment, force his way into the narrow,
fire-ringed passage of Hell,
and to do it serenely,
even if it ends in annihilation!

Come down to me now, long-forgotten chalice,
out of your ancient case.
My mind floods with memories of family gatherings and
guests who did their duty in making toasts,
amusing us all with rhymes
to explain your artful decorations,
and then drain the bowl at a single draught.

I have no friend of my youth to pass it on to,
nor any reason now for rhyming.
This is a drink that soon intoxicates,
a drink I prepared myself and now
pour its dark liquid into your brimming cup.
I pledge it now, with all my heart,
to the new day.

(As he puts the goblet to his lips, church bells and a choir are heard.)

CHOIR OF ANGELS:

> Christ is ascended!
> Hail the glad token,
> True was it spoken,
> Sin's fetters are broken,
> Man's bondage is ended!

FAUST:

> What deep resonance, what clear, shining note
> has such power to drag this chalice from my lips?
> Muted bells announce the Easter festival,
> and choirs sing their song of consolation
> first sung by angels at that darkened tomb—
> proclamation of a new faith, a new covenant.

CHOIR OF WOMEN:

> With myrrh and with aloes
> We balmed and we bathed Him,
> Loyally, lovingly,
> Tenderly swathed Him;
> With cerecloth and band
> For the grave we arrayed Him;
> But, oh, He is gone
> From the place where we laid Him!

CHOIR OF ANGELS:

> Christ is ascended!
> The love that possessed Him,
> The pangs that oppressed Him,

To prove and to test Him,
In triumph have ended!

FAUST:
Heavenly tones, so gentle, so strong,
why do you seek me here in the dust?
Send your sounds to weaker men.
I hear your message,
but lack the faith that fathers the miraculous.
I don't aspire to those spheres
that peal out your message of salvation.
I wouldn't dare.

And yet,
I've known these sounds from my earliest youth,
and even now they call me back to life.

Time was when in the stillness of the Sabbath
the kiss of heavenly love descended upon me.
Pealing bells then were full of promise,
and prayer a rapturous delight.
An unknown sweet yearning
would lure me to rove the woods and fields
where floods of tears gave birth to a new world.
This is the hymn that announced the games of childhood
and the untroubled joy of springtime celebrations.
It is this memory that holds me back from
taking this last, this solemn step.

Sweet and heavenly songs, ring out!
My tears well up and earth wins me back again.

CHOIR OF DISCIPLES:
Now He who was buried
On high has ascended;
He lives there in glory,
Divinely attended;
He in the joy of birth
Close to creating light;

We on the breast of earth
Lost in frustrating night;
Lord God, we languish
In pain and annoy;
Lord, in our anguish
Lamenting Your Joy.

CHOIR OF ANGELS:

From the lap of corruption,
Christ has ascended!
Rejoice, now, the fetters
That bound Him are rended!
Praise Him unceasingly,
Show love increasingly,
Giving alms brotherly,
Break bread in sanctity,
Spread the Word wanderingly
To all who will hear,
The Master is near you,
The Master is here!

V ✒ OUTSIDE THE CITY GATE

A variety of strollers come from the city.

SOME APPRENTICES:
Where're you off to?

OTHERS:
Hunter's Lodge.

FIRST GROUP:
We'll be out at the Mill.

ONE APPRENTICE:
It's livelier out at the River Inn.

SECOND APPRENTICE:
Ah, but what an ugly walk.

SECOND GROUP:
> What about you?

THIRD APPRENTICE:
> I'll be with them.

FOURTH APPRENTICE:
> Ah, come with us to Burgdorf's.
> Prettier girls and the best beer in town.
> The fights aren't bad either, you know?

FIFTH APPRENTICE:
> What a lunatic!
> Your ass itching for another hiding?
> The place spooks me.

SERVANT GIRL:
> No, I'll be going back to town.

ANOTHER:
> He's sure to be over there by the poplars.

FIRST GIRL:
> That's all very well for you to say!
> You're the one he'll walk and dance with,
> and what about me?

SECOND GIRL:
> But he's bringing a friend.
> He crossed his heart that Curly'd be with him.

FIRST STUDENT:
> Jesus, look at the strut on those girls!
> They look like they could use some company.
> What do you say?
> Do we give it a try?
> A good strong beer, some weed with a bite,
> and a servant girl decked out in her Sunday best!
> Sounds good to me!

FIRST CITIZEN'S DAUGHTER:

> Over there? Do you see?
> Those college boys?
> They can have the pick of the lot,
> but all they chase is servant girls!

SECOND STUDENT: *(To the FIRST.)*

> What's the rush?
> Take a look behind us. See those two,
> all dressed up and out for a stroll?
> And one lives next door! O God,
> look at her! Isn't she something!
> They may look shy,
> but they'll come around.

FIRST STUDENT:

> No way. I like my game wild.
> Get a move on, we'll lose the scent.
> They know more than sweeping floors.
> On Sunday those tiny hands go roaming.

FIRST CITIZEN:

> No, I *don't* like the new mayor, no!
> Arrogant fellow if you ask me!
> Gets worse every day!
> And what's he ever done?
> Thinks he can dictate our every move!
> *And* raises taxes!

A BEGGAR: *(Sings.)*

> > Fine gentlemen and lovely ladies,
> > Rosy-cheeked in such fine dress,
> > Look at me and show some pity,
> > Be kind to me in my distress.
> > Let me not grind away for nothing.
> > Only the one that gives is gay.
> > A day when all the world is joyous
> > Should be for me a harvest day!

SECOND CITIZEN:

>What can be nicer on Sundays and holidays
>than to talk of war or rumors of it,
>while far off somewhere,
>maybe in Turkey,
>they're pounding each others' heads together.
>You stand at the window, draining your glass,
>and watch bright ships sail downstream,
>and then at twilight wend your way back home
>and thank God for the blessings of peace.

THIRD CITIZEN:

>Right you are! There I agree!
>Let them bust each others' heads and
>turn the world all topsy-turvy, as long as we're
>true to our good old German customs.

OLD WOMAN: *(To the CITIZENS' DAUGHTERS.)*

>Mercy! Aren't we all decked out!
>What fine young things you ladies look!
>Who wouldn't love to win prizes like you?
>Now, now, not so snooty!
>It's all right, believe me, dearies,
>I know how to get you what you want.

FIRST CITIZEN'S DAUGHTER:

>Come, Agatha!
>I refuse to be seen in public places
>with these dreadful witches.
>All the same, last Halloween
>she showed me my future lover in the flesh.

SECOND CITIZEN'S DAUGHTER:

>She showed me mine in a crystal ball;
>a soldier with all his bold comrades.
>I look around for him everywhere,
>and yet I never seem to find him.

SOLDIERS: *(Sing.)*

Castles with lofty
Walls and high towers,
Wenches with arrogant
Hearts must be ours,
Win them we must,
And win them we will,
Whatever the struggle,
We'll win them still.
The effort is daring,
And lordly the pay!

The trumpets woo us
To joy or to danger,
To love or to battle,
To strife I'm no stranger.
They all must be mine!
Castle with high walls
And wenches so fine.
Ah, what a life!
All must be mine!
The effort is daring,
And lordly the pay!
And soldiers go marching,
Marching away!

(Enter FAUST and WAGNER.)

FAUST:

River and stream are freed from ice
by lovely spring's life-giving glance,
and every valley trembles with hope.
Ancient winter,
losing his strength,
withdraws to the mountains' rugged terrain,
sending back in his flight
weak showers of sleet that speckle the plain.
But the sun, always impatient with whiteness,
stirs all things to life with his shafts, and

turns the earth to a riot of colors.
And since no flowers dot the landscape,
he dapples the earth with colorful crowds of
joyous people in all their finery.

Turn around;
look back toward the town from this hilltop.
You can see them there,
streaming out through the gloomy gate:
a throng of many colors,
eager to sun themselves today of all days,
the day of the Lord's resurrection,
for they, too, are resurrected:
from the damp rooms of their humble homes,
from the manacles of mills and factories,
from the dismal oppression of stuffy attics,
from the crush of narrow, crowded streets,
from the churches' venerable night,
they have been raised into joyous light.

Look!
Look there!
How quickly the fields and gardens
are sprinkled with thronging crowds,
and boats and pleasure craft on the river
dance along all its length and breadth.
And there!
Do you see?
The last barge takes the current,
loaded near to sinking!
And there!
On the mountains!
Colors flashing on every pathway,
a rainbow of clothes dazzles our sight.

Already I hear the bustle and hum of the village.

Here, here is their heaven,
the people's heaven,

everyone shouting, great and small,
happy with life.
It's here I feel, I dare to feel,
human again.

WAGNER:

To take a stroll with you, Doctor,
is a real privilege, and a profit, too.
But I'd never choose to lose my way alone here,
sworn enemy of everything vulgar.
I look around at this fiddling, screaming,
bowling hubbub and think how detestable.
It's a devil-driven riot, if you ask me,
and they call it pleasure, they call it song.

(PEASANTS sing and dance under the linden tree.)

PEASANTS:

The shepherd decked out in his Sunday best,
Ribbons flying and flowered vest,
Oh, what a sight was he!
Under the linden tree they danced,
Man and maid, how high they pranced.
Yoo-hoo! Yoo-ho!
And a hey-nonny-no!
And the fiddler played, yo-hee!

He pushed his way on into the swirl,
Dancing on up to the prettiest girl,
And jabbed her with his elbow.
The sturdy lass turned round and said:
"How'd you like a knock on the head?"
Yoo-hoo! Yoo-ho!
And a hey-nonny-no!
"Show some manners, you know?"

He danced in a circle and she held tight,
They danced to the left, they danced to the right,
And every skirt went flying.

They were red in the face, they got so warm,
And rested, breathless, arm in arm.
Yoo-hoo! Yoo-ho!
And a hey-nonny-no!
Breast on breast soft lying!

"Keep your hands to yourself," said she,
"I know how girls, young brides-to-be,
Are stood up by no-goods like you!"
But soon he'd coaxed her to the side,
And the music rang out far and wide:
Yoo-hoo! Yoo-ho!
And a hey-nonny-no!
And the fiddler, he played too!

OLD PEASANT:

How good it is of you, Doctor,
not to scorn our holiday,
but come to mingle with us folk,
scholar that we know you are.
Take this, now, this jug,
this handsome jug,
filled at the tap with our freshest brew.
I give it to you with our wish
that it not only quench your thirst,
but every drop that it contains
should lengthen your life by another day.

FAUST:

Thank you, old man,
and health and happiness to you.

(The people gather round him.)

OLD PEASANT:

It's kind of you, truly kind,
to visit us on this happy day.
In years gone by,
in very dark times,

you proved yourself the people's friend.
Many a man among us has your father
to thank for his life.
When burning fever raged, your father
snatched many of us from the grip of death
when he put an end to the pestilence.
Young as you were,
you entered each house,
no matter the danger;
and though many a corpse left feet first,
you always emerged from every dwelling,
safe and sound,
and shouldered many bitter trials,
the helper helped by the Helper on high.

PEASANT CROWD:

    Let's drink health to this trusty man!
    Long may he live to help in our need!

FAUST:

    Bow your heads to Him
    Who teaches us to help the helpless!

(FAUST and WAGNER go on.)

WAGNER:

    Great man, what a joy you must feel
    to have such reverence from the masses!
    Happy the man who from his talents
    can reap so grand a reward!
    Fathers point you out to their sons,
    all ask questions,
    crowd around you,
    jostle for room,
    the fiddles stop,
    the dancers pause,
    and as you pass on by
    they stand in rows and caps go flying.
    It wouldn't take much to make them kneel
    as if the Host were seen approaching.

FAUST:

A few more steps to that rock and we'll rest.
—How often I've sat here alone in thought,
tormenting myself with prayer and fasting.
Rich in hope, firm in faith,
with tears and sighs and wringing of hands
I tried to extort from the Lord an end to that plague.
The crowd's applause sounds to me now like mockery.
If only you saw in my innermost soul
how little that father and son deserve such fame!

My father was an honorable man groping in darkness.
In all good faith, he brooded on Nature
and her sacred spheres,
but always in his odd capricious way—
never without honesty,
never without sincerity of heart—
but with tedious and fantastic means,
and that was the problem.
In the company of other adepts,
he locked himself in the black kitchen of necromancy,
where, with interminable recipes,
he mixed the mutually incompatible.

Patients died,
and no one bothered to count the survivors.
And so, armed with these hellish powders,
we raged through the region,
these mountains, these valleys,
more devastating than even the plague!
I myself gave the poison to thousands
who withered away; and now I must live to hear
the murderers praised to the skies.

WAGNER:

But how can you let such matters trouble you?
An honest man
who works at the art he received from others,
and does so punctiliously with a clear conscience—

what more can he do?
In your youth you honor your father
and take from him what he teaches you.
As a man, you, too, add to this knowledge,
and your own son will add even more.

FAUST:

That man is happy who has any hope
of rising out of this sea of confusion!
What we need most is just what we don't have,
and what we have is of no use whatever.

Ah,
but why spoil the beauty of this blessèd moment
with such melancholy thoughts?

Look there! Do you see?
Cottages nestled in their beds of greenery,
shimmering in the rays of the setting sun.
The sun retreats, moves on, and day is done,
scurrying off to nourish new life elsewhere.

Oh, how I wish for wings to lift me from earth and
strive forever after him! Below me the world
in eternal sunset, peaks flaring in the glow,
valleys tucked in slumber, and silver brooks
flowing into golden streams.
No savage mountain, no gorges then could check
my godlike flight.

And there, look!
The ocean and its sun-warmed bays
opening out to my wondering eyes!
At last the god seems near to sinking,
and a new impulse wakens in my breast:
I hurry after to drink his eternal light,
the day before me,
and behind me the night,
above me the heavens,
and below me the waves.

A lovely dream—until he fades from view.
But where do I find them, where, those earthly wings,
companions to the wings of the spirit?
Yet everywhere, in each of us,
we harbor the desire to rise above,
to surge, to soar along,
when high in the blue immensity of heaven
the lark pipes its trilling song;
when high above pine-clad crags
the eagle hovers on wings wide spread;
when at evening the crane flaps slowly homeward
over sleepy ponds and marches.

WAGNER:

Yes, well,
I've had my aberrant moments, too,
but I must confess I've never felt such an urge.
You see one field and forest you've seen them all,
and soon enough, too.
And as for envying a bird its flight,
no no, not me, glad to say.

How differently the spirit's pleasures
bear us from book to book,
from page to page!
How bright and beautiful winter nights are then,
every limb snug and warm.
Ah, and then you unroll an ancient parchment
and heaven spreads out before you!

FAUST:

Yes, and this is the force that drives you.
You know only the one urge,
never strive to know the other!

Ach!
Two souls cohabit in my breast,
each one struggling to tear itself from the other!
The one, like a coarse lover,

clings to the earth with every sensual organ;
the other struggles violently from the dust and
soars to the fields of great departed spirits.

O spirits! if there *are* spirits!
You mediating powers between heaven and earth!
Come to me,
·come down from your golden mists,
and carry me off to a new and motley life!
Oh, if only I held in my hand
some magic cloak that would sweep me off to
unknown lands, I would never exchange it
for the costliest robes,
no, not for a king's mantle!

WAGNER:
No, you mustn't!
Don't summon that swarm,
that throng of demons
that streams through the murky air,
threatening a thousand evils from every quarter!
We've known them far too often!
Sharp-toothed spirits that ride the northern winds
with tongues like arrows;
on withering eastern winds they feed on your lungs;
and if on southern winds
they swarm from the desert with paralyzing waves
of searing heat, from the west
they will come on a wind to revive you with showers,
and drown you then in floods with fields and meadows.
They prick up their ears,
because they're made of mischief;
they gladly obey, the better to betray us;
they pretend to be heaven's angels
while lying with a vengeance.

But it's time to be going now;
the world's grown gray.
There's a chill in the air, mist falling.
It's only at evening we appreciate our homes.

But why do you stand there staring?
What's there to startle you in the twilight?

FAUST:

Do you see that black dog
ranging through the grain and stubble?

WAGNER:

I saw it awhile back.
It's only a dog.

FAUST:

Observe him closely.
What do you make of the brute?

WAGNER:

A poodle like every other poodle,
sniffing out its master's tracks.

FAUST:

Yes, but he's circling us, closer and closer.
And unless I'm very much mistaken,
he's trailing a whirlpool of fire in his wake.

WAGNER:

I see a black poodle and nothing but.
As for you, Master, your eyes are playing tricks.

FAUST:

I'd say that, with some sly and subtle magic,
he's drawing snares round our feet for future reference.

WAGNER:

It's confused is all, leaping around, timid,
two strangers instead of its master.

FAUST:

The circle is narrowing,
he's already near!

WAGNER:

Yes, and what have we but a dog, no more,
no phantom here. It growls, hangs back,
grovels on its belly in the grass, wags its tail.
What more could you want from a dog?

FAUST:

Come! Come join us! Here! Come!

WAGNER:

It's a stupid beast of a poodle.
You stop, he stops;
you speak, he jumps up;
you lose something, he finds it;
throw your stick in the water,
he'll leap in after it.

FAUST:

Right you are.
No sign of any spirit here.
Just doing what he was taught.

WAGNER:

A dog as well trained as this
might well win a philosopher's favor.
I'd say he deserves you, sir.
His student masters have made him an apt scholar.

(They enter the city gate.)

VI ✒ FAUST'S STUDY (a)

FAUST enters with the poodle.

FAUST:

Dark night has settled now on fields and meadows,
waking my soul with awe and sacred dread.
Wild, ungoverned longings and unguarded acts are

sleeping now, and the love of humankind revives,
the love of God.

Quiet there, poodle!
What's this running about!
What are you sniffing there at the threshold?
Come, lie behind the stove here.
You'll have my best cushion.
You entertained us out there on the mountain
with your canine antics, so now
let me welcome you as my guest,
but a quiet one, you hear?
No noise!

How clear the mind becomes,
sitting here in one's own narrow cell,
the lamp lighted and burning with a friendly glow,
the heart growing brighter with self-knowledge.
Reason once more raises its voice,
and hope blossoms.
We yearn, we long, for the springs of life,
for the very source of being.

All right now, poodle,
that's enough whining and growling!
This beastly racket is out of tune
with the sacred harmonies gripping my soul.
We all know men who jeer at things
they don't understand, who grumble at the
Good and the Beautiful because it embarrasses them.
Are we now to hear dogs growl, too?

Ah, but already I feel it beginning to fail,
that inner contentment,
no matter how much I long for it.
Why must the stream run dry,
why so soon,
and leave us thirsting once more?
How many times this has happened to me!

And yet there's another way to satisfy this want.
We learn to prize the things of the spirit,
to long for revelation which nowhere burns more nobly
and with greater beauty than in the New Testament.
I must open that fundamental text;
I must, now, with all honorable dedication,
turn that holy original
into my beloved German.

(He opens a large volume and prepares to begin.)

It is written:
"In the beginning was the *Word!*"

Already I'm stuck.
Who will help me?
Who?
Someone!
How can I rate the *Word* so highly?
I must translate it otherwise
if I'm truly enlightened by the spirit.

It is written:
"In the beginning was the *Mind!*"

Not so fast.
Let's not rush over that first line!
Is it truly the mind that creates all things?

Surely it ought to read:
"In the beginning was the *Force!*"

And yet I've scarcely written it and
immediately something tells me it's not right.

But, yes, now the spirit's helping,
helping me,
and all at once I have it, and write:

"In the beginning was the *Deed!*"

If we're to share this room, poodle,
you'll have to put an end to this howling and growling!
I can't manage so distracting a companion.
One of us will have to leave.
And as much as I hate to be an ungracious host,
there's the door, it's open, you're free to go.

But what's this?
What am I seeing?
Can it be? Is it real?
Is it an illusion?
How long and broad my poodle's growing!
It rises a monstrosity!
This is no longer the shape of a dog!
What sort of specter have I taken in?
He's already the size of a hippopotamus,
eyes like torches,
terrible fangs!

Ah! I know you now!
The key of Solomon's the thing to handle you.

(SPIRITS are heard in the corridor outside.)

SPIRITS:

> One we know well
> Is caught fast within there.
> Mind what you're doing,
> No one go in there!
> An old lynx of Hell,
> Like a fox in a gin, there
> Is quaking and stewing.
> Have a care! Have a care!
> Unseen, through the air,
> Flit now and hover,
> To and fro, round about,
> Now under, now over,

And he will get out!
Aid him, if aid you may!
He's done us before today
Great pleasures and rare!
Help him, then, in his despair!

FAUST:
First to encounter the beast,
I'll use the Incantation of the Four.

(He reads from the conjurer's book.)

Salamander, glow,
Undine, coil,
Sylph, disappear,
Goblin, toil!

He who knows not the four Elements,
their power, their potencies,
will never master the spirit world.

Vanish in flame,
Salamander!
Flow swirling together,
Watery Undines!
Burn like meteors,
Sylphs of the air!
Bring housely help,
Incubus, Incubus!
Come forth
And make an end!

None of the four is in the beast.
Look at him there, quietly grinning!
I haven't yet harmed the brute at his core.
But now I'll conjure with a mightier spell.

(He shows the beast a magic sign.)

You! Are you
A thing from Hell?
Behold this sign
That black angels bow to!

Look how he swells, his hair bristling.

Accursed creature!
Do you know Him, then,
The never-begotten,
The ineffable one,
The everywhere-present,
The wickedly transfixed?

Trapped behind the stove, it swells,
elephant-high, the room is crammed,
and he about to melt into mist.
No, not up to the ceiling, no!
Lie down, lie here at your master's feet!
You can see my threats are not in vain.
I'll set you aflame with sacred fire!
Don't dare the glare of the thrice-holy light!
Don't dare the scare of my mightiest spells!

*(As the mist falls, MEPHISTOPHELES appears from behind the stove
dressed as a vagabond scholar.)*

MEPHISTOPHELES:
What's all the racket?
How can I serve you, sir?

FAUST:
So this was at the poodle's core!
A vagabond scholar!
Very amusing, I must say.

MEPHISTOPHELES:
I salute you, sir, you're well versed.
That was quite a sweat you put me through.

FAUST:

    What's your name?

MEPHISTOPHELES:

    I'd call that a rather petty question,
    especially from one with such contempt for words,
    who scorns appearance
    and digs down deep for the core of things.

FAUST:

    The essence of the likes of you, sir,
    can usually be read in their name,
    Lord of the Flies, say,
    or Destroyer, Liar.
    It's really quite transparent.
    So, then, who are you?

MEPHISTOPHELES:

    A part of the Power that always wills evil,
    but always works the good.

FAUST:

    What is this riddle?

MEPHISTOPHELES:

    I'm the spirit that always negates!
    And rightly so, since all that is
    deserves to perish. How much better
    If nothing ever existed. And therefore,
    all that you call sin, destruction,
    in a word, evil,
    is my proper element.

FAUST:

    A part, you say?
    You call yourself a part,
    and yet you stand there as whole as can be?

MEPHISTOPHELES:

I speak only the modest truth, sir.
And yet men,
that foolish congregation of petty microcosms,
insist on calling themselves whole entities.
As for me,
I'm a part of that Part that at first was All,
a part of the darkness that gave birth to light,
arrogant light that competes with Night
for her ancient rank and ancient space.
But it won't succeed, struggle as it may.
Light is one with objects.
Light flows from bodies,
it gives bodies beauty,
and yet bodies check it in its course.
And so, I trust, it won't be long
till light and the physical world
go down to dark destruction.

FAUST:

Yes, I begin to grasp it,
your worthy occupation!
Unable to annihilate wholesale,
you've made a stab at it retail.

MEPHISTOPHELES:

Yes, and a lot of good it's done me.
Empty hands is all I have.
This Something, this lump of a world, this mess,
for all the inroads I've made on it with my Nothing,
does nothing but oppose me tooth and nail.
What good have flood and fire,
earthquake and storms done me?

Nothing!

Land and sea are as unshaken as ever.

And as for that damnable brood of men and animals,

there's no getting at them!
How many millions I've buried,
and still not made a dent.
There's always new fresh blood in circulation;
it never stops!
It's enough to drive you to distraction!
Earth, air, water give birth,
a thousand thousand germinations,
in wet and dry,
in heat and cold.
If I hadn't held back fire for myself,
what in Hell could I call my own?

FAUST:

And so, in rage,
you raise your cold devil's fist
in malice at creation's power
and the life force that never ceases!
Give it up, you curious son of Chaos,
or try something new!

MEPHISTOPHELES:

Yes, we'll look into it next time we meet.
But for now, would you mind if I go?

FAUST:

Why do you ask?
Now we're acquainted, come when you like.
Here's the window, there's the door,
or, if you prefer, the chimney.

MEPHISTOPHELES:

Yes, well, I must confess, you see,
a minor obstacle inhibits my leaving the premises.
That witch's foot in the doorway.

FAUST:

Is it the pentagram pains you?
Is that it? Then tell me,

you misbegotten son of Hell,
how the devil did you get in,
if now you can't get out?
How did I manage to delude so vast an intellect?

MEPHISTOPHELES:

Look closely. Do you see?
It's improperly drawn. The corner that
points outward has a break in it.

FAUST:

That was some piece of luck!
And so you're my prisoner.
What an opportunity!

MEPHISTOPHELES:

The poodle never noticed when he bounded in,
but now it's taken on a new complexion.
The devil can't get out.

FAUST:

Then why not go out through the window?

MEPHISTOPHELES:

Yes, well, ghosts and devils have rules, too.
Where they slip in, they have to slip out.
Going in, we choose; going out, we don't.
And that's the law.

FAUST:

Aha, so even Hell has it's laws.
Yes, I like that. Who knows,
perhaps we'll make a pact,
a binding one, at that.

MEPHISTOPHELES:

Whatever we promise you'll enjoy to the full.
You'll have full purchase.
And yet these matters aren't easily settled.
We'll talk it over next time, shall we?

For the present, I bid you—
no, I implore you—
to give me my leave.

FAUST:

No, stay another moment, won't you?
Tell me what other news you have.

MEPHISTOPHELES:

Let me go for now. I'll come back soon.
You can ask me then to your heart's content.

FAUST:

You must admit, I didn't trap you.
You did it yourself.
Once you've got the Devil in hand,
never let go; it won't be so easy
the second time around.

MEPHISTOPHELES:

All right, then, if you like,
I'm prepared to stay and keep you company;
but only on one condition:
you'll let me entertain you with my arts
in some worthy fashion.

FAUST:

I'd like that. Yes. It's up to you.
As long as your arts are amusing.

MEPHISTOPHELES:

Your senses, my friend,
will know more stimulation in this hour
than in a year of academic monotony.
The songs these gentle spirits sing,
the lovely images they bring,
are no mere empty sorcery.
Smell and taste and touch
will be ravished with delight.
No preparation needed, let us begin!

SPIRITS: *(Sing.)*

> Disappear, disappear,
> Drear arches above him!
> Let the blue sky of heaven
> Look in on us here,
> The beautiful blue sky
> With friendliest cheer!
> Away, clouds, away,
> Clouds gloomily darkling!
> Behold now the little stars
> Glimmering and sparkling,
> Mellower suns
> Shine in on us here.
> Heaven's sons, bright
> In spiritual beauty,
> In hovering flight
> Are bending and swaying,
> And souls with a passionate
> Longing, aspiring,
> View them, pursue them,
> Soaring untiring!
> And ribbons gay
> Are flashing and gleaming
> Where lovers stray,
> Musing and dreaming,
> Stray on by grove
> And meadow, requiting
> Love with return of love,
> Life for life plighting!
> Arbor on arbor,
> Tendrils run rife!
> Grapes in huge clusters
> Piled over and over,
> Under the winepress
> Spurting their store.
> Seething and foaming,
> Wines gush into rills,
> Over smooth stones
> Rush from the hills,

Broaden to lakes, that
Are mantled in green.
And birds of all feather,
Pure rapture inhaling,
Sunwards are sailing,
Sailing together,
On to the isles,
That lie smiling and dreaming,
Where the bright billows
Are rippling and gleaming;
Where we see jocund bands
Dance on before us,
Over the meadow lands
Shouting in chorus,
All in the free air
Every way rambling;
Some up the mountains
Climbing and scrambling;
Some over lakes and seas
Floating and swimming,
Others upon the breeze
Flying and skimming;
All to the sources
Of life pressing onward,
Flushed by the forces,
That carry them sunward;
On to the measureless
Spaces above them,
On where the stars bless
The spirits that love them.

MEPHISTOPHELES:
   Asleep!
   Well done, you dainty, airy lads!
   You've done your best and sung him to sleep.
   I'm in your debt for this concert.

   You're not the man yet, Faustus,
   to hold the Devil in his grasp.

Play upon him now, Spirits,
ring him round with lovely phantom forms,
plunge him into a sea of delusion!

But first a rat's tooth to shatter this threshold's magic.
No need to conjure long;
I hear one scampering near who'll hear me soon.

> The Lord of Rats, the Lord of Mice,
> Master of Frogs and burrowing Lice,
> Of Flies and Bedbugs, commands you appear
> And gnaw away this oil-dotted smear!

Ah, and here you come hopping, old friend!
That's the way! And now to work!
A gnaw or two here at the point, and it's done!
I'm free!

Dream away, Faust, till we meet again!

(Exit.)

FAUST: *(Waking.)*
Ah!
Have I been duped a second time?
How can such a throng of spirits
vanish into thin air, telling me
it was only a dream,
a lying dream of the Devil,
and that a poodle ran off?

VII ✌ FAUST'S STUDY (b)

FAUST:
A knock? Come in!
Who's bothering me now?

MEPHISTOPHELES: *(Outside the door.)*
Only me.

FAUST:
Come in!

MEPHISTOPHELES:
You have to say it three times.

FAUST:
All right, come in, then!

MEPHISTOPHELES: *(Entering.)*
That's the way!
I like you better already!
I suspect we'll hit it off famously.
Yes, I'm certain we will.
Besides,
to sweep away your melancholy moods,
I've come this time as a noble cavalier,
scarlet doublet trimmed in gold,
a cloak of splendid rustling stiff silk,
a fashionably long rapier at my side,
and a cock's feather stuck in my hat.

Take my advice, friend, dress as I'm dressed,
free yourself, let yourself go,
throw off the yoke that holds you in check,
and discover for the first time
the adventure that life can be.

FAUST:
Whatever I wear,
what is this earth but a prison,
a narrow, confining cell that denies me liberty!
Too old to do anything but play,
too young not to burn with desire,
what satisfaction can life offer?

Do without!
Do without!

There's the world's advice!
There's the song that sings eternally,
that rings in our ears, year in, year out,
hour after hour, minute by minute,
singing hoarsely till the day we die!

I wake each morning in terror,
horrified,
wishing I could shed hot, bitter tears
for the day that will give me nothing,
not one wish fulfilled,
not one satisfaction,
not *one!*
the day that will drag down to defeat
every faint promise of pleasure with its
constant, capricious carping,
that with a thousand petty impediments,
with life's ugliness, its mockery, will
lay to waste my soul's creative urge.
And then when night draws close,
and I lie on my bed,
I expect no rest, but anxiety to haunt me,
desperation, and wild, ungoverned dreams to terrify me.
The divinity that rules my heart,
that governs my powers,
can shake my soul to its depths,
but is helpless where the world is concerned.

And so,
Life is an enemy,
Being a burden,
and only Death to be wished for.

MEPHISTOPHELES:
    And yet, not even Death
    is a wholly welcome guest.

FAUST:

    Happy the man whom Death crowns
    with the bloodstained wreath in the blaze of victory!
    Or he whom Death finds in the arms of a girl
    after the night's wild revelry!
    Oh, how I wish I'd dropped lifeless in purest rapture
    overcome by the power of that great spirit!

MEPHISTOPHELES:

    And yet, if I'm not mistaken,
    a certain someone failed to drink down a drink,
    a brown elixir he'd prepared?

FAUST:

    Spying, it appears, is second nature to you.

MEPHISTOPHELES:

    I'm not omniscient, but I know a thing or two.

FAUST:

    I admit it, yes,
    I was dragged from my soul's tumult by music so sweet
    it deluded that remnant of childhood in me
    with echoes of a happier time.
    But I curse it now,
    curse it,
    all that binds the soul with lures and trickery,
    and with lies and flattery confines it to this fleshly cavern,
    the miserable valley of despair!
    I curse first the mind and its prideful self-exaltation!
    I curse the dazzling stab of appearance
    that assaults our senses!
    I curse the dreams we dream, dreams that lie,
    dreams of fame and an enduring name!
    I curse property we use to flatter ourselves,
    wife and child, man and plow!
    I curse Mammon when with the promise of riches
    he incites us to rash deeds,
    or fluffs our pillows for a sensuous diversion!

I curse the purple juice of the grape!
I curse the transcendent flight of love!
Curse hope,
curse faith,
and above all else curse patience!

CHORUS OF INVISIBLE SPIRITS:
Aiiii! Aiiii!
You have destroyed
The beautiful world
With a merciless blow!
It totters, it crumbles,
It shatters, it tumbles,
A demigod has dashed it.
The ruins we trail
Back into Nothingness,
Ah, and wail
The loss of beauty.
Mightiest of men,
Of the sons of earth,
Build it again,
Give it new birth,
Raise it more splendidly
In your own breast!
Begin again!
Begin!
A new life!
A life of cheer!
A life of new vision,
With a mind that is clear!
And new songs
To welcome it in!

MEPHISTOPHELES:
These are mine, these little minions.
Notice how sagely they urge you on to pleasure,
urge you on to action!
They long to lure you into the wide world,
to abandon your solitary life where
sense and sap stagnate and stand still.

But enough of this mooning, this dabbling in
grief and misery that gets you nowhere but
gnaws at you like a vulture!
Why, even in the worst of company
you'd feel alive and a part of life.
And, no,
I'm not about to thrust you into the hoi polloi.
I may not be on the highest echelon of devils,
but I'm not the shabbiest, either;
and if you'd be content we join forces for life,
I'd oblige you anything on the spot.
We'll be brothers-in-adventure,
and, if I suit you,
I'll even be your servant—your slave.

FAUST:

And what's *your* reward for all of this?

MEPHISTOPHELES:

Oh, I wouldn't worry;
your credit's in good order.

FAUST:

No, not a bit of it, no!
The Devil's an egoist.
He doesn't work for free to benefit man.
He's out for himself is what he is.
Lay it out. Your terms.
Servants like you don't come without trouble.

MEPHISTOPHELES:

I pledge myself to you in *this* life,
no matter what. Over *there*,
when we meet in the next,
you'll do the same for me.

FAUST:

Over *there?*
Over there means nothing to me.

Shatter this world first, turn it into rubble,
and then let the other world come.
This is the earth my joys well out of;
this is the sun shines down on my sorrows.
Part me from them and what will may take its course.
What happens happens.
Let there be love and hate in those other spheres,
let there be top and bottom,
it means nothing to me.

MEPHISTOPHELES:

With an attitude like that you can risk anything.
Be bold! Bind yourself to me!
Begin a new life!
You'll see soon enough what I can do!
You'll see spectacles no man has ever seen!

FAUST:

What, poor devil, what, what can you show me?
Was the mind of man in its exalted striving
ever grasped by the likes of you?
What is it you offer?
Food that gives no satisfaction?
Red gold that runs like quicksilver through my fingers?
A game no one can win?
A girl who, while I'm lying in her arms,
has already, with a wink, chosen another?
Or honor worthy of the gods,
that flares and is gone like a shooting star?
All these things you have and what are they worth?
Fruit that rots before it's picked!
Trees that shed their leaves and grow new ones daily!

MEPHISTOPHELES:

What you ask is no great task for a devil.
Such treasures are for the taking.
And yet, my friend, the time will come
when we'll choose to enjoy something special
in peace and tranquility.

FAUST:

> If ever I lie down in a bed of ease,
> let that be my end!
> If ever you so delude me with your flattery
> into feeling self-satisfied,
> or deceive me with pleasure,
> let that day be my last!
> This is my wager!

MEPHISTOPHELES:

> Done!

FAUST:

> And done again! My hand!
> If ever I say to the moment:
> "Linger awhile, you are so fair!"
> then cast me in chains, for I'll be glad to die!
> Let the bell toll for me then;
> then you'll be freed of your service;
> let the clock stop,
> let its hands fall,
> and time for me will be at an end!

MEPHISTOPHELES:

> Consider well what you're doing;
> it won't be forgotten.

FAUST:

> And that's your right.
> This has been no rash decision.
> Once I stand still,
> once I begin to stagnate,
> I'm a slave.
> Whose makes no difference,
> yours or another's.

MEPHISTOPHELES:

> There's a faculty dinner tonight.
> I'll be there, and begin my service as your servant.

Ah, but there's another small matter,
if you don't mind!
Just to cover all contingencies,
do you think you could manage a few lines in writing?

FAUST:

Is the written word the only thing
with meaning for you, you pedant?
Have you never known a man who was
true to his word? Isn't my word
enough to dispose of my days to all eternity?

Oh, I know!
You see the world flow past like a raging torrent,
and wonder why a mere promise should bind me.

But that's the way we are.
It's an illusion we cherish and refuse to resign.
It's inscribed in every heart. It keeps us honest,
keeps us clear and pure spirited and responsible,
and no sacrifice in its name is too great.
But a parchment signed and sealed
is a ghost that everyone dreads.
The written word dies as the ink dries,
and leather and sealing wax tyrannize us.

So what do you want of me, you devil?
Bronze, marble, parchment, paper?
Name it.
The choice is yours.

MEPHISTOPHELES:

Oh, come now, let's not overdo it, shall we?
Is all that rhetoric necessary?
Any scrap of paper will do—
and sign it with a drop of blood.

FAUST:

Fine.

If all this nonsense meets your requirements,
let's get on with the farce.

MEPHISTOPHELES:
Yes, well, blood is a very special juice.

FAUST:
You needn't worry.
I'm not about to break our bargain!
Never to give up striving with all my energy
is what I promise.
I aimed too high.
I'm only fit to be with the likes of you.
The great Spirit rejects me,
Nature shuts her gates against me,
the thread of thought is snapped, and for ages now
I've loathed the blight of knowledge.
Let us satisfy our passions in the throws of sensuality.
Surround me with your wonders
and I'll never ask to know what's behind them.
Let us plunge ourselves into the roar of time,
the maelstrom of chance,
hit or miss,
pain or pleasure,
however it comes,
never ceasing,
always doing.
There's no other way.

MEPHISTOPHELES:
You're free.
Do as you please.
No restrictions.
Every delight is yours for the taking,
every pleasure yours to be snatched at will.
And may they agree with you.
Just be certain of one thing:
Be bold.
Take what you want!

FAUST:

Don't you hear?
Pleasure means nothing to me.
I dedicate myself herewith
to the frenzy of dissipation,
to joy that is pain, and pain joy,
to adoring hatred, and hatred that is love,
to torments that refresh, and refreshing exhaustion.
My soul healed of the lust for knowledge,
I lay myself open to the world's pain and suffering.
In my innermost self
I will experience all that humankind experiences,
the heights and the depths,
the sorrows and delights,
and doing so expand myself to encompass
all of humanity, and, in the end,
shatter like a ship in a storm.

MEPHISTOPHELES:

Oh, believe me,
I've gnawed away at these iron rations for millennia
and have learned only one thing:
there's no man, none, from womb to tomb,
has ever digested this bitter dough!
Take it from one of us,
this totality of creation, the universe,
is made only for a god!
It's *he* who dwells in eternal light,
us he casts into darkness,
while *you* must make do with day *and* night.

FAUST:

But I will!

MEPHISTOPHELES:

Good!
I like your spirit!
But there's only one thing frightens me:
Time is short, my friend, and art is long.

Search out some poet for your journey,
someone whose mind can range at will;
have him heap all noble virtues on your honored skull:
the lion's courage, the swiftness of the stag,
the hot blood of the Italian,
and the Northerner's steadfast endurance.
Have him solve for you the riddle
of combining magnanimity with cunning,
and how to plan an impulsive young man's love affair.
I'd like to meet such a man myself.
I'd call him Mr. Macrocosm.

FAUST:

What am I, then,
if I fail to gain the crown of all humanity,
the end that all my senses struggle to achieve?

MEPHISTOPHELES:

You are in the end—just what you are.
Deck your head with a wig of countless curls,
walk around in shoes a yard high,
you will never be anything—
but what you are.

FAUST:

What a waste!
I feel it now!
I've heaped on myself
all the treasures of the human mind,
and for what?
When finally I sit down, there's nothing new
wells up from within me,
no new force, no new strength.
I'm not a hairsbreadth taller,
no single step closer to the Infinite.

MEPHISTOPHELES:

You perceive all this too conventionally, dear friend.
We must see to reforming that

before all of life's joys escape us.
What the Hell!
You've got hands and feet,
a head and a pair of balls!
Use them!
Just because I enjoy something,
does that mean it's any the less mine?
If I can afford to keep six stallions,
doesn't that mean their strength is a part of me?
I race along, and what a man I've become,
all twenty-four feet of me!

So wake up, why don't you?
Let's put rumination to bed,
and come with me!
I'll introduce you to the world!
All this theorizing makes you like a donkey
on a barren heath, led round and round
by an evil spirit,
while splendid green meadows surround you on every side.

FAUST:

How do we go about it?

MEPHISTOPHELES:

By leaving. It's that simple.
By escaping this torture chamber.
What kind of a life is this,
boring yourself and those
poor young men, your students?
From here on you leave that to your
potbellied neighbor!
Why waste time threshing straw?
Besides, all the best things you know
they wouldn't let you tell the poor lads in any case.
Which reminds me,
I hear one outside in the hall.

FAUST:

No, I can't possibly see him.

MEPHISTOPHELES:

The poor boy's waited too long;
we can't send him away disconsolate.
Here now, give me your cap and gown.
Yes, this disguise will suit me well.

(He puts them on.)

Just trust to my wits, won't you?
I'll only be a quarter of an hour.
In the meantime,
prepare yourself for our Grand Tour.

(Exit FAUST.)

And so it goes.
But keep it up, you sorry son of earth.
Go on, go,
go on scorning knowledge and reason,
those highest of man's powers;
let the Spirit of Lies seduce you
with his ravishing necromancy, let him blind you
with his magic arts of illusion and deceit,
and then I'll have you,
and no escape.
Fate endows him, this Faust, this striver,
with a spirit that won't desist,
a mind that refuses to know defeat,
and in his overhasty headlong struggle
he overleaps the earth, its joys, its pleasures.

But I'll have him yet.
I'll drag him through a riotous life
of numbing insignificance. I'll make him
flounder, stiffen, stick fast in my lime.
I'll dangle food and drink before his
greedy and insatiable lips and he'll
beg for refreshment,
but it will do him no good.

And even if he hadn't come to terms with the devil,
he'd still know defeat in the end.

STUDENT: *(Entering.)*
Excuse me, sir, I'm new here,
just barely arrived—and, well,
longed to make the acquaintance of a man
the world respects and honors.

MEPHISTOPHELES:
Your courtesy flatters me.
Thank you. And yet,
I'm a man like many another.
Have you called on any of my colleagues?

STUDENT:
Please, sir, take me under your wing.
I come with the best of intentions,
a fair amount of money, and a healthy body.
My mother—
well, she almost didn't let me leave—
but I'm eager to learn, it's why I'm here.

MEPHISTOPHELES:
Then I'd say you've come to the right place.

STUDENT:
To be honest, sir, I wish I could escape right now.
It's so cramped. These walls, these halls,
they intimidate me. It's so bleak—no green,
no trees, no grass. And the lecture halls,
the benches!
I can't hear or see or think!

MEPHISTOPHELES:
Yes, well, that comes with practice.
The child at first is hesitant at the mother's breast,
but soon it feeds with gusto; and so with you.
You'll find as you suck daily at Wisdom's breasts,

you'll do so with greater pleasure.
So suck away, my boy!

STUDENT:

Oh, sir, I'll embrace her, and gladly!
But do tell me how to find my way?

MEPHISTOPHELES:

Tell me first, what major have you chosen?

STUDENT:

I want to be really learned!
I want to master everything!
Heaven, earth, science, nature!
I want it all!

MEPHISTOPHELES:

Ah, yes! You're on the right track, my boy;
just never let distraction lead you astray.

STUDENT:

Well, I mean—
however set on this I may be,
I'd still like a bit of recreation now and again,
an outing on summer holidays, and such.

MEPHISTOPHELES:

Time slips away so fast, you must never waste it.
But method will teach you that, my boy.
Order. System.
And so I advise you first to take up Logic.
It will put your mind in fine fettle,
drill it into submission,
lace it into iron boots, and from then on
it will creep and shuffle ponderously down the path
of thought, never again go will-o'-the-wisping,
flitting about this way and that,
crisscrossing hither and yon.

We'll teach you, we will,
we'll pound it into your head,
that things you once did without thinking,
like eating, drinking,
things you did freely, spontaneously,
with the ease of unknowing,
you've been doing all wrong,
and that now they must be done in regimental order:
One and two and three,
and so on into infinity.

Fact is, this thought machine of ours
is like a masterpiece on a weaver's loom.
One pedal stirs a thousand threads,
shuttles shooting back and forth,
threads flowing unseen,
and then a single stroke,
and a thousand knots are tied.

Yes, yes, and then in comes the philosopher,
sure as rain, explaining, explaining:
it had to be so, how else could it be?
First comes one,
and then comes two,
and then the three and four come due;
and if the one and two hadn't come,
three and four would come undone!

What a round of applause that gets from the students—
and yet, not one of them ever became a weaver.

When scholars want to describe a living thing,
they must kill it first. Only then do they
have the parts in the palm of their hand,
but they've lost the whole—
the spirit that binds it!
Chemists call it manipulating nature,
and come out looking fools,
but don't know why.

STUDENT:

    I'm not sure I understand.

MEPHISTOPHELES:

    You'll get the hang of it in time,
    once you've learned to analyze and classify.

STUDENT:

    All this confuses me so.
    I feel as if a millwheel were turning in my head.

MEPHISTOPHELES:

    Next, and before all else,
    you must tackle metaphysics—
    metaphysics that will put in your head ideas
    too vast for the human brain to consider.
    And whether they fit or whether they don't,
    doesn't matter, really;
    you'll always come up with some
    pompous word or other
    you can use to describe them.

    Now:
    this first semester you must work
    according to an ironbound schedule.
    You'll attend five classes daily;
    you'll be there at the stroke of the bell,
    and no absences;
    you'll be prepared;
    you'll do your homework beforehand,
    and that way you'll know,
    without consulting the text,
    that the professor's not adding things that aren't in the book.
    And be certain you write down his every syllable
    as if it came straight from the Holy Ghost.

STUDENT:

    That you won't have to tell me twice!
    I can see the use of it.

When you've got it down in black and white,
you can take it home and not have to worry.

MEPHISTOPHELES:

But tell me about your major.

STUDENT:

Well, at least I know it won't be Law.

MEPHISTOPHELES:

Ah, well, I can't blame you there.
I know a few things about that discipline.
Laws and statutes,
passed down from generations like inherited diseases,
slowly pass from one land to another,
and what once was reason becomes nonsense,
and blessings turn into curses.
I pity you that you are someone's descendant!
As for the rights and privileges we're born with,
they're never mentioned, not a word.

STUDENT:

You've made me hate it even more than I thought.
How I envy the fortunate student who has you for a teacher.
I almost think I'd like to take on Theology.

MEPHISTOPHELES:

Far be it from me to lead you astray,
but it's hard to keep to the straight and narrow
where that science is concerned.
All the poison hidden away in it,
you can't tell what's deadly and what's the cure.
But even there it's best to choose one teacher,
and swear by his every word.
In general, though, stick to words;
they'll lead you on through the Gate of Certainty
and into the Temple of Total Security.

STUDENT:

    But mustn't a word mean?
    Mustn't there be a concept behind it?

MEPHISTOPHELES:

    Of course, of course!
    But don't let that bother you overmuch.
    When the well of concepts runs dry,
    a word in the nick of time will bring on a deluge.
    Words will help you get up an excellent argument,
    devise a system, even. They're beautiful things,
    words are, matters of faith, you know,
    and they're not to be robbed of even an iota.

STUDENT:

    I'm sorry to plague you with all these questions,
    but there's one thing more.
    Tell me something about Medicine.
    Something pertinent. I'm certain you can.
    Three years is such a short time and, Lord!
    it's so vast a field.
    Just a hint from you could be a great help.

MEPHISTOPHELES: *(Aside.)*

    I've had it with this academic pose;
    it's time again for the devil to interpose.

    (Aloud.)

    Medicine, my boy, is an art easily grasped.
    You study the world,
    the great as well as the small,
    and end up letting it take its own sweet way,
    just as God intended in the first place.
    And don't waste time dabbling in sciences;
    it won't help.
    Each of us learns what he can.
    Just be certain you don't fritter away opportunity.
    Make the most of it.
    Seize it!

Then you'll be the man!
Then you'll be the clever one!
You're well built—well enough, at least—
you're not backward, not lacking in sense,
so trust yourself and others will trust you.

But above all else, learn to manage women!
Their eternal moaning and groaning,
their thousand pains and complaints,
so multifarious in their variety,
can be cured with a bit of pressure at the right point.
A soupçon of discretion,
and you'll have them eating out of your hand.

First, of course, it helps to be an M.D.;
it makes them assume your skill
and you win their confidence.
You'll have opened for you all the riches of the Orient,
luxurious gardens vast in number,
that ordinary men spend years trying to conquer.
No delay for you, though:
a fumble here, a fumble there,
you finger the merchandise.
You'll know just where to squeeze that little pulse,
then clasp her round her slender hips
to see how tightly she's laced.

STUDENT:

That's more like it!
At least you know what you're after.

MEPHISTOPHELES:

Dear friend, theory is a gray affair,
and the golden tree of life is green.

STUDENT:

It's all like a dream, I swear.
May I trouble you again,
and truly get to the bottom of your wisdom?

MEPHISTOPHELES:

　I'm glad to do what I can.

STUDENT:

　Would you mind?
　I really can't leave without you signing my album.
　It would mean a lot.

MEPHISTOPHELES:

　By all means.

　(He writes in the book and returns it.)

STUDENT: *(Reads.)*

　"Eritis sicut Deus, scientes bonum et malum."

　(He reverently closes the book and leaves.)

MEPHISTOPHELES:

　Follow my motto and my ancient old aunt the Serpent,
　and one day your likeness to God will be cause for alarm.

FAUST: *(Entering.)*

　Where do we go now?

MEPHISTOPHELES:

　Wherever you like.
　We'll tour the little world first,
　and then the great. Just think,
　you're auditing this course for free,
　and the pleasure you'll have
　you can't yet even imagine.

FAUST:

　But this beard! What to do with it!
　How do I appear sophisticated?
　It's certain to be a disaster.
　I don't adjust well to people, never have.
　I feel so small out in the world, so naked.
　I'll never be at my ease.

MEPHISTOPHELES:
>   Time will see to that, my friend.
>   Trust yourself and you'll be just fine.

FAUST:
>   But how do we leave here?
>   Where's the coach, the horses, the coachman?

MEPHISTOPHELES:
>   Just wait!
>   We'll simply spread out this cloak—
>   like so—
>   and fly through the air.
>   Remember,
>   this is no petty venture,
>   so go light on the luggage.
>   A little hot air, that I'll provide,
>   and off we go, flying high.
>   Once we're buoyant, away we'll soar.
>   Congratulations on your new career!

VIII ๛ AUERBACH'S WINE CELLAR IN LEIPZIG

A rowdy student drinking party well underway.

FROSCH:
>   Liven it up, men!
>   Why so glum? Bend an elbow,
>   for Chrisake! Set the place on fire,
>   you soggy noodles!

BRANDER:
>   Us! Hell! *You!*
>   You haven't shown us shit!
>   Where's that bag of tricks you're always touting,
>   you old fart! Show us something gross!

FROSCH: *(Pours a glass of wine over his head.)*
>   There! How's that? Two in one!

BRANDER:

And you're a double pig-assed swine!

FROSCH:

What you ask for is what you get!

SIEBEL:

Start a fight, you're out on your ass!
Come on! Sing! A round! Let's go!
Swill and shout, men! Hip-hip-hooray!

(Sings at the top of his voice.)

Yohoyohoyohooo!

ALTMAYER:

Stop! I can't take anymore!
Cotton! Where's the cotton!
You're splitting my goddamn ears!

SIEBEL:

Listen to that bass ring round the vault!

FROSCH:

You can't take a joke, there's always the door!

(Sings.)

With a do-re-me!

ALTMAYER: *(Sings.)*
And a la-di-da-di-do!

FROSCH:

Quiet! We're tuned! Let's go!

(Sings.)

Alas, our Holy Roman Empire,
How do we get her out of the mire?

BRANDER:

> Ah, miserable, a miserable song!
> Foul! Political! Claptrap! Phui!
> Pitiful, nasty, filthy song!
> Think yourselves lucky, lads,
> you don't have to worry your heads
> over the Roman Empire!
> Thank God I'm no emperor or chancellor.
> But we still need a man in charge.
> How about we elect a pope!
> And we all know what it takes to be that, don't we?
> A man who'll sit on high and snort and souse!

FROSCH: *(Sings.)*

> > Fly away, fly away,
> > Mistress on wings,
> > Take to my true love
> > My tenderest greetings!

SIEBEL:

> Not to *that* true love you won't!
> Not a chance! Try it and see!

FROSCH:

> And *you* try and stop me!
> With this I send her my love and kisses!

> *(Sings.)*

> > Unbolt the gate
> > In the stilly night!
> > Unbolt the gate,
> > My love awakes!
> > Bolt fast the gate
> > When fair dawn breaks!

SIEBEL:

> Go on! Sing!
> Sing yourself hoarse over the tart!

Praise her to the skies! Who cares?
I'll have the last laugh, at least.
She led me on the same as she'll lead you.
Oh, I wish her a randy goblin for a sweetheart,
who'll plow her field all night where two roads cross!
I wish her a goat to bleat her a fond goodnight
with a fart on his way home from the witches' jamboree!
A decent man of flesh and blood's
too good for that crusty bitch.
The only greeting she'll have from me
is a brick aimed straight at her window!

BRANDER: *(Pounding the table.)*

Gentlemen! Gentlemen! Your attention!
Order in the house, if you please!
Admit, gentlemen, I've an inside track
on patching things up: I know what's right.
Now! Here we have a pair of lovelorn losers,
and it's for me to send them off as friends.
All right, now, pay attention!
It's brand new,
and join in loud as you can at the chorus.

(Sings.)

> In a cellar once
> There lived a rat,
> A rat that ate nothing
> But lard and fat.
> So fat he grew
> That he had a pot
> As big as Doctor
> Luther's got.
> The cook spread poison
> Around one night,
> And that rat's world
> Closed in so tight,
> He thought he had love in his belly.

CHORUS: *(Shouting.)*
> He thought he had love in his belly!

BRANDER: *(Sings.)*
> He scampered in,
> He scampered out,
> He lapped up puddles
> With his fuzzy snout;
> He tore up the house,
> He gnawed at the door,
> He scratched and rolled
> Around on the floor.
> He hopped and pranced,
> His pain was so great,
> But it did him no good,
> Early or late.
> He thought he had love in his belly.

CHORUS: *(Shouting.)*
> He thought he had love in his belly!

BRANDER: *(Sings.)*
> In terror he ran straight
> Into the kitchen
> In the light of day,
> Twistin' and twitchin',
> And lay on the hearth,
> And started to shake,
> As if his little
> Rat's heart would break.
> The murderess rose up
> And started to gloat:
> "Ha, he's tuning
> His last note!
> As if he had love in his belly."

CHORUS: *(Shouting.)*
> As if he had love in his belly.

SIEBEL:

    Look at the louts!

    A noble art, I must say,

    poisoning rats, the poor devils!

BRANDER:

    Partial to them, are you?

ALTMAYER:

    Old beer gut with his shiny noggin's

    been beaten once too often;

    he sees his spitting image in a bloated rat.

(Enter FAUST and MEPHISTOPHELES.)

MEPHISTOPHELES:

    First I'll introduce you to some merry company.

    You'll see how easily life can be lived.

    Being students, these boys make every day a holiday.

    They may not be the brainiest,

    but they know the art of enjoyment,

    and each dances round in his own little circle,

    like a kitten chasing its tail just for the fun of it.

    As long as their credit's still good,

    and their hangover's not too fierce,

    they're happy as larks.

BRANDER:

    Those two over there?

    Travelers, I'd say. You can tell

    by their foreign ways.

    They haven't been in town an hour.

FROSCH:

    I suspect you're right.

    Here's one to Leipzig! Prost!

    A Paris in small, and refines us all.

SIEBEL:
>Who do you think they are, those strangers?

FROSCH:
>Leave it to me. A good tall drink and I'll have
>wormed out of them their darkest secret.
>My guess is they're nobles,
>what with their haughty discontent.

BRANDER:
>I think they're quacks.

ALTMAYER:
>Could be.

FROSCH:
>Watch me. I'll get it out of them.

MEPHISTOPHELES: *(To FAUST.)*
>These simpletons wouldn't recognize the Devil
>if he had them by the throat.

FAUST:
>Good evening, gentlemen!

SIEBEL:
>And the same to you, sirs!

>*(In an undertone, eyeing MEPHISTOPHELES askance.)*

>Look at that, would you?
>He limps with one foot.

MEPHISTOPHELES:
>May we join you?
>In place of a decent drink,
>which of course can't be had here,
>we'll at least enjoy your company.

ALTMAYER:
>My, aren't we particular!

FROSCH:

    You were late in leaving Rippach, I take it.

    Did you have dinner first with Signor Bumpkin?

MEPHISTOPHELES:

    No, we passed through without stopping.

    But we did speak last time.

    He asked if we'd give his best to his many

    Bumpkin cousins here in Leipzig.

    (He bows to FROSCH.)

ALTMAYER: *(In an undertone.)*

    See there? He's on to us!

SIEBEL:

    The crafty devil!

FROSCH:

    Just you wait. I'll get him yet.

MEPHISTOPHELES:

    Am I wrong, gentlemen,

    or did we hear in passing

    a well-trained chorus in song?

    A vaulted ceiling like this

    must make a wonderful echo.

FROSCH:

    Are you a virtuoso perhaps?

MEPHISTOPHELES:

    Oh, no, my talent's not much,

    though my liking is great.

ALTMAYER:

    Give us a song!

MEPHISTOPHELES:

    As many as you like.

SIEBEL:

> Just make it something new!

MEPHISTOPHELES:

> We've only recently returned from Spain,
> that lovely land of wine and song.

> *(Sings.)*
>> There once was a king
>> Who had a great flea—

FROSCH:

> Ah! Hear that! A flea!
> I find a flea's a fine kind of fellow!

MEPHISTOPHELES: *(Sings.)*

>> There once was a king
>> Who had a great flea,
>> He loved him so tender,
>> Like a son, loved he.
>> He called for his tailor,
>> Who came on the run:
>> "Make jacket and trousers,"
>> He said, "for my son!"

BRANDER:

> Just remind the tailor his head's on the block
> if the measurement's wrong or the trousers wrinkle!

MEPHISTOPHELES: *(Sings.)*

>> Sir Flea in satin and
>> Silk was now dressed,
>> With ribbons flowing
>> And a cross on his breast.
>> At once he was made
>> A Minister of State,
>> And all his flea kinsfolk,
>> Too, grew great.

But the lords and ladies of
Court started itching,
The Queen and her Ladies-in-
Waiting were bitching;
But nobody dared give those
Fine fleas a smack.
Let them come biting us,
We'll give them a crack.

CHORUS: *(Shouting.)*

Let them come biting us,
We'll give them a crack.

FROSCH:

Bravo! Bravo! Well done!

SIEBEL:

That should be the fate of every flea!

BRANDER:

You get them between your finger and thumb
and nip them nicely!

ALTMAYER:

Long live freedom!
Long live wine!

MEPHISTOPHELES:

I'd gladly drink a glass to freedom
if your wines weren't quite so—awful.

SIEBEL:

Let's hear no more of that!

MEPHISTOPHELES:

If the host didn't mind, I'd treat our worthy guests
with a marvelous something from our own fine cellar.

SIEBEL:
  Bring it on!
  I'll take the blame!

FROSCH:
  Give us a drink to remember
  and we'll praise you to the skies.
  Just be generous with the sample.
  I need a full mouth to make a judgment.

ALTMAYER: *(Softly.)*
  I was right. They're from the Rhine.

MEPHISTOPHELES:
  Anyone have an auger?

BRANDER:
  Auger? What for?
  You got your kegs outside?

ALTMAYER:
  There's a box of tools back there.

MEPHISTOPHELES: *(Takes the auger; to FROSCH.)*
  All right now, what's your wish?

FROSCH:
  I don't get it.
  You have different kinds?

MEPHISTOPHELES:
  Each gets his choice.

ALTMAYER: *(To FROSCH.)*
  Aha, you're already licking your lips!

FROSCH:
  All right, then, if I've a choice, I'll take Rhine.
  The Fatherland always delivers the best.

(MEPHISTOPHELES bores a hole in the table where FROSCH is sitting.)

MEPHISTOPHELES:
> I'll need wax for the stoppers.

ALTMAYER:
> Ah, another old conjuring trick!

MEPHISTOPHELES: *(To BRANDER.)*
> And you?

BRANDER:
> Champagne for me; and really sparkling,
> so it tickles my nose!

(MEPHISTOPHELES bores; in the meanwhile someone has made the stoppers and plugs the holes.)

BRANDER:
> Not everything good is from home;
> some good things come from afar.
> No good German can stand the French,
> but we don't mind drinking their wines.

SIEBEL: *(As MEPHISTOPHELES approaches his seat.)*
> I confess I don't like the dry stuff,
> so give me something really sweet.

MEPHISTOPHELES: *(Boring.)*
> Tokay's on the way!

ALTMAYER:
> Gentlemen! No! I've had enough!
> You're making fools of us!

MEPHISTOPHELES:
> No, no, gentlemen, come now!
> Come now!

With worthy guests like you,
that would be taking things too far.
Very well, then.
Now. Hurry! What can I serve you?

ALTMAYER:
Whatever you like!
Just don't waste time asking questions!

(After all the holes have bored and plugged.)

MEPHISTOPHELES: *(With strange gestures.)*
Wine grapes of the vine are born,
The billy-goat's head sprouts a double horn;
The wine is juicy, the vines are wood,
The wooden table gives wine as good.
Here's a truth for all that see;
Gaze into Nature's mystery.

Now pull the stoppers and enjoy yourselves!

(As they draw the stoppers wine flows into each one's glass.)

ALL:
O lovely fountain that flows for us all!

MEPHISTOPHELES:
Be careful you don't spill a drop!

(They drink repeatedly.)

ALL: *(Singing.)*
Things are about as
Good as can be,
We're like a whole pack of
Pigs on a spree!

MEPHISTOPHELES:
See that? How free they are?
They're lapping it up!

FAUST:

I think I'd like to leave now.

MEPHISTOPHELES:

No, stay! Another moment!
You'll see how splendidly swinish they can be!

(SIEBEL drinks carelessly, spilling the wine on the floor that turns into flame.)

SIEBEL:

Help! Fire! Help! Hell's on fire!

MEPHISTOPHELES: *(To the flame.)*
Peace, friendly element, down!

(To the DRINKERS.)

This time it was only a spark from Purgatory.

SIEBEL:

What's all this? Just you wait!
You'll pay! You'll pay dearly!
I dare say you don't know who you're dealing with!

FROSCH:

Don't try that again!

ALTMAYER:

Let's get rid of them on the sly.

SIEBEL:

How dare you, sir! How dare you play
your monkey shenanigans on us!

MEPHISTOPHELES:

Quiet, you old tub of lard!

SIEBEL:
>   And you, Signor Beanpole!
>   Insult us now, too, will you?

BRANDER:
>   I say we beat him to a pulp!

(ALTMAYER pulls a stopper and fire leaps out at him.)

ALTMAYER:
>   I'm burning!
>   I'm burning!

SIEBEL:
>   Sorcery!
>   Run him through!
>   He's outside the law!

(They draw knives and advance on MEPHISTOPHELES.)

MEPHISTOPHELES: *(With solemn gestures.)*
>   False sound,
>   Delude ear,
>   False sight,
>   Appear, appear,
>   Be there, be here!

(They stand astonished and look at each other.)

ALTMAYER:
>   Where am I?
>   What a lovely land!

FROSCH:
>   Vineyards!
>   Am I seeing right?

SIEBEL:
>   And grapes at my grasp!

BRANDER:
>   Here's a green arbor!
>   Look, what a vine!

(He seizes SIEBEL by the nose and the others with their raised knives do the same.)

MEPHISTOPHELES: *(With a solemn gesture.)*
>   Error, remove the blindfold from their sight!
>   And you, remember how the Devil jests.

(He disappears with FAUST. The others leap apart.)

SIEBEL:
>   What was that?

ALTMAYER:
>   What!

FROSCH:
>   Was that your nose?

BRANDER: *(To SIEBEL.)*
>   And look, here I'm holding yours!

ALTMAYER:
>   There was a shock! It went right through me!
>   Quick! A chair! I'm about to faint!

FROSCH:
>   No, what happened, tell me!

SIEBEL:
>   Where is he? Where's he gone? That bastard!
>   He won't get away from me alive!

ALTMAYER:
>   I saw him leave by the cellar door.
>   On a keg! He was riding it!
>   Ah! My feet! My feet are heavy as lead!

(Turning toward the table.)

Jesus! I wonder if the wine's still flowing!

SIEBEL:
  It was all a trick, a sham, a lie.

FROSCH:
  And yet I thought I was drinking wine.

BRANDER:
  And what was all that with the grapes?

ALTMAYER:
  And they say there's no such thing as miracles!

IX ⚡ WITCH'S KITCHEN

*A low hearth with a large cauldron over the fire. Various apparitions,
scorpions, salamanders, etc., are seen in the steam rising from it.
A FEMALE MONKEY sits beside the cauldron, skimming it, taking
care it doesn't boil over. A MALE MONKEY sits nearby with the young
ones, warming himself. Walls and ceiling are decorated with the strangest
implements of witchcraft. Enter FAUST and MEPHISTOPHELES.*

FAUST:
  I'm sick of it!
  Sick of this insane witchcraft!
  You promise me I'll recover in this chaotic madness.
  How?
  By begging for aid from some ancient hag's remedy?
  A filthy brew will take thirty years off my back?
  I pity myself if you can think of nothing better.
  No, I've already lost hope.
  Is there no natural way to this end?
  Has no noble mind discovered some healing balm?

MEPHISTOPHELES:

Ah! You see? You're talking sense again! Yes,
there *is* a natural means to recover youth,
but that's a chapter in another book,
and a very curious one at that, I may say.

FAUST:

Tell me! I insist.

MEPHISTOPHELES:

Good!
It calls for neither money, magic, nor medicine!
Get yourself out into a country field,
start hoeing,
start digging,
confine yourself and your thoughts
to a narrow sphere of reference,
eat the simple foods you raise,
live with your beasts of burden as a beast,
be proud to manure the fields with your own dung.
Believe me, there's no better way
to keep yourself young at eighty.

FAUST:

No, I could never do that.
I'm just not used to such things.
Dig with a spade?
I could never manage so narrow an existence.

MEPHISTOPHELES:

Well, then, the witch it will have to be.

FAUST:

But why the old hag?
Can't you brew it yourself?

MEPHISTOPHELES:

Oh, that would be a splendid pastime!
In the time it would take I could build a thousand bridges.

It isn't just science is needed,
but infinite patience.
A quiet spirit
nurses it year after year for ages,
for time alone
makes the subtle ferment potent.
And then there's all the marvelous things go in it.
True, the Devil taught her to make it,
and yet the Devil can't make it himself.

(He sees the MONKEYS.)

Now there's a petite crew!
That one's the maid,
and that the houseboy.

(To the MONKEYS.)

It seems your mistress is away.

MONKEYS:

> Out,
> Roundabout,
> Up the chimney spout!

MEPHISTOPHELES:
How long does she go gadding about?

MONKEYS:
Long as it takes to warm our paws.

MEPHISTOPHELES: *(To FAUST.)*
What do you think of our dainty menagerie?

FAUST:
I've never seen anything so gross.

MEPHISTOPHELES:
But little chats like this are great fun.

(To the MONKEYS.)

Tell me, you accursed creatures,
what are you stirring in that stew?

MONKEYS:
Watery soup for beggars.

MEPHISTOPHELES:
It's sure to go over well.

*(The MALE MONKEY comes over and fawns on
MEPHISTOPHELES.)*

MALE MONKEY:
Throw the dice, sir,
And so be nice, sir;
Things are vile,
So win me a pile.
To be rich in pence
Is to have sense.

MEPHISTOPHELES:
How lucky this monkey would think himself
if only he could play the lottery.

*(Meanwhile the YOUNG MONKEYS have been playing with a large
ball, which now they roll forward.)*

MALE MONKEY:
This is the world,
Forever twirled
Round and about.
It rings like glass,
And is, alas,
Hollow, no doubt,
And so it will shatter,
And will little matter
In the round and about.

Here it's bright,
There brighter to sight.
I'm alive! Watch out!
Take care, my boy!
This is no toy!
It's made of clay
And will crumble away!

MEPHISTOPHELES:
Why the sieve?

MALE MONKEY: *(Taking it down.)*
If you were a thief,
I could tell without grief.

*(He scampers over to the FEMALE MONKEY and makes
her look through it.)*

See through the sieve!
You know the thief well,
Though his name you won't tell!

MEPHISTOPHELES: *(Going to the fire.)*
And this pot?

BOTH MONKEYS:
The crack-brained sot
Knows not the pot,
Knows not the kettle!

MEPHISTOPHELES:
Discourteous beasts!

MALE MONKEY:
Here, take this whisk!
Sit down on the settle!

*(He makes MEPHISTOPHELES sit down. FAUST in the meantime
has been standing in front of a mirror, now approaching it, now
drawing back.)*

FAUST:

What is this vision?
What heavenly form do I see in this magic glass?
O Love, Love,
lend me your swiftest wings and
guide me to her,
lead me to her presence!
Ah, if I move from this spot,
if I dare to approach her by only a step,
it's as if I saw her only in a mist.
How beautiful,
how unspeakably beautiful!
Can woman be so lovely?
I see in this reclining figure
the quintessence of all the heavens.
Does earth have anything to show more fair?

MEPHISTOPHELES:

Of course!
When God slaves like a dog for six whole days
and then on the seventh cries *Bravo!*
there's got to be something mighty clever there!
But go on, don't let me stop you,
gaze away, look your fill for now.
I know just how to hunt down such a darling for you.
And happy the man lucky enough
to lead her home as his bride!

(FAUST continues to look in the mirror, as MEPHISTOPHELES stretches out in the chair, plays with the whisk, and continues talking.)

Here I sit like a king on his throne,
scepter in hand,
and all that's lacking is a crown.

(The MONKEYS, who have been performing all sorts of odd antics, bring a crown to MEPHISTOPHELES with a great outcry.)

MONKEYS:

Oh, be so good, sir,

With sweat and blood, sir,
The crown to belime.

(They handle the crown so clumsily that it breaks into two pieces, which they then scamper about with.)

It's done! He-he!
We speak and we see,
We hear and we rhyme—

FAUST: *(Looking into the mirror.)*
Aiii! I think I'm going mad!

MEPHISTOPHELES: *(Pointing to the MONKEYS.)*
Now even *my* head's beginning to reel.

MONKEYS:
And if the rhymes fit,
We've made a lucky hit,
And there's a thought in it!

FAUST: *(Still looking in the mirror.)*
My heart's on fire!
Let's leave here! Quick!

MEPHISTOPHELES: *(In the same posture as earlier.)*
Let's admit first, though,
that some poets are honest.

(The cauldron that the FEMALE MONKEY has failed to watch begins to boil over and a great flame leaps out and shoots up the chimney and down comes the WITCH through the flame with a horrible shriek.)

WITCH:
Ow! Ow! Ow! Ow!
Damn you! Damn you!
Blasted bitch!
You forgot the kettle
And burned the Witch!

(Seeing FAUST and MEPHISTOPHELES.)

> What do I see here?
> Who may you be here?
> What do you seek here?
> How did you sneak here?
> May fire pangs fierce
> Your marrow pierce!

(Dipping the ladle in the cauldron she sprays flames out at FAUST, MEPHISTOPHELES, and the MONKEYS. The MONKEYS whine and whimper. Reversing the whisk in his hand, MEPHISTOPHELES lashes out smashing pots and glassware.)

MEPHISTOPHELES:

> In two! In two!
> There lies your stew!
> There lies your glass!
> A joke, my lass!
> A bright tattoo
> To your tune, foul shrew!

(The WITCH recoils in rage and horror.)

MEPHISTOPHELES:

> Do you recognize me now, old bag of bones?
> Abomination!
> Do you recognize your lord and master?
> Why don't I just lash out and crush
> you and your monkey brood?
> Have you so little respect for this scarlet doublet?
> Is this cock's feather unknown to you?
> Have I come in disguise?
> Or perhaps you'd like me to introduce myself!

WITCH:

> O master, forgive my rude reception!
> But I don't see your horse's hoof?
> And your two ravens! Where are they?

MEPHISTOPHELES:

>All right, then, well, this once I'll let you off.
>I admit, it's been a while since last we met.
>Besides, civilization is on the warpath,
>tidying up here and there and everywhere.
>It's even got as far as the Devil.
>And as for that Nordic phantom we're used to,
>he's gone, vanished, a thing of the past.
>No more horns, no more claws,
>no tapering tail that ends in a dart.
>And the foot, my cloven foot,
>which I really can't do without,
>how would I ever explain it in social circles?
>And so, you see, like many a young buck,
>I've indulged in false calves for quite a few years now.

WITCH: *(Dancing.)*

>Ah, I'm near to losing my mind
>to see Squire Satan back in town!

MEPHISTOPHELES:

>Woman, don't use that name to me!

WITCH:

>But why? Why not? What's wrong with it?

MEPHISTOPHELES:

>It's been demoted—to fairy tale status.
>A scary something to frighten the children with.
>But humans are no better off.
>They're rid of the Evil One,
>but evil ones are still among them.
>So call me *Baron,* that will do nicely.
>A cavalier like all the others.
>And if there's any doubt about my noble birth,
>here's my coat-of-arms.

(He flips a finger.)

WITCH: *(Laughing immoderately.)*
    Hahaaaaaa!
    Just like you!
    Once a rogue, always a rogue!
    You rascal!

MEPHISTOPHELES: *(To FAUST.)*
    Friend, I hope this teaches you something.
    How to get along with witches.

WITCH:
    Very well, gentlemen, what can I do for you?

MEPHISTOPHELES:
    A generous glass of your fabled liquor.
    And be certain it's the oldest you've got.
    The older it is, the greater its power.

WITCH:
    Gladly.
    Now, here's a bottle, a fine brew,
    I nip at it myself from time to time—
    so old it's lost whatever stink it had.
    Yes, I'm happy to give you a small glass.

    (Aside to MEPHISTOPHELES.)

    You realize that if he drinks this unprepared,
    he won't live an hour.

MEPHISTOPHELES:
    He's a friend, it will do him good,
    so give him your best.
    Draw your circle now,
    speak your spells,
    and give him a full cup.

    *(Making curious gestures, the WITCH draws a circle and puts
    strange and wondrous things inside it; meanwhile the glasses begin*

to ring and the kettle to sound, making music. In conclusion she brings a large volume and arranges the MONKEYS in the circle to serve as a lectern and to hold the torches. She beckons FAUST to approach her.)

FAUST: *(To MEPHISTOPHELES.)*
    What's the meaning of this?
    What good will it do?
    I've seen this all before,
    the insane apparatus,
    the idiotic gestures,
    the nauseating absurdity of it all!
    It's a fraud! I despise it!
    I despise it to my heart's core!

MEPHISTOPHELES:
    Well, of course, it's nonsense!
    Relax, it's a joke, can't you see that?
    She's a doctor, after all;
    she needs the hocus-pocus to make it work.

(He forces FAUST into the circle.)

WITCH: *(After all the holes are bored and plugged.)*
                    Hear me and see!
                    Out of one make ten,
                    Let two go, then
                    Make an even three,
                    And you'll be rich.
                    Since four won't mix,
                    Out of five and six,
                    So says the witch,
                    Make seven and eight.
                    And then it's straight.
                    And nine is one,
                    And ten is none,
                    And there's the witch's
                    One-times-one.

FAUST:
    I suspect the old crone's having a fit.

MEPHISTOPHELES:
> You haven't heard the half of it yet.
> There's more.
> I know it backwards and forwards,
> it's all like that.
> Ah, the time it's cost me!
> A waste!
> A perfect contradiction, you see,
> the totally nonsensical is as deep a mystery
> to wise men as to fools.
> It's a game, my friend,
> a game they've made an art,
> as old as it is new.
> Its purpose is always to spread lies instead of truth,
> all by proclaiming the Three-in-One and
> One-in-Three. It's a safe choice.
> You can chatter and teach in the same breath,
> and no one to bother you.
> Who wants to waste his time on fools?
> Besides, people hear words,
> and what's their first thought?
> That behind every word there must be sense.

WITCH: *(Continuing.)*
> > The lofty light
> > Of science's might
> > From all the world is hidden!
> > Refuse to think,
> > It comes in a wink,
> > It flies on wings unbidden!

FAUST:
> What's this drivel she's babbling at us?
> My head's about to split. It's like hearing
> a hundred thousand fools in chorus.

MEPHISTOPHELES:
> Enough, enough, excellent sibyl!
> Bring on your potion and be sure to fill the cup full.

The drink won't harm him; we're friends;
and he's a man of many degrees of imbibing,
a man who's taken many a healthy swallow.

*(With considerable ceremony, the WITCH pours the potion into a bowl,
and as FAUST brings it to his lips a faint flame rises from it.)*

MEPHISTOPHELES:
All the way now!
Do it, down we go!
There! It'll do your heart good.
You claim to be friends with the Devil,
and you're afraid of a little fire?

(The WITCH breaks the circle. FAUST steps out.)

Quickly now!
Let's go!
You mustn't rest.

WITCH:
May that little swallow do you much good!

MEPHISTOPHELES: *(To the WITCH.)*
If ever I can do you a favor,
mention it to me some Walpurgis Night.

WITCH: *(Handing FAUST a song on a broadsheet.)*
Here's a song you might enjoy singing, sir.
For when you do,
you'll notice a certain tingling here and there.

MEPHISTOPHELES: *(To FAUST.)*
Hurry now, come with me! You must
work up a sweat so the potion's force will
work on you inside and out. I'll teach you then
to treasure the life of noble idleness,
and soon you'll feel the deep delight of Cupid
stirring and leaping in you every which way!

FAUST:

Yes, but just one more glance in the glass.
That woman's image was too beautiful for words!

MEPHISTOPHELES:

No, no! You'll see her soon in the flesh,
that paragon of all earthly beauty.

(Aside.)

With that swill in his belly,
every housewife will look a Helen to him.

X ☞ STREET

FAUST advances on GRETCHEN as she passes by.

FAUST:

Lovely lady,
may I offer you my arm
and be your escort?

GRETCHEN:

I'm neither lovely nor a lady.
And I can get home without your help, thank you.

(She disengages herself and goes out.)

FAUST:

Great Heaven, what a beautiful child!
I've never seen anything like her.
Modest, virtuous, unspoiled,
but not without some snap in her, too.
The red of her lips, her cheeks' glow—
can I ever forget them?
And the way she cast down her eyes
stirred me to the core.
And the way she cut me short!
Enchanting!

(Enter MEPHISTOPHELES.)

Listen, I want you to get me that girl!

MEPHISTOPHELES:
  Girl? Which girl?

FAUST:
  She just passed by.

MEPHISTOPHELES:
  Oh, her! Yes, well, I mean,
  she's just come from confession, you know.
  The priest absolved her of her sins,
  every last one, no less.
  I crept up close to hear and, well—
  she's an innocent, a young thing
  with nothing to confess.
  How could I have power over *her?*

FAUST:
  She's over fourteen, isn't she?

MEPHISTOPHELES:
  Ah! There!
  The down-and-dirty libertine speaks!
  Your kind believes every blossom
  blows for him alone; you flatter yourself
  that there's no honor or favor
  that isn't yours for the reaping.
  It's just that things don't always fall out that way.

FAUST:
  I suggest to *you,* Most Mighty Master Moralist,
  that you come down off your pulpit
  and spare me your sermons.
  And let me be brief and to the point. Either
  that sweet lovely thing is in my arms tonight,
  or at midnight you and I are quits.

MEPHISTOPHELES:

>And I suggest *you* try using your head for a change!
>I need two weeks at minimum to sniff out opportunities.

FAUST:

>Give me seven hours free
>and I assure you I'd need no Devil
>to help me seduce that little creature.

MEPHISTOPHELES:

>Ah, you almost sounded like a lascivious Frenchman!
>Just don't let it get the better of you.
>Why rush into pleasure like any fool?
>You need to work it,
>this way, that way,
>knead your little puppet into shape,
>work her up with all sorts of wonderful nonsense,
>get her going—
>that's when pleasure comes like a flood,
>as in the tales those randy Italians tell.

FAUST:

>I have appetite enough without all that.

MEPHISTOPHELES:

>All right, let me give it to you bluntly.
>This little beauty of yours can't be rushed;
>you don't take her kind by storm.
>So what do we do?
>We use our wits.
>We stoop, as they say, to strategy.

FAUST:

>Get me something of hers, that angelic creature!
>Take me to her room!
>Bring me the kerchief she wears at her breast,
>a garter to excite my passion!

MEPHISTOPHELES:

>To prove how well I serve your anguish,

we'll waste not another moment.
This very day I'll take you to her room.

FAUST:
Will I see her?
Will I have her?

MEPHISTOPHELES:
No! She'll be at a neighbor's.
Meanwhile, all alone, you can
bathe yourself in the aura of her fragrance,
and feast on the promise of future joys.

FAUST:
Can we go now?

MEPHISTOPHELES:
It's still too soon.

FAUST:
Then find me some present to give her.

(Exit.)

MEPHISTOPHELES:
Presents? So soon?
Ah, well, that's my boy!
He'll succeed, no question about it! Besides,
I know the location of many a buried treasure.
Now for a bit of reconnoitering.

XI 🖝 EVENING

A neat, well-kept little room.
GRETCHEN braiding and binding up her hair.

GRETCHEN:
Hm.

I wonder who that gentleman was today.
I'd give a lot to know, I would.
He looked such a valiant sort;
I'm certain he's of noble blood.
You could see it in his face.
Otherwise he'd never have been so bold.

(*She goes out. FAUST and MEPHISTOPHELES enter.*)

MEPHISTOPHELES:
Come in, come, just do it quietly!

FAUST: (*After some moments of silence.*)
I beg of you, please, leave me alone here!

MEPHISTOPHELES: (*Snooping about.*)
Not all girls keep their room this tidy.

(*Exit.*)

FAUST: (*Looking around.*)
Welcome, sweet twilight,
hovering in this holy sanctuary!
Seize on my heart, sweet pain of love,
you that live and languish on the dews of hope!
About me here I feel the breath of peace,
of order, contentment.
What fullness I sense in this poverty!
What blessèdness in this narrow prison!

Dear girl,
I feel your spirit of order and abundance
murmuring around me in the air,
the spirit that, like a mother, instructs you daily
to spread the clean cloth on the table and
strew the sand in patterns on the floor.

Dear hand, dear heavenly hand!
You've turned this lowly cottage into a paradise.

And here!

(He lifts one of the bed curtains.)

What a shiver of joy comes over me!
I could linger here for hours.

It was here, blessèd Nature,
that in gentle dreams you
formed her into the angel she was born to be.
Here lay the child,
the warmth of life filling her tender body,
and here, by God's pure and holy weaving,
the image of divinity took form.

But *you!*
What brings *you* here?
How deeply my soul is stirred!
What do you want?
Why is your heart so heavy?
Poor Faust, I no longer know you.
Am I the prisoner of some magic fragrance?
I came here driven by lust for immediate pleasure,
and now feel myself dissolved in a dream of love.
Are we the prey of every breath of air?
If she were to enter at this instant,
how you would suffer for your offense!
The swollen braggart, so petty now,
would lie here, melting, at her feet.

MEPHISTOPHELES: *(Entering.)*
    Quick!
    I see her coming down below!

FAUST:
    Away! Away!
    I'll never come again!

MEPHISTOPHELES:

    Here's a small casket I picked up for you—
    rather weighty, I'd say—
    just don't ask where.
    Put it there in the clothespress. She'll see it
    and go out of her mind with joy.
    I've put in certain trinkets that would
    win a woman of quite another stamp.
    But, then, a girl's a girl,
    and a game is always a game.

FAUST:

    Should I? I don't know—

MEPHISTOPHELES:

    Now what's the trouble?
    Or perhaps you mean to keep it yourself?
    In which case, I advise Your Greediness
    not to waste the lovely light of day,
    not to mention my time.
    Oh, I do hope you're not a miser.
    I rack my brains, I work my fingers to the bone—

(He places the casket in the clothespress and locks it again.)

    All right, let's go! Now!—
    all for the sake of winning this sweet young thing
    to bend to your every wish;
    and *you* stand there gloomy faced
    as if you'd just entered the lecture hall
    and seen there in all their drab reality
    Physics and Metaphysics
    staring you in the face!
    Let's go!

(Exeunt.)

GRETCHEN: *(Enters with a lamp.)*

    How close and stuffy it is in here.

(She opens the window.)

And yet it's not all that warm outside.
I feel so—I don't know—
I wish mother would come home.
I'm shivering head to toe.
What a foolish, frightened thing I am.

(She sings while undressing.)

> There was a king in Thulë
> Faithful to the grave,
> To whom his dying sweetheart
> A golden goblet gave.
>
> At every bout he drained it,
> It was his fondest prize;
> And every time he drank from it
> Tears sprang to his eyes.
>
> And then when Death came calling,
> He tallied his towns and his lands,
> Bequeathing them to his loved ones,
> All but the cup in his hands.
>
> He sat at feast with his vassals
> In his castle by the sea,
> In the great hall of his forebears,
> For their last revelry.
>
> The old man stood there draining
> His life's last sunset glow;
> And tossed that holy goblet
> Into the sea below.
>
> He saw it fall and founder
> And sink down deep in the sea.
> His eyelids closed and thereafter
> Not another drop drank he.

(She opens the clothespress to put in her clothes and sees the casket of jewels.)

How did this pretty box get in here?
I'm certain I locked the press.
How strange!
What could be in it, I wonder?
Perhaps someone left it as a pledge
and mother made a loan on it.

Here's a small key on a ribbon.
I think I'll open it.

What's this?
Dear God in Heaven! Look!
I've never seen the like in all my life!
Jewels!
Why, these are things a woman of the nobility
could wear on the highest holidays.

I wonder how this necklace would look on me?
Who could possibly own such splendors?

(She puts on the necklace and looks in the mirror.)

If only just the earrings were mine!

Goodness, what a difference it makes!
What good are youth and beauty?
It's all very fine if you have them,
but even so, who really cares?
People praise you half in pity.
It's gold that counts,
money that matters.

And then there's us poor people!

XII ✒ PROMENADE

FAUST walking up and down in meditation.
MEPHISTOPHELES joins him.

MEPHISTOPHELES:

By love scorned!
By the fires of Hell! Ah,
if only I knew something worse to curse by!

FAUST:

What is it? What's eating you?
I've never seen such a face!

MEPHISTOPHELES:

If I weren't the Devil myself,
I'd say "Devil take me!"

FAUST:

Have you lost your mind?
On second thought, it suits you!
A raving lunatic!

MEPHISTOPHELES:

Imagine!
Those jewels I got for Gretchen?
Some priest's just come along and snapped them up!
No sooner her mother's eye spies them,
she goes all jittery with some secret horror.
Some nose that woman's got!
Always sniffing her prayer book.
One whiff
and she knows if something's holy or unholy.
She knew on the spot
there wasn't much blessing in those jewels.

"Child," cries she, "ill-gotten goods
ensnares the soul and corrupts the flesh.
We'll offer these up to God's own Mother,
and she'll shower down manna from Heaven on us."

Our little Gretchen pulls a long face, and thinks:

"It's a gift horse, after all;
and how can the man nice enough to bring it,
whoever he is, be bad?"

So off her mother sends for one of those priests,
and no sooner he understands the joke
and likes what he sees, he says:

"That's the spirit!" he says.
"Who conquers his greed wins big.
The church has a marvelous digestion:
it's gobbled up whole countries,
and never been glutted.
The church alone, dear ladies,
can digest ill-gotten goods."

FAUST:

Nothing new there;
a king can do it the same as any Jew.

MEPHISTOPHELES:

With that,
he pockets the necklace, brooches, and rings
as if they were so many mushrooms,
thanking them neither more nor less
than if he'd pocketed a bag of nuts.
Promising them their reward in Heaven,
he left then feeling edified.

FAUST:

And Gretchen?

MEPHISTOPHELES:

She sits there restless,
not knowing what to do or how,
thinking day and night of the jewels,
but even more about him who brought them.

FAUST:

>I can't bear to know my darling's sad.
>Get her another set at once!
>The first wasn't worth much, anyway.

MEPHISTOPHELES:

>Yes, of course!
>You think this is all just child's play!

FAUST:

>Go on! Do as I say!
>And get something going with that neighbor of hers.
>Damn you, get a move on!
>And bring me a new set of jewels!

MEPHISTOPHELES: *(Ironically.)*

>Whatever you say, Your Lordship!
>With all my heart!

(Exit FAUST.)

>It's lovesick fools like this
>who'd puff out sun, moon, and stars,
>only to amuse their lady loves!

(Exit.)

XIII ⚹ THE NEIGHBOR'S HOUSE

MARTHA:

>God forgive him, that dear husband of mine—
>but he really didn't do right by me.
>Off he goes into the wide world,
>leaving me to fend for myself.
>And why?
>I never gave him cause.
>God knows I loved him so.

(She weeps.)

Who knows, he may be dead!
Oh, dear!
If only I had a death certificate.

GRETCHEN: *(Entering.)*
Martha!

MARTHA:
What is it, Gretchen dear?

GRETCHEN:
My knees are shaking so, I can't stand!
I found another, in the clothespress,
another casket, this one of ebony,
and filled with such beautiful things,
far grander than the first.

MARTHA:
Not a word to your mother, hear?
She'd only give it to the priest again.

GRETCHEN:
Look at them!
Oh, just look!

MARTHA: *(Putting them on her.)*
Oh, you lucky, lucky thing, you!

GRETCHEN:
I wouldn't dare wear them on the street.
Nor in church, either.
Oh, what a pity!

MARTHA:
You can come here often as you please,
bring them with you and wear them in secret.
You'll stroll up and down in front of the mirror
for an hour or so,
and won't we be happy!
And finally there'll come a holiday

and you can show them off, one at a time,
first a necklace,
then a pearl earring,
and your mother will never notice,
and if she does, we'll think up something.

GRETCHEN:
But who? Who in the world could have
brought them? Both of them?
There's something just not right about it!

(A knock at the door.)

Dear God, don't let it be my mother!

MARTHA: *(Peeking through the curtains.)*
It's a strange gentleman.
Come in!

MEPHISTOPHELES: *(Entering.)*
Do excuse me, ladies, for barging in like this!

(He steps back deferentially at the sight of GRETCHEN.)

I've come to see Frau Martha Schwerdtlein.

MARTHA:
Why, that would be me.
What did you want?

MEPHISTOPHELES: *(Aside to her.)*
It's enough for now that I know you.
And I see you have a distinguished visitor.
Do pardon me the liberty,
I'll return this afternoon.

MARTHA: *(Aloud.)*
Oh, dear child, of all things!
The gentleman thinks you're a lady of rank!

GRETCHEN:

    Oh, but, sir,
    I'm nothing but a poor young girl.
    You're far too kind.
    Besides,
    the jewels and things aren't mine.

MEPHISTOPHELES:

    No, it's not only the jewels are splendid.
    There's an air about you,
    a look in the eye.
    I'm delighted to be able to stay.

MARTHA:

    But tell me, what brings you?
    I very much want—

MEPHISTOPHELES:

    I wish I had happier news,
    and I trust you won't hold it against me.
    But your husband's dead,
    and he sends you his best.

MARTHA:

    Dead? He's dead?
    Oh, that poor faithful soul!
    O God! My husband's dead!
    Let me die!

GRETCHEN:

    Dear, dear Martha, don't despair!

MEPHISTOPHELES:

    Listen, then.
    I'll tell you the whole mournful tale.

GRETCHEN:

    I hope I never love, ever;
    such a loss would kill me.

MEPHISTOPHELES:

> Joy must have sorrow, and sorrow joy.

MARTHA:

> Tell me about his life's end.

MEPHISTOPHELES:

> His grave is in Padua, by St. Anthony's Church.
> He lies there, forever cool, in holy ground.

MARTHA:

> Is this all you've brought me?

MEPHISTOPHELES:

> Ah, yes, right, a request, and a grave one, at that!
> You're to have three hundred masses sung!
> Except for that, my pockets are bare.

MARTHA:

> What! No lucky coin? No jewel?
> Every journeyman has something he'd sooner
> starve or die for than part with!
> Some keepsake?

MEPHISTOPHELES:

> Dear madam, I'm heartily sorry;
> I am, indeed;
> but he didn't fritter his money away, believe me!
> He repented his sins, to the very last one,
> and even more, bewailed his wretched luck.

GRETCHEN:

> How terrible to have such misfortunes.
> I'll pray many a Requiem for him, I promise.

MEPHISTOPHELES:

> A sweet and gentle girl like you
> deserves a husband without delay.

GRETCHEN:

    No, it's much too soon for that.

MEPHISTOPHELES:

    If not a husband, a lover, then.
    To hold such a man in your arms
    is Heaven's greatest gift.

GRETCHEN:

    That's not the custom around here.

MEPHISTOPHELES:

    Custom or not, it happens all the same.

MARTHA:

    Tell me more!

MEPHISTOPHELES:

    I stood beside his deathbed. Half-rotten straw,
    but at least better than a bed of manure.
    He also died Christian, knowing he deserved worse.
    "I hate myself, " he cried, "from the depths of my soul!
    How could I forsake my trade like that,
    how forsake my wife?
    The thought of it is killing me.
    If only she'd forgive me in this life!"

MARTHA: *(Weeping.)*

    Oh, the poor dear man!
    I forgave him long ago.

MEPHISTOPHELES:

    "And yet, God knows,
    she was more to blame than me!"

MARTHA:

    That's a lie! The liar!
    To lie like that on the brink of the grave!

MEPHISTOPHELES:

    If I'm any judge of such things,
    his mind wandered wildly as he gasped his last.
    "I never had time to kill," said he;
    "first to get children for her,
    and then bread for them all—
    bread in the very broadest sense—and then
    not have time to eat my share in peace."

MARTHA:

    He forgot, did he, my loyalty to him, my love,
    slaving away for him day and night?

MEPHISTOPHELES:

    Not so, no, never, he thought of you fondly.
    Said he: "When I sailed out from Malta,
    I prayed hard for wife and children;
    and then Heaven blessed us:
    we captured a Turkish vessel that had in its hold
    a treasure of great Sultan himself.
    Bravery's reward then came due,
    and I got my share."

MARTHA:

    What's that?
    What? Where?
    Did he bury it?

MEPHISTOPHELES:

    Who knows where the four winds have blown it?
    One day as he strolled through Naples,
    a lovely young miss took him to her heart.
    She showed him so much love and loyalty
    that he felt it till the day he died.

MARTHA:

    Oh! The scoundrel! The wretch!
    Stealing from his own children, he did!
    No misery, no poverty
    could check his scandalous life!

MEPHISTOPHELES:
Yes! Well! But just think!
It killed him off!
Now, if I were in your shoes,
I'd spend the next year decently mourning,
and in the meantime shop around
for a replacement sweetheart.

MARTHA:
God knows, I'll never find another like my first!
What a sweet little fool that rascal was.
He was just too fond of foreign ports,
of foreign wines, *and* foreign women,
and then those blasted dice.

MEPHISTOPHELES:
Yes, well, how nice it might have been
if he'd overlooked as many peccadilloes
in you as you did in him.
With that as a condition, madam,
I wouldn't mind taking you on myself.

MARTHA:
Oh, sir, how you do jest!

MEPHISTOPHELES: *(Aside.)*
I'd best get out of here before it's too late!
She'd hold even the Devil to his word.

(To GRETCHEN.)

And how are things with your heart, dear?

GRETCHEN:
What do you mean, sir?

MEPHISTOPHELES: *(Aside.)*
Sweet innocent child!

(Aloud.)

Good-bye, ladies!

GRETCHEN:
   Good-bye!

MARTHA:
   Oh, but one thing more, sir!
   Tell me, won't you? Quickly?
   Is there a witness to when, where and how
   my poor darling died,
   and where he was buried?
   I'm an organized person, you see;
   I so like order.
   And I *would* like to read the account
   in the weekly journal.

MEPHISTOPHELES:
   Of course, good woman!
   The truth demands two witnesses.
   I have an excellent companion
   I'll take to the judge for you,
   then bring him here.

MARTHA:
   Oh, yes, please do!

MEPHISTOPHELES:
   And the young lady?
   Will she be here, too?
   He's a fine young man! Well traveled,
   and shows every politeness to young ladies.

GRETCHEN:
   I'd blush just to meet him.

MEPHISTOPHELES:
   Blush?
   No king could make *you* blush, dear child.

MARTHA:

This evening, then, in the garden behind the house.

XIV ✒ A STREET

FAUST.
MEPHISTOPHELES.

FAUST:

How's it going?
You getting anywhere?
How much longer will it be?

MEPHISTOPHELES:

Ah, bravo! All on fire, are we?
She'll be yours in just a bit.
You'll see her this evening at neighbor Martha's.
If ever a woman was born to be a Gypsy bawd,
she's it!

FAUST:

Fine!

MEPHISTOPHELES:

She'll expect a small favor of us, though.

FAUST:

One good turn deserves another.

MEPHISTOPHELES:

We're to swear a deposition that her husband's bones
rest in consecrated ground.
Ah, in Padua, yes!

FAUST:

Very clever!
Except that first we'll have to go there!

MEPHISTOPHELES:

>*Sancta simplicitas!*
>Who cares?
>Sign it and you're done with it.

FAUST:

>If this is the way you operate,
>your scheme's as well as done itself in.

MEPHISTOPHELES:

>Ah, the sanctity of the man!
>It's you all over!
>It's the first time, is it,
>you've borne false witness?
>You haven't, I suppose,
>with your oh so great and mighty powers,
>propounded definitions of God and the world
>and the forces that move it at its inmost core,
>of man and man's heart,
>man's head and soul,
>and what goes on there?
>Done so, I dare say,
>without a qualm or a blush?
>And yet, if you looked
>deep and hard in your own soul
>you'd have to confess you knew as much about that
>as you know of Schwerdtlein's death.

FAUST:

>Sophist and liar you are and always will be!

MEPHISTOPHELES:

>Yes, well; at least I won't be lonely.
>For tomorrow, in all sincerity,
>you'll be proving our little Gretchen a fool
>with vows of love and other such nonsense.

FAUST:

>Yes, and with all my heart!

MEPHISTOPHELES:
>All very fine, I'm sure!
>Undying faith and eternal love will come next?
>And then incomparable and all-consuming passion!
>Will that, as well, be from your heart?

FAUST:
>Stop it!
>It will! It will! Yes!
>When I *feel*,
>when I sense this frenzy in me,
>and try to find a name for it and cannot,
>when I rove the world with all my senses,
>seeking the most exalted words to express it,
>and call this blaze burning inside me infinite,
>eternal—eternal—
>is this no more than a devilish game of lies?

MEPHISTOPHELES:
>And still I'm right!

FAUST:
>Listen!
>And remember this, I beg you,
>and spare my lungs:
>A man who insists on being right,
>and still has a tongue,
>that man is right.
>
>But come, I'm sick of talking.
>And you're right
>Do I have a choice?

XV ↝ GARDEN

GRETCHEN on FAUST'S arm.
MARTHA with MEPHISTOPHELES walking back and forth.

GRETCHEN:

    I feel you're only sparing me, sir;
    that you're being considerate
    so as not to embarrass me.
    Travelers are very good in that way;
    they make the best of it just out of kindness.
    I know that my poor chatter
    could never amuse a man of your experience.

FAUST:

    One look, one word from you means more to me
    than all the wisdom of the world.

    (He kisses her hand.)

GRETCHEN:

    Oh, you mustn't put yourself out!
    No!
    How could you even want to kiss it?
    A hand so rough and ugly!
    When I think of all the work it's done!
    My mother's much too particular.

    (They walk on.)

MARTHA:

    And you, sir, are you always on the go?

MEPHISTOPHELES:

    Yes, business, duty!
    Hard taskmasters, you know.
    It's with no great pleasure we leave certain places.
    And yet, there's no other way.

MARTHA:

    It's all very well when you're young and eager
    to wander the world and take it for all it's worth;
    but let the sour years come,
    and what choice is there but to drag on to the grave,

a bachelor—
and what good has that done anyone?

MEPHISTOPHELES:
It makes me shudder.

MARTHA:
In that case, sir, consider before it's too late.

(They walk on.)

GRETCHEN:
Yes, out of sight is out of mind.
But courtesy comes easily to you.
You have many friends much more clever than I—

FAUST:
No, my dear, what the world calls clever
is often nothing more than
vanity and narrow-mindedness.

GRETCHEN:
I don't understand.

FAUST:
How is it that simplicity, that innocence,
never recognize their sacred worth?
That meekness and humility,
loving, bountiful Nature's greatest gifts should—

GRETCHEN:
If only you'll think of me for one brief moment,
I will have time enough to think of you.

FAUST:
I take it you're often alone.

GRETCHEN:
Yes. And even though our household's

small, it still needs tending.
We have no household help,
and so I cook and sweep,
knit and sew,
and run errands—
I'm always on my feet—
and mother *will* be so strict about just everything!
Not that we have to be, you know,
we could be freer with money than most.
My father left us a tidy sum,
and a cottage and garden just outside town.
But I live mainly a quiet life now.
My brother's a soldier,
my little sister's dead.
I had some difficult times with her,
but I'd gladly live them all over again,
I loved her so.

FAUST:

She must have been an angel if she was like you.

GRETCHEN:

I brought her up myself.
Oh, she loved me so!
She was born after my father died.
We gave up mother for lost,
she was so badly off. But then,
little by little she began to come round.
Still, of course, she couldn't dream of
nursing the poor thing, she was so weak,
so I made do feeding it with milk and water,
and that's how she came to be mine.
And so she grew big,
in my arms, on my lap,
squirming, kicking, smiling.

FAUST:

That must have been the sheerest happiness for you.

GRETCHEN:

> Yes, but many bad hours, too.
> The cradle was beside my bed at night,
> and every time she moved I woke,
> one time to give her a drink,
> another to take her in beside me,
> and when she wouldn't stop crying I'd
> dandle her, walking back and forth,
> and the next morning, bright and early,
> I'd be at the washtub—
> after which came marketing and cooking.
> And so it went, day in, day out,
> every day no different from the one before.
> Life was no bed of roses,
> but your food tastes all the better,
> and rest is sweeter, too.

> *(They walk on.)*

MARTHA:

> Women are in a bad way, poor things;
> it's no easy task converting a confirmed bachelor.

MEPHISTOPHELES:

> It would take only one of you to convert me, madam.

MARTHA:

> Come now, admit it, sir:
> haven't you found anyone?
> Has your heart never found a haven?

MEPHISTOPHELES:

> As the proverb has it:
> "A man's hearth and a good woman
> are worth their weight in pearls and gold."

MARTHA:

> I mean: Have you never felt the urge?

MEPHISTOPHELES:

>I've always been treated with the greatest courtesy.

MARTHA:

>What I'm trying to say is:
>Have you never thought seriously—

MEPHISTOPHELES:

>It never pays to trifle with women.

MARTHA:

>Oh, why can't you understand!

MEPHISTOPHELES:

>For that I'm terribly sorry!
>But I do understand—
>you are kindness itself.

>*(They walk on.)*

FAUST:

>Did you know me again, little angel,
>the moment I entered the garden?

GRETCHEN:

>Didn't you notice?
>I lowered my eyes.

FAUST:

>And you forgive me the liberty I took,
>my impudence,
>that day you came from the cathedral?

GRETCHEN:

>I was confused—
>it came as a shock.
>No one had ever had anything
>bad to say about me.
>I began asking myself if I'd

done something immodest,
something unbecoming.
It seemed you'd acted with no hesitation,
as if you never questioned you could
get somewhere with—with me.
Still,
I must confess that from the start
there was a part of me on your side,
so quickly.
But I was angry, too,
angry that I wasn't angrier with you.

FAUST:
You dear sweet love!

GRETCHEN:
No, wait!

(She picks an aster and pulls off the petals one after another.)

FAUST:
What's that for?
A bouquet?

GRETCHEN:
No, it's only a game.

FAUST:
Game? What?

GRETCHEN:
No, don't. You'd make fun of me.

(She pulls off the petals and murmurs to herself.)

FAUST:
What are you murmuring?

GRETCHEN: *(Half aloud.)*
He loves me—loves me not—

FAUST:
>You sweet lovely vision!

GRETCHEN: *(Continuing.)*
>Loves me—not—loves me—not—

>*(Pulling off the last petals, joyfully.)*

>He loves me!

FAUST:
>Yes, dear child!
>Let this flower's decision
>be an oracle from the gods!
>He loves you!
>Do you know what that means?
>He loves you!

>*(He takes both her hands in his.)*

GRETCHEN:
>I'm shivering!

FAUST:
>No, no, don't be frightened!
>Look at me—look—and let our
>hands say what can never be expressed:
>To surrender yourself totally,
>give yourself over to rapture that can only be eternal!
>Eternal!
>Its end would be despair.
>No, no end! No end!

>*(GRETCHEN presses his hands, frees herself, and runs off. FAUST stands thoughtfully for a moment, then goes after her. Enter MARTHA and MEPHISTOPHELES.)*

MARTHA:
>Night's coming on.

MEPHISTOPHELES:

    Yes. And we must be going.

MARTHA:

    I'd ask you to stay longer,
    but this is such a busybody town,
    you'd think people had nothing better to do
    than to spy on their neighbors' every move.
    Do what you will, they'll talk and talk.
    Now where are our lovebirds off to?

MEPHISTOPHELES:

    They fluttered up that path.
    Naughty little butterflies!

MARTHA:

    He seems rather fond of her.

MEPHISTOPHELES:

    And she of him.
    It's the way of the world.

XVI ✒ A SMALL SUMMER ARBOR

GRETCHEN runs in, hides behind the door, and finger at her lips she peeks through the crack.

GRETCHEN:

    He's coming!

FAUST: *(Entering.)*

    Little rascal!
    So that's how you tease me!
    Now I've got you!

(He kisses her.)

GRETCHEN: *(Grasps him and returns the kiss.)*
Sweet man!
I love you with all my heart!

(MEPHISTOPHELES knocks.)

FAUST: *(Stomping his foot.)*
Who's there?

MEPHISTOPHELES:
A friend!

FAUST:
A beast!

MEPHISTOPHELES:
I think it's time to go.

MARTHA: *(Entering.)*
It's really late, sir.

FAUST:
May I see you home?

GRETCHEN:
My mother—no, good-bye!

FAUST:
Do I have to go, then?
Good-bye!

MARTHA:
Adieu!

GRETCHEN:
See you soon.

(Exeunt FAUST and MEPHISTOPHELES.)

GRETCHEN:
>   Dear God, the thoughts a man like that must think!
>   He puts me to shame.
>   All I can do is stand there and say yes.
>   What a poor stupid girl I am.
>   I can't imagine what he sees in me.

(Exit.)

XVII ✏ FOREST AND CAVERN

FAUST: *(Alone.)*
>   Exalted spirit, you gave me all,
>   all I prayed for, everything.
>   It wasn't for nothing
>   you turned your gaze on me from the flame.
>   You gave me glorious Nature for my kingdom,
>   the power to feel and enjoy her;
>   not merely cold and wondering visits,
>   but the privilege to gaze deeply into her being
>   as into the heart of a friend.
>   You parade before me endless lines
>   of living creatures, and teach me
>   to know my brothers in the silent
>   thicket, in air, in water.
>   And when the stormwind roars and rages through the forest,
>   and the giant fir tumbles and crashes,
>   crushing neighboring limbs and trunks,
>   and its fall echoes like thunder through the mountains,
>   then, oh, then you lead me to this sheltered cavern
>   and reveal to me the secret depths
>   and wonders of my heart.
>
>   And when, as now, the pale moon rises and
>   gently limns the landscape,
>   I see rising before me silvery shapes
>   slipping from rocky cliffs and marshy thickets
>   tempering the austere joy of contemplation.

But I know now that nothing
perfect is given to man.
You gave me this rapture that leads me nearer
and nearer to the gods,
but you gave me also the companion
I can't do without, even though
he degrades me in my own eyes,
cold, impudent, and in a single breath
reduces your gifts to nothingness.
He fans inside me incessantly the raging passion
for that woman's bewitching image.
So I stagger from desire to pleasure,
and having that,
languish once more for desire.

MEPHISTOPHELES: *(Entering.)*
Haven't you had enough of this?
How much longer can it please you?
Trying something once is understandable,
but then it's time to go on.

FAUST:
I wish you had something more to do than
plague me on one of my better days.

MEPHISTOPHELES:
Oh, well, let's make no mistake!
I'd gladly just wash my hands of you!
Just be careful not to say that to me in earnest.
You aren't exactly an ideal companion, you know.
You're rude, ill-tempered, and, what's more, a lunatic.
I'm never done with dealing with you!
Nor can I ever tell from looking at you
what you want and don't want!

FAUST:
Ah! There! Now!
There you've got it!
Just the right tone!
He wants to be thanked for boring me!

MEPHISTOPHELES:

    What would your life have been without me,
    you miserable son of earth?
    For how long now have I cured your mind
    of the nonsense you call imagination?
    Besides, if not for me, you'd have
    strolled your way right off planet Earth.
    But here you squat in holes and caverns like a hoot owl,
    sucking strength, like a toad, from sodden moss
    and dripping stones!
    What a charming pastime!
    There's still the Doctor creaking in your bones!

FAUST:

    Have you any notion of the renewed and vital power
    this wandering in the wilderness has given me?
    No, for if you had, you'd be devil enough
    to begrudge me my very happiness.

MEPHISTOPHELES:

    Ah! What transcendental gratification!
    To lie around on some dewy mountain in the dark,
    to enfold earth and sky in rapturous embrace,
    to puff yourself up till you think you've achieved the godhead,
    to burrow through the bowels of earth with urgent intuitions,
    to feel the creative labor of those first six days,
    to enjoy in your new-found strength, ah!
    who knows what! and then,
    having left the earthbound mortal behind,
    to merge blissfully with the universal All!
    Consummating then your lofty intuition

    (Mimes a gesture of masturbation.)

    I mustn't say how!

FAUST:

    Shame on you!

MEPHISTOPHELES:
Aha!
I see that doesn't suit you!
Well, you have the right, of course,
politely, to say so.
The modest ear must never hear
what the modest heart can't do without.
In a word, feel free to indulge yourself
in the occasional lie, but just be aware
that you can't hold out much longer.

You're already exhausted.
This fear and trembling of yours will drive you
to distraction and madness before long.

Enough of this!

Your sweetheart sits at home feeling trapped and sad.
You're never out of her thoughts;
she loves you insanely. It was as if you
drowned her in your love's frenzy—
like a brook swollen to a torrent with melting snow.
You poured it into her heart,
but now your brook's run dry again.

I'd suggest that instead of presiding
here in the woods as if you were somebody
you reward the poor young thing for her affection.
Time drags unbearably for her;
she stands at the window
watching clouds drift past
over the old city wall.
"If I were only a little bird" she sings
all day and half the night.
Sometimes she's up, but mostly down,
and at times she's wept herself dry.
She's calm then, or appears so,
but always, always in love.

FAUST:
Serpent! Serpent!

MEPHISTOPHELES: *(Aside.)*
Yes, and I'll get you, too.

FAUST:
Monster! Get away!
Don't ever mention that lovely creature to me!
Never again waken to my half-crazed senses
my desire for her sweet body!

MEPHISTOPHELES:
Well, then, what do you suggest?
As far as she's concerned,
you've run off,
and that's not too bad a guess.

FAUST:
No, not true.
I'm near her now;
no matter how far,
I can never forget her.
I envy the Body of our Lord the touch of her lips
when she receives it in Communion.

MEPHISTOPHELES:
Splendid! Well said!
And I've often envied you that pair of
twins that feeds among the lilies.

FAUST:
Pimp!
Get out of my sight!

MEPHISTOPHELES:
Fine!
Scold all you like,
it only makes me laugh.

When God created boys and girls,
He tipped his hat to this noblest of professions.

He knew the value of creating opportunities.
Let's go. It's time.
This is a sorry business.
It's your lover's bedroom you need,
not your grave.

FAUST:

What good is heaven's joy in her arms;
what good warming myself at her breast,
when all I feel is her need, her misery, always?

What am I, what, but a homeless fugitive,
a monster who without peace or purpose
plunges like a cataract in greedy rage from
rock to rock into the abyss?
And there, at the side, in her little hut,
on her tiny Alpine meadow, dreaming
childlike dreams in her little world,
she knows nothing, nothing of the world outside.
And I, hated of God, couldn't be satisfied
with seizing the rocks and smashing them to bits—
I had to ruin her peace!

You, Hell, you, you had to have this sacrifice!
Devil, Devil, help me cut short this anguish!
Let happen what has to happen,
let it happen now!
Let her fate be my fate,
let it fall crushingly down upon me,
and hurl us to a single doom!

MEPHISTOPHELES:

Mercy, what a stew he's in,
all hot and bothered!
Go on, go, go comfort her, you fool!
Let a blockhead arrive at his wits' end

and he thinks it's the end of the world.
More power to the man who lives dangerously!
Aha, but there's a devil in you somewhere.
It's just that a devil in despair is an oxymoron!

XVIII 〜 GRETCHEN'S ROOM

GRETCHEN alone at her spinning wheel.

GRETCHEN: *(Sings.)*

My peace is gone,
My heart is sore,
I'll find it never
And never more.

Where he is not,
Is a grave to me,
The world is changed,
Ah, bitterly.

I sit, I ponder
One only thought,
My senses wander,
My brain's distraught.

My peace is gone,
My heart is sore,
I'll find it never
And never more.

I look through my window
The livelong day,
I go out to meet him,
If meet him I may.

His noble form,
His bearing high,
His mouth's sweet smile,
His mastering eye,

And the magic flow
Of his talk, the bliss
In the clasp of his hand,
And oh! his kiss!

My peace is gone,
My heart is sore,
I'll find it never
And never more.

My heart cries out,
My sad heart pines,
To hold him fast,
And keep him mine,

And kiss him, kiss him,
Night and day,
And on his kisses
Die away!

XIX ⁓ MARTHA'S GARDEN

GRETCHEN.
FAUST.

GRETCHEN:
Promise me, Heinrich!

FAUST:
Whatever I can.

GRETCHEN:
Well—religion.
How do you feel about it?
You're such a kind,
such a good-hearted man,
and yet it seems not to
matter much to you.

FAUST:

>My dear,
>let's not talk about that.
>I love you,
>and that's all that counts.
>I'd give my life for you.
>Why would I rob anyone
>of his church and faith?

GRETCHEN:

>But that's not right.
>You have to believe!

FAUST:

>Do I?

GRETCHEN:

>Oh, if only I could make you listen!
>And you also don't honor the sacraments.

FAUST:

>But I do.
>I do honor them.

GRETCHEN:

>Yes, but you don't long for them.
>And you don't go to Mass or Confession.
>I know you don't.
>Not for a long time.
>Do you believe in God?

FAUST:

>My dear,
>who would dare to say:
>"I believe in God"?
>Ask a priest or philosopher that
>and his answer will only
>seem to mock you.

GRETCHEN:
>So you don't believe?

FAUST:
>Don't mistake me, my dear.
>Who can name him?
>Who?
>Who can testify:
>"I believe in him"?
>And who with life and feeling still in his body
>can with any honesty say:
>"I don't believe in him"?

>The All-Embracing,
>the All-Sustaining,
>doesn't he embrace and
>sustain you, me, himself?
>Doesn't the sky arch above us?
>Doesn't the earth stand firm beneath us?
>And the stars,
>the eternal stars,
>don't they look kindly down upon us?
>And when we look into each other's eyes,
>doesn't all this press in on your heart and mind,
>weaving a presence around you,
>seen and unseen,
>an eternal mystery?

>Let it in,
>fill your heart with this to overflowing,
>and when it's reached its peak,
>when your bliss can grow no stronger,
>then call it what you will!
>Love!
>Happiness!
>Soul!
>God!
>I have no name for it.
>Feeling is everything.

Name is sound and smoke
clouding heaven's light.

GRETCHEN:

Yes, that's all fine and good.
Our priest says the same thing, almost,
except he puts it differently.

FAUST:

It's what we all say,
every human heart under the sun,
each in his own way.
So why not I in mine?

GRETCHEN:

It all sounds so nice,
so fine when you say it;
and yet it's still not right,
something wrong.
You have no Christianity.

FAUST:

Dear child!

GRETCHEN:

It's hurt me for a long while now,
seeing you in such company.

FAUST:

How so?

GRETCHEN:

That person,
the one who's always with you—
I hate him,
I hate him from the depths of my soul.
Nothing in my life
has ever pained me so deeply
as the sight of that man's loathsome face.

FAUST:

    You pretty little thing,
    you mustn't let him frighten you.

GRETCHEN:

    His presence makes my blood run cold.
    I try to be nice to everyone;
    and I so long to see you,
    but I'm secretly horrified by that man.
    Besides, I think he's a scoundrel.
    God forgive me if I misjudge him!

FAUST:

    It takes all kinds to make a world.

GRETCHEN:

    I wouldn't like living with a man like him.
    He no sooner comes in the door
    than he looks around in mockery and half in a rage.
    He has no interests;
    he's interested in nothing;
    it's written all over his face.
    And there's not a living soul he can love.
    With you I'm so free and easy,
    so happy and content in your arms;
    but just his presence strangles my very soul.

FAUST:

    What a foreboding little angel you are!

GRETCHEN:

    He has only to come near
    and I feel overwhelmed,
    almost as if I don't love you anymore.
    And I can't pray with him in the room,
    and that nearly breaks my heart.
    Dear Heinrich,
    you must feel that, too!

FAUST:

It's just a dislike you've taken toward him.

GRETCHEN:

I have to go now.

FAUST:

Can we never have a quiet hour,
bodies pressed together,
soul to soul?

GRETCHEN:

Oh, if only I slept alone!
I'd leave the bolt drawn for you tonight.
But mother's such a light sleeper,
if she caught us I'd die on the spot.

FAUST:

Sweet angel, there's no need of that.
Here, take this flask.
Three drops in her drink
and she'll sleep a deep and happy sleep.

GRETCHEN:

What wouldn't I do for you!
I hope it won't harm her.

FAUST:

Would I give it to you if it did?

GRETCHEN:

Just looking at you, my sweet,
and I do whatever you say.
I've done so much already,
there isn't much left undone.

(Exit.)

MEPHISTOPHELES: *(Entering.)*

Has the little monkey left?

FAUST:

Been spying again?

MEPHISTOPHELES:

Yes, every juicy detail.
And you were catechized, Doctor,
make no mistake.
Let's hope it does some good.
Girls these days insist on knowing
if a man's simple and pious
in the good old fashioned way.
They think if he gives in on that score,
he can be brought round to yield on everything.

FAUST:

Can't you understand, you monster,
how this dear and loving creature,
so filled with her faith that's it's her only salvation,
can be terrified to think her love is a lost soul?

MEPHISTOPHELES:

Aha, the transcendental sensualist!
Led around by the nose by some little chit!

FAUST:

You misbegotten monster of fire and shit!

MEPHISTOPHELES:

As for her,
she knows her physiognomy like a pro.
In my presence she's struck by—well,
she doesn't know quite what.
She finds some hidden meaning
behind this phiz of mine:
that I'm at least an evil genius,
and maybe even the Devil.

So.

And tonight—?

FAUST:
    What's it to you?

MEPHISTOPHELES:
    Oh, I get my kicks out of it, too!

XX 🙪 AT THE WELL

GRETCHEN and LIESCHEN carrying water jugs.

LIESCHEN:
    You've heard about Barbara?

GRETCHEN:
    No. I don't get out much.

LIESCHEN:
    It's true.
    Sibyl told me this morning.
    Finally made a fool of herself, she did.
    That's what comes from putting on airs.

GRETCHEN:
    How so?

LIESCHEN:
    It smells to high heaven!
    As they say,
    she's feeding for two now.

GRETCHEN:
    Oh, no!

LIESCHEN:
    Serves her right, if you ask me.
    She's been leading that good-for-nothing
    around by the nose for years.
    All that gallivanting around town

so everyone could see her,
the music, the dances,
always had to be first,
and him,
always wheedling her with pastries and wine.
And the way she put on,
you'd think she was some real beauty.
The brass of the girl,
hadn't the decency to be ashamed!
The presents he was always throwing at her!
Disgusting, the way they petted and
slobbered over each other!
So that's another cherry off the tree.

GRETCHEN:

Poor thing!

LIESCHEN:

You're sorry for her?
God!
Nights when girls like us were indoor spinning,
our mothers never taking their eyes off us,
there she was on the bench by the door,
or in some dark passageway,
with you-know-who.
Time didn't seem to matter for her then.
So now she'll just have to pay up—
Sunday in church in her sinner's shift!

GRETCHEN:

But surely he'll marry her.

LIESCHEN:

And be a fool?
Smart lad like him?
With all those other fish in the sea?
Not likely! Besides,
he's long gone.

GRETCHEN:

But that's not fair!

LIESCHEN:

And even if she gets him,
it'll be no picnic for her.
The boys'll rip off her bridal garland,
and we'll strew straw at her
door for the shame of her.

(Exit.)

GRETCHEN: *(Walking home.)*

Time was I'd rail with the best of them
about some poor girl who went wrong.
There were never words enough for the sins of others.
They seemed so black,
and I made them even blacker;
but even then it wasn't black enough for me.
I'd bless myself then and feel so proud—
and now I'm just as bad as them.
And yet,
everything that drove me to it—
O God! How good it was,
how good, how sweet!

XXI ⚘ BY THE CITY WALL

*An image of the Mater Dolorosa set in the niche of a wall with pots
of flowers in front of it. GRETCHEN puts fresh flowers into them.*

GRETCHEN:

Mother of Sorrows,
behold me in my distress!

Your heart pierced by the sword
knows unending pain
as you look on your Son dying.

You send up sighs to the Father on high
for your agony and for His.
But who can know, who can feel,
the rage that tears me?

Who can know my fear
and the tremble of my heart?
Who but you, sweet Mother?

Wherever I go,
what woe, what woe, what woe,
I feel in my heart!

Alone,
I weep, I weep, and I weep,
till my heart is torn.

At dawn when I picked these flowers,
the pots at my window were wet with my tears.

The sun shines into my room so brightly,
and I sit on my bed engulfed in agony.

Lady! Mother! Help me!
Save me from disgrace and death!
Mother of sorrows, behold me in my distress.

XXII ⚡ NIGHT

The street in front of Gretchen's door.
VALENTINE, a soldier, Gretchen's brother.

VALENTINE:
Time was I'd sit drinking with the boys,
listening to them boast about their girls,
and wash it down with another drink or two.
There I sat, smiling,
stroking my chin at all their big talk.

"Chacun à son gout!" I cried,
raising my glass.
"Show me a girl to match my Gretchen!
Show me a better sister!"
We all clinked glasses at that.
And the braggarts sat there like bumps on a log.

But they scorn me now,
sneer at me,
call me names!
I sit there ashamed, taking it all,
and I can't call one of them a liar!

Who's that coming?

Two of them, slinking toward her door.
If that's the bastard, I'll kill him!
I'll kill him!

(Enter FAUST and MEPHISTOPHELES.)

FAUST:
    I see the sanctuary lamp in the sacristy,
    its gleam shoots upwards, then, fainter and fainter,
    fades away, swallowed by darkness and gloom,
    the same gloom that has captured my heart.

MEPHISTOPHELES:
    And I'm like any old alley tomcat
    out on the prowl, up the fire escape,
    hugging close along the wall, always
    looking, primed for the pounce.
    And to be quite honest,
    I feel rather virtuous about it, I do.
    A touch of thievery,
    a soupçon of lechery.
    Every tingling limb
    looks forward to Walpurgis Night.
    The glory of it, two more days,
    that's when you learn what it means to be alive!

FAUST:

   Haven't you any jewelry for her?

MEPHISTOPHELES:

   Oh, I think I might have.
   A string of pearls?
   Who knows?

FAUST:

   It pains me to go without a gift.

MEPHISTOPHELES:

   Silly boy,
   what makes you think you always have to pay?
   But look!
   There's a sky full of stars!
   I'll sing you a masterpiece!
   A moral song, just for her,
   the better to seduce her by.

   (He sings to a zither.)

                  Katie, dear Katie,
                   At break of day
              You stand at your true love's door.
                    O never begin,
                    No, never give in!
                   He'll lift the pin
                   And a maid goes in,
              But a maid, no, nevermore.

                   Young men will do it,
                    If they come to it,
              And good girls do not linger!
                   So, Katie, be wise,
                   Believe no lies,
                   Hide your prize
                   From lovers' eyes,
              Till you have a ring on your finger!

VALENTINE: *(Comes forward.)*
  Bastard, what do you want here?
  I swear, you goddamned rat catcher,
  I'll first send your instrument to perdition,
  and then the singer!

(He smashes the zither.)

MEPHISTOPHELES:
  Well, now you've broken it, what good is it?

VALENTINE:
  And now for a little skull splitting!

MEPHISTOPHELES: *(To FAUST.)*
  Hold your ground, Professor!
  Quick, now! Stick close to me,
  do as I do. Now,
  out with your feather duster!
  You thrust, I'll parry.

VALENTINE:
  Parry that!

MEPHISTOPHELES:
  Why not?

VALENTINE:
  And that!

MEPHISTOPHELES:
  Be my guest!

VALENTINE:
  What's this?
  The Devil fighting me?
  My hand's gone lame!

MEPHISTOPHELES: *(To FAUST.)*
  Let him have it!

(FAUST thrusts. VALENTINE falls.)

VALENTINE:
> O God!

MEPHISTOPHELES:
> That settles him, the bastard!
> It's time, let's go, let's disappear.
> They're already screaming bloody murder.
> I get on famously with the police,
> it's criminal courts get my goat.

(Exeunt MEPHISTOPHELES and FAUST.)

MARTHA: *(At the window.)*
> Help! Help!

GRETCHEN: *(At the window.)*
> Help! Bring a light!

MARTHA: *(As before.)*
> They're cursing, scuffling,
> shouting and fighting!

PEOPLE:
> A dead man, lying here, look!

MARTHA: *(Coming out.)*
> Have the murderers escaped?

GRETCHEN: *(Coming out.)*
> Who's that lying there?

PEOPLE:
> Your mother's son.

GRETCHEN:
> Dear God!
> What have they done!

VALENTINE:
I'm dying!
Quickly said and quickly done.
Why are you standing there howling?
Come here.
Listen.

(They all gather round him.)

Listen to me, Gretchen—
you're young,
young but not very clever where it counts,
and you've made a real mess of things.
Let me tell you something.
You're a whore,
so you might as well play it to the hilt.

GRETCHEN:
My brother!
Dear God!
What are you saying?

VALENTINE:
Leave God out of this!
What's done is done.
You began on the sly with one,
but there'll be more, count on it,
and when you've had a dozen
the whole town can come calling.

Shame's birth is a secret thing,
her little ears and head
are hidden by night in a veil of darkness,
and all would like to kill and forget her.
But she grows, she grows,
and parades around brazenly
in broad daylight,
and not any prettier.
And the uglier she grows,
the more she seeks out daylight.

Time will come when all good people
will shrink from you, you whore,
as though you were a rotting,
plague-ridden corpse.
They'll look you in the eye,
and your heart will break.
No more golden necklaces for you!
No more standing by the altar! No more
fun at the dance in a fine lace collar!
You'll hide away in some miserable
hole among beggars and cripples,
and even if God forgives you,
you'll be damned here on earth forever!

MARTHA:

Commend your soul to God's mercy!
Will you burden yourself with slander, too?

VALENTINE:

You shameless pandering bitch!
If only I could get at your withered body
my soul would be wiped clear of sin!

GRETCHEN:

My brother!
Oh, the agony!

VALENTINE:

No more tears!
I've had enough!
The day you destroyed your honor
was the day you stabbed me to the heart.
I'm going to God—
a soldier good and true.

(He dies.)

XXIII ↝ CATHEDRAL

Service, organ and choir.
GRETCHEN in the midst of many people.
The EVIL SPIRIT behind her.

EVIL SPIRIT:
   How different it once was, Gretchen,
   when you came here to the altar,
   still full of innocence,
   and out of your little prayer book,
   well thumbed by generations,
   stammered your prayers,
   and in your heart half play, half God!
   Gretchen!
   What are you thinking?
   What crime is in your heart?
   Is it for your mother's soul you're praying?
   Your mother who slipped sleeping into endless torment?
   Because of you?
   Whose blood is that on your doorstep?
   Yes, and beneath your heart is there something
   stirring, swelling, torturing you and itself
   with its foreboding presence?

GRETCHEN:
   Dear God! Dear God!
   Free me of the thoughts that
   attack me from every side
   in spite of myself!

CHOIR:
            Dies irae, dies illa,
            Solvet saeclum in favilla.

(Organ music.)

EVIL SPIRIT:

> God's wrath seizes you!
> The trumpet sounds!
> The graves quake!
> And your heart,
> roused from its ashes to suffer
> the tormenting flames,
> leaps up in agony!

GRETCHEN:

> O God, to be out of here!
> I feel the organ suffocating me,
> the choir dissolving my soul to its very depths!

CHOIR:

> *Judex ergo cum sedebit,*
> *Quidquid latet adparebit,*
> *Nil inultum remanebit.*

GRETCHEN:

> I'm stifling!
> The columns closing around me!
> The ceiling crashing down on me!
> Air!

EVIL SPIRIT:

> Hide yourself!
> Sin and shame cannot stay hidden.
> Air? Light?
> Woe to you!

CHOIR:

> *Quid sum miser tunc dicturus?*
> *Quem patronum rogaturus?*
> *Cum vix justus sit securus.*

EVIL SPIRIT:

> The Blest turn their
> faces from you.
> The Pure shudder

to reach out to you.
Woe!

CHOIR:

Quid sum miser tunc dicturus?

GRETCHEN:
Neighbor!

Your smelling salts!

(She faints.)

XXIV ⚡ WALPURGIS NIGHT

The Harz Mountains, near Schierke and Elend.
FAUST and MEPHISTOPHELES.

MEPHISTOPHELES:
Don't you wish you had a broomstick to ride?
I could do with a randy goat for a mount.
It's a long way before we get there.

FAUST:
As long as I'm fresh on my legs,
this knotted staff will do.
But why shorten the route?
These valleys are a labyrinth;
let's see them first;
let's creep our way through;
then we can climb to the rocky heights.

But look there!
That spring gushing from the mountain!
Plunging downward in its everlasting spray!
It's a great joy seeing such sights.
Spring's already stirring in the birches,
even the firs feel it already.
No wonder our bodies thrill to the same feeling.

MEPHISTOPHELES:
> Frankly, I feel nothing!
> My body's a wintry thing.
> I'd rather be trudging
> through ice and snow.
>
> And that humpbacked moon rising reddish and late,
> how sadly it climbs and gives no light,
> while we bump trees and crack our shins on rocks.
> Excuse me while I call on a will-o'-the-wisp.
>
> There's one there, shining ever so brightly!
>
> You there! Friend!
> May I have a word?
> Why do you keep burning in vain?
> Be so kind as to light our way up the mountain.

WILL-O'-THE-WISP:
> Perhaps in respect
> I can harness my wayward disposition.
> I usually travel in a reckless zigzag.

MEPHISTOPHELES:
> Listen to him!
> Doing his best to imitate humans.
> Just keep going straight, in the Devil's name,
> or I'll blow out your flickering life!

WILL-O'-THE-WISP:
> Since you're the boss here, sir,
> I'll do my best. Just remember,
> tonight the mountain's mad with magic,
> and if a will-o'-the-wisp's to guide your way,
> you'd better not be too particular.

FAUST: *(Sings.)*
> > Now we're in the sphere, it seems,
> > Of enchantment and of dreams.
> > Lead us on, fair meteor gleam,

Lead us speedily in our race
To the deserts of vast space!

WILL-O'-THE-WISP: *(Sings.)*
See them, see, tree after tree,
How thick and swift behind they drift,
And crag and cliff bow down, bow low,
And the long-snouted crags below,
Listen, listen, they snort, they blow!

FAUST: *(Sings.)*

Over moss and over stone,
Brook and brooklet race along.
What noise is that, around, above?
Listen, listen! The sounds of song,
Lovers' sweet lamenting moan,
Loosing their happy hearts in sighs,
Voices we knew in days now flown,
When to live and love were paradise?
All that we hope for, all that we love,
Throbs in the heart and thrills in the brain,
And Echo, Echo, like the tale
Of ancient days, over hill, over dale
Reverberates the strain!

MEPHISTOPHELES: *(Sings.)*
Tu-whit! Tu-whoo! More near, more near!
The jargon rises shrill and clear.
The owl, the peewit, and the jay,
All awake and abroad are they.
Can those be salamanders there,
Long in leg, and huge in paunch,
Striding onward through the brakes?
Behold, the great roots gaunt and bare,
How from rock and sand they branch,
Wreathed fantastical like snakes,
In weirdest coils, which through the air
They stretch to scare and to ensnare us,
From wartlike knots, with life instinct,

Darting polyp fibres, linked
To enmesh and overbear us!
And see! see mice of every hue,
How they crowd, and how they speed
Through the moss and through the heather!
Up and down the fireflies, too,
Flit and flicker, thronged together,
To bewilder and mislead!

FAUST: *(Sings.)*

But tell me, are we standing? Say,
Which is moving, we or they?
All about us seems to spin,
Rocks and trees grimace and grin,
And, swollen and puffed, on either side,
Will-o'-the-wisps are multiplied.

MEPHISTOPHELES:

Grab my coattail and hang tight!
This middle summit gives us a grand view
of Mammon, Lord of Wealth,
glowing in the mountain.

FAUST:

How strange!
Down there, far down,
a dull reddish glow,
like dawn's first light,
feeling its way into the deepest chasms of the abyss.
Fumes rise, vapors drift,
a cloud of mist takes sudden fire,
creeping along, a slender thread,
then gushes up like a fountain of flame and
streams its way to the valley in numberless veins,
only there, there at the narrow turn,
to unite again in a single flow.

And there, nearby, sparks, like golden sand,
are strewn about.

Oh, but look!
Now the cliff's whole height
is a mighty flaming firebrand!

MEPHISTOPHELES:
Lord Mammon spares nothing
in lighting his palace for the festivities!
You're lucky to have seen such a sight!
But now I hear his unruly guests arriving.

FAUST:
Listen to the whirlwind rage!
Beating my neck like a powerful fist!

MEPHISTOPHELES:
Grab tight those ancient rock ribs
or be flung into a bottomless chasm.
The mist is making the night more dense.

Listen!

Do you hear?

Trees crashing in the forest far off!
Frightened owls scurry in terror.
Pillars of eternally green palaces splinter!
Branches creak and snap, and
mighty tree trunks groan in their depths!
Roots gape and moan with the strain, and
trees fall in tangled heaps,
littering the valleys with confusion,
as through the rubble the wild winds howl!

Do you hear them?
Voices?
High in the air?
Near and far?

Yes, and the whole mountain roars
with the frenzied song of incantation!

WITCHES: *(In chorus.)*

> The witches to the Brocken are bound—
> The stubble is yellow, the corn is green—
> A mighty throng will there be found,
> And Old Nick on his throne be seen.
> Hurry, we're off; we'll make a start;
> A billy goat stinks and a witch can fart!

VOICE:

> Old Mother Baubo's coming now,
> riding high on a farrowing sow.

WITCHES: *(In chorus.)*

> Let honor be given where honor is due!
> Forward, Dame Baubo, and lead our crew!
> A sturdy sow, and a mother, too,
> Is a proper guide! We'll follow you!
>
> The way is wide, the way is long.
> Ah, what a lively, jolly throng!
> The broom straw scratches, the pitchfork pokes,
> The mother pops open, the little tyke chokes.

WARLOCKS: *(First half chorus.)*

> We crawl like snails, so far behind
> Have we been left by womankind;
> For woman, when to Hell she rides,
> Outstrips us by a thousand strides.

WARLOCKS: *(Second half chorus.)*

> That's not at all the way we view it.
> She takes a thousand strides to do it,
> But let her scamper fast as she can,
> It's done in a single bound by man.

VOICE: *(From above.)*

> Come up from the lake!
> Come up, join us!

VOICES: *(From below.)*

>We'd love to join you.
>We're all washed,
>clean as can be,
>but we're barren eternally.

WARLOCKS AND WITCHES: *(In chorus.)*

>The wind is still, the star's in flight,
>The wan moon hides herself from sight,
>Whizzing along, the magic choir
>Scatters a thousand sparks of fire.

VOICE: *(Below.)*

>Stop! Stop!

VOICE: *(Above.)*

>Who's calling from down in the rocky cleft?

VOICE: *(Below.)*

>Take me along,
>oh, take me, take me!
>I've climbed this climb
>for three hundred years,
>and still haven't reached the top.
>I want to be with the likes of me!

WARLOCKS AND WITCHES: *(In chorus.)*

>Fly on a broom, fly on a stick,
>Fly on a billy goat, but do it quick;
>Who tonight can't make the climb
>Is forever lost to the end of time.

HALF-WITCH: *(Below.)*

>I've trudged behind
>for how long I don't know,
>and look how far the others have come!
>But I can't stay home.
>I find no peace there,
>nor here do I find peace.

WITCHES: *(In chorus.)*

> Their magic salve makes witches hale,
> And any old rag will do for a sail,
> Any old tub can fly through the sky,
> You either fly now, or you'll never fly.

WARLOCKS AND WITCHES: *(In chorus.)*

> And when we've sailed around, around
> The peak, then sweep along the ground,
> And scour the heath to its farthest reaches
> With endless swarms of lowering witches.

(They alight.)

MEPHISTOPHELES:

> They jammer and jolt, they jabber and justle,
> They whiz and whirl, babble and bustle,
> They flash and spark, stink, and burn,
> And all things topsy-turvy turn!
> The truly hurly-burly which is
> Mother's milk to hovering witches!

Stick close to me now
or we'll be swept apart.
Where are you?

FAUST: *(In the distance.)*
Here!

MEPHISTOPHELES:

What, dragged off so far already?
I guess I'll have to show them who's master here.
Make way!
Squire Nick is coming through!
Make way there, make way, good people!

—Here, Doctor, hold on tight!
One grand leap and we're free of this mob
that's too wild even for me.

Ah! Look there,
over there,
that weird light!
Do you see?
It draws me toward those bushes.
Come, come, we'll slip in over there.

FAUST:
What a spirit of contradiction!
But, yes, lead on, I'll follow.
What a marvelous idea!
We climb the Brocken on Walpurgis Night,
only to hide in the bushes and watch!

MEPHISTOPHELES:
Look there, at that merry campfire!
A club for fun and games, it seems.
One's never alone in a select cabal.

FAUST:
Yes, but I'd rather be at the top!
I already see the fire's glow and
swirls of smoke, and crowds streaming
to see the Evil One.
Many a riddle will be solved here tonight.

MEPHISTOPHELES:
And many another evolved here, too.
Let the great world run riot if it likes,
I'll stay here in peace and quiet.
It's said—and tradition has it—
that out of the great world
men make their own snug little worlds.
And so we will.

Look at those young witches there,
naked as the day they were born,
and the older ones wise enough
to know what not to show.

Be nice to them, if only for my sake;
it's little trouble and great fun.

But what's that racket of instruments I hear?
Blasted noise!
Just have to get used to it, I guess.

Come, come along now!
You've no choice. Let's go in.
I'll make the introductions, and, doing so,
put you in my debt a soupçon deeper.
What do you say to that, my friend?

Look!

No small space, this!
You can hardly see to the end.
A hundred bonfires blazing in a row!
And dancing, and chatter, and
drinking, cooking, making love!
I ask you now, what could be better?

FAUST:

When you introduce me,
what role will you be playing,
sorcerer or Devil?

MEPHISTOPHELES:

I'm likeliest to go incognito,
though on gala days one can show one's decorations.
Unfortunately, I haven't a garter to distinguish me,
but my horse's hoof garners high honor here.

Do you see that snail crawling this way?
With her groping face
she's already sniffed out something special in me.
I couldn't deny my identity here if I wanted to.

Come!

We'll go from fire to fire,
I'll play pimp to your lover.

HUCKSTER WITCH:

Gentlemen, not so fast!
Slow down!
Pass by and you miss the opportunity!

Here, take a look, do,
inspect my merchandise.
Quite a variety, wouldn't you say?
And yet there's nothing in my little stall—
nothing like it in the whole wide world—
that hasn't done malicious harm,
sometime, somewhere,
to mankind and to the world at large.
You'll find here no dagger that hasn't dripped blood,
no goblet that hasn't poured destructive hot poison
into a sturdy, healthy body,
no jewel that hasn't seduced some lovely girl,
no sword that hasn't severed some pact
or with guile stabbed an enemy in the back.

MEPHISTOPHELES:

Old Auntie, I'd say you're behind the times.
What done is done, what's past is past.
Deal in novelties.
Only novelties appeal today.

FAUST:

I could lose myself if I don't take care!
This is a marvelous fair, I must say!

MEPHISTOPHELES:

This whirlpool of a mob
is struggling to get to the top.
You think you're shoving
when you're being shoved.

FAUST:
 Who's that?

MEPHISTOPHELES:
 Take a good look!
 That's Lilith.

FAUST:
 Who?

MEPHISTOPHELES:
 Adam's first wife.
 Beware her beautiful hair,
 there's magic in it.
 She needs no other ornament.
 Let her snare a young man with it,
 and she won't soon let him loose.

FAUST:
 Look at those two,
 one old witch, one young;
 they've done their share of dancing, all right!

MEPHISTOPHELES:
 No one gets enough tonight.
 There's another dance starting.
 Let's get in on it.

FAUST: *(Dancing with the young one.)*
              A lovely dream once came to me;
              In it I saw an apple tree,
              And on it two fair apples grew,
              I climbed to pluck them, one and two.

THE PRETTY ONE:
              You men have thought such apples nice
              Since ancient days in Paradise.
              How pleased I am to let you know
              Such apples in my garden grow.

MEPHISTOPHELES: *(Dancing with the old one.)*

> A wildish dream once came to me;
> In it I saw a cloven tree.
> It had a monstrous hole so big
> I humped and pumped like a rutting pig.

THE OLD ONE:

> I greet the knight of the cloven hoof.
> There's a place for him beneath my roof.
> Prepare to stop my monster hole
> With your randy rutting monster pole.

MEPHISTOPHELES: *(To FAUST, who has left the dance.)*

> That pretty creature,
> why did you let her go?
> She sang so sweetly as she danced.

FAUST:

> Ach!
> While she was singing,
> a little red mouse sprang from her mouth!

MEPHISTOPHELES:

> So? Why so fussy?
> Be glad it wasn't gray.
> Such things don't matter
> when your making love.

FAUST:

> And then I saw—

MEPHISTOPHELES:

> What?

FAUST:

> Mephisto, look!
> Over there in the distance!
> Do you see that girl?
> So pale and lovely, all alone?

The way she drags her feet you'd
think they were chained.
I must confess, she seems so very like
my dear good Gretchen.

MEPHISTOPHELES:

Keep away!
That's bad news for anyone!
It's a lifeless apparition, a phantom.
Nothing good can come from such a meeting.
Its staring eyes can freeze a man's blood
till he's almost turned to stone.
You've heard the story of Medusa.

FAUST:

Yes, eyes of a dead girl
not closed by a loving hand.
This is the breast Gretchen gave me,
the sweet body I enjoyed.

MEPHISTOPHELES:

It's sorcery, you gullible fool!
She appears to every man in the guise of his love.

FAUST:

What ecstasy!
What agony!
How can I tear myself from this vision!
How strange that lovely throat should be
adorned by one thin red thread
no wider than the blade of a knife.

MEPHISTOPHELES:

Right you are! I see it, too.
She could just as well carry her head
tucked under her arm; after all,
Perseus cut it off for her.
Ah, but this hankering of yours for illusion!

XXV 〜 GLOOMY DAY. A FIELD

FAUST and MEPHISTOPHELES.

FAUST:

    In misery! In despair!
    Pitiably wandering the earth for so long,
    and now, now, imprisoned,
    a criminal!
    Confined in a dungeon,
    that lovely ill-fated creature,
    suffering unspeakable torments!
    To have come to this!
    To this!

    Treacherous, abominable spirit,
    how could you have done this to me?

    How?
    To have kept it from me?
    How?

    Yes! Stand there!
    Stand!
    Stand rolling your hellish eyes in rage!
    Stand and defy me with your unendurable presence!

    In prison! Ruined!
    In miserable, hopeless ruin!
    Abandoned to evil spirits
    and to the judgment of heartless humanity!

    And all this
    while you lulled me with vulgar diversions,
    hiding from me her growing wretchedness,
    and letting her go helpless to destruction!

MEPHISTOPHELES:

    She's not the first.

FAUST:

   Beast! Detestable monster!—
   Transform him, transform this reptile,
   oh, you, you Infinite Spirit of Earth!
   Change him into the dog that he once was,
   cavorting on evening walks,
   rolling at the feet of the unsuspecting wanderer,
   bounding onto his shoulders when he falls.
   Change him back into his favorite form,
   to grovel before me in the sand on his belly,
   so I can trample him,
   trample the depraved creature!

   "Not the first"!

   O grief,
   grief not to be grasped
   by human soul,
   that more than one creature
   has reached this depth
   of misery;
   that that first failed
   to atone for all others
   in her death agony
   before the eyes of the
   ever-forgiving God!
   The misery of this *one,*
   her,
   cuts me to the marrow of my being!
   And you stand there grinning coolly
   across the doom of thousands.

MEPHISTOPHELES:

   So, then!
   Here we are!
   Again!
   At the farthest reaches
   of our wits' end.
   The point where the mind of you men

goes stark raving mad.
Why do you do it?
Why make common cause with us
when you can't stand the heat?
You say you want to fly,
and yet your head goes all dizzy.
Did we make inroads on you,
or you on us?

FAUST:

Don't bare your teeth at me!
It disgusts me!

Great and glorious Spirit
who deigned to appear to me,
you who know my heart and soul,
why do you chain me
to this abominable creature
who feeds on misery
and gluts himself
on destruction?

MEPHISTOPHELES:

Finished?

FAUST:

Save her,
or be damned and suffer for ages!

MEPHISTOPHELES:

What's that?
Loose the avenger's chain's?
Undo his bolts?
I can't!
Powerless!

"Save her!"

Who was it destroyed her?
You or I?

(FAUST looks frantically about him.)

Reaching for a thunderbolt, are you?
A good thing they weren't given
to you wretched mortals.
Annihilate the innocent objector.
That's the way to smooth the path.
The tyrant's way.
Gets you past embarrassing obstacles.

FAUST:

Take me to her! She shall be free!

MEPHISTOPHELES:

And the danger to you?
What of that?
There's bloodguilt on this town,
the work of your hand,
and avenging spirits
still hover over the place
awaiting the murderer's return.

FAUST:

That, too, from you.
May the murder and death of all the world
descend upon you, you monster!
You listen!
Take me there!
Set her free!

MEPHISTOPHELES:

I'll take you there. Yes.
And once I get there
I'll tell you what I can do.
Do you think I'm omnipotent?
That I hold power over heaven and earth?
Ha!

Tell you what I'll do.
I'll cloud the jailer's senses,
you get his keys and
lead her out with a human hand.
I'll stand watch.
The magic horses are ready.
I'll carry you both away.
That I can do.

FAUST:
Hurry!

XXVI 🖎 NIGHT. OPEN COUNTRY

FAUST and MEPHISTOPHELES fly wildly past on black horses.

FAUST:
There, at the Ravenstone!
What are they weaving?

MEPHISTOPHELES:
Who knows?
Brewing and doing.

FAUST:
They're soaring, swooping,
bowing, scraping.

MEPHISTOPHELES:
A witches' cabal.

FAUST:
They strew and hallow.

MEPHISTOPHELES:
Gone by! Gone by!

XXVII ✗ DUNGEON

FAUST with a bunch of keys and a lantern, in front of a narrow iron door.

FAUST:
   What a shudder runs through me.
   How long it's been.
   I thought I'd forgotten.
   All the misery of mankind grips me.
   She's here, here where she lives,
   behind this dripping wall,
   yet her crime was no more than a fond illusion.
   And now you, Faust, you,
   now you think twice about going to her.
   Afraid?
   Afraid to see her again?
   Go, go on, you fool!
   Your timidity only brings death closer!

(He takes hold of the lock.)

GRETCHEN: *(Singing from within.)*
                   My mother, the whore,
                   She took my life,
                   My father, the rogue,
                   Ate me up with his knife!
                   My sister, wee tyke,
                   She picked up my bones,
                   And laid them to cool
                   Down under the stones.
                   Then I turned to a woodbird
                   So pretty to see;
                   Fly away, fly away
                   To the woodland with me!

FAUST: *(Unlocking the door.)*
   She doesn't know her lover
   can hear her chains rattle,
   and the rustle of the straw.

(He enters the dungeon.)

GRETCHEN: *(Trying to hide in her bed.)*
    O! O!
    They're coming!
    Bitter death!

FAUST: *(Softly.)*
    Hush! Hush!
    I've come to set you free.

GRETCHEN: *(Writhing at his feet.)*
    If you're human,
    think of me in my misery.

FAUST:
    Don't scream, you'll waken the guards!

(He begins unlocking the chains.)

GRETCHEN: *(On her knees.)*
    Hangman,
    who gave you this power over me?
    It's only midnight,
    and here you've come.
    Have pity on me,
    let me live.
    I'll die tomorrow,
    tomorrow morning,
    it's soon enough.

(She rises.)

    I'm young,
    still young,
    so young,
    and now have to die!
    And I was beautiful, too,
    and that was my ruin.

My lover was near,
but he's far away now;
and the garland torn,
blossoms scattered.

Not so rough!
Take hold gently!
Spare me!
Don't let me beg in vain!
What did I ever do to you?
I never saw you before!

FAUST:

How can I bear this misery!

GRETCHEN:

I'm in your hands now,
at your mercy.
But first let me nurse my baby.
I cuddled it all last night, you know,
and then they came
and took it away,
to grieve me,
grieve me,
and now they say I murdered it.
And I'll never be happy again.
And they make up songs about me,
they do,
and they sing them,
and it's bad of them,
wicked!
There's an old tale that ends like that—
but why mix it up with me?

FAUST: *(Throwing himself at her feet.)*

A lover lies here at your feet,
come to free you of this captive misery!

GRETCHEN: *(Throwing herself down beside him.)*

Yes, oh, yes,

let us kneel,
let us kneel
and call on the saints!
You see?
Do you see, here,
under these steps?
Here?
Hell seethes!
Hell's cauldron's boiling!
The Evil One,
with rage in his voice,
makes a terrible din!

FAUST: *(Loudly.)*
Gretchen! Gretchen!

GRETCHEN: *(Listening.)*
That was my lover's voice!

(She jumps up. The chains fall from her.)

Where is he?
I heard him call to me.
I'm free! No one can stop me!
I'll fly to him, his arms!
Hold him so tight!
He called "Gretchen!"
There on the threshold!
And through all the howling
and clanking of Hell,
through the furious rage
of devilish mockery,
I recognized his dear, sweet voice.

FAUST:
It's me!

GRETCHEN:
You!
Oh, say it again, again!

(Clasping him.)

It's him! It's him!
Where is all my agony now?
My misery, these chains,
this dungeon?
It's you! Come to save me.
I am saved!
I see it,
see the street again now
where I first saw you,
the pleasant garden where I
waited for you with Martha.

FAUST: *(Urging her to leave with him.)*
Come with me!
Come with me!

GRETCHEN:
Oh, stay!
Linger with me awhile.
I love it where you are.

(Caressing him.)

FAUST:
Hurry! Now!
Hurry or we're lost.

GRETCHEN:
What is it?
Can't you kiss anymore?
My love,
parted for so short a time,
and you've forgotten how to kiss?
Why am I so afraid in your arms when,
once, only a word,
only a glance from you,
and all Heaven descended upon me
and you kissed me as if to smother me?

Kiss me!
Or I'll kiss you!

(She embraces him.)

Oh—oh, your lips—
they're cold—
cold and silent.
Where has your love gone?
Who's stolen it from me?

(She turns from him.)

FAUST:
    Come! Follow me!
    Oh, my love, be brave!
    I'll love you a thousand times over
    if only you'll follow me!

GRETCHEN: *(Turning to him.)*
    And is it you, then?
    And is it really you?

FAUST:
    It is! But come!

GRETCHEN:
    You undo the chains,
    you hold me again in your arms,
    but how is it you aren't afraid of me?
    And do you know, my love,
    do you really know
    who it is you're setting free?

FAUST:
    Come!
    Night's giving way to dawn.

GRETCHEN:
    I killed my mother,

I drowned my baby.
Wasn't it given to you and me?
To you, too?
Oh, it *is* you!
I can hardly believe it.
Give me your hand!
It's not a dream!
Your dear, sweet hand!
Oh, but it's damp!
Wipe it! It's blood. I see it.
O God, what have you done!
Put up your sword, I beg you.

FAUST:

Let what's done be done!
Forget it!
You're killing me!

GRETCHEN:

No, no, *you* must go on living!
I'll tell you about the graves,
because tomorrow,
first thing tomorrow,
I want you to see to them.
Give mother the best place,
and put my brother beside her,
and me a little to the side,
just not too far!
And the little one put at my right breast.
No one else will ever lie beside me.
It was such sweet dear joy
snuggling next to you!
Now I'll never do it again.
It's as if now
I have to force myself on you,
as if you're pushing me away.
And yet it's you,
and how kind and good you look.

FAUST:

>If you feel it's me, then come with me!

GRETCHEN:

>Out there?

FAUST:

>Into the open!

GRETCHEN:

>If the grave's out there
>and death is waiting, then come!
>From here to my eternal rest
>and not one step beyond—
>You're going now?
>Oh, Heinrich, if only I could, too!

FAUST:

>You can!
>Just *want* to!
>The door is open.

GRETCHEN:

>I don't dare.
>There's no hope for me.
>What good is running away?
>They're waiting out there to catch me.
>It's miserable having to beg,
>and even worse with a guilty conscience!
>It's miserable
>wandering around some foreign country.
>Besides, they'd catch me in the end.

FAUST:

>I'll never leave you.

GRETCHEN:

>Quick! Quick!
>Save your poor child!

Run! Keep on the path by the brook,
over the bridge,
into the woods,
on the left,
there,
by the fence,
in the pond!
Grab it! Hurry!
It's trying to rise!
Kicking!
Save it! Save it!

FAUST:

Come to your senses!
One step and you're free!

GRETCHEN:

If only we were past the hill!
My mother sits there on a stone,
a cold hand grabs me by the hair!
My mother sits there on a stone,
wagging her head.
She doesn't wave,
doesn't nod,
her head's so heavy,
she slept so long she'll never wake up.
She slept so we could enjoy ourselves.
Those were happy times.

FAUST:

If pleading and reasoning do no good,
I'll carry you off by force.

GRETCHEN:

Don't touch me, don't!
I won't have violence!
Don't grab me so murderously!
You know I once did everything you asked.

FAUST:
My love! My love!
A gray day is breaking!

GRETCHEN:
Day!
Yes, dawn.
My last day
pressing in on me!
It was to have been my wedding day.
Now that you've been with Gretchen,
you mustn't tell.
No one.
Oh, and my poor garland's spoiled!
What's done is done!
We'll meet again, but not at the dance.
The crowd's pressing in,
but there's no sound.
The square, the streets can't hold them all.
The bell tolls,
the staff is broken.
They seize and bind me,
drag me to the bloody block.
Each of them feels at their neck
the sharp blade meant for mine.
The world lies silent as the grave.

FAUST:
I wish I had never been born!

MEPHISTOPHELES: *(Appears outside.)*
Let's go, or you're lost!
All this delay, this nonsense,
this babbling!
My horses are shivering,
it's almost day.

GRETCHEN:
What's that rising from the ground?

It's him! It's him!
Send him away!
What does he want in this holy place?
He wants me!

FAUST:
You're to live!

GRETCHEN:
Judgment of God,
I give myself over to you!

MEPHISTOPHELES: *(To FAUST:)*
Let's go, let's go,
or I'll leave the two of you!

GRETCHEN:
Father, I'm yours! Save me!
Angels!
You hosts of Heaven!
Gather round me, guard me!
Heinrich, I shudder to see you!

MEPHISTOPHELES:
She is doomed!

VOICE: *(From above.)*
She is saved!

MEPHISTOPHELES: *(To FAUST.)*
Let's go!

(He vanishes with FAUST.)

VOICE: *(From within, dying away.)*
Heinrich! Heinrich!

FAUST

⤙ PART TWO ⤚

ACT I

XXVIII ✒ A PLEASANT LANDSCAPE. TWILIGHT

FAUST, bedded on a flowery meadow, exhausted, restless, trying to sleep.
Graceful little SPIRITS hover over him in a circle.
ARIEL sings accompanied by Aeolian harps.

ARIEL:

> When the rain of new spring blossoms
>   Blesses every hill and glen,
> When green meadows, bright with showers,
>   Gladden all the sons of men,
> Elvin creatures, great in power,
>   Run to help where help they can,
> Whether he be good or evil,
>   They sorrow for the luckless man.

You spirits, elves,
who hover in broad circles above his head,
show him now the noble nature of elves.
Ease his heart,
root out the fierce strife that tears him,
withdraw the bitter, burning arrows
of self reproach and purge his soul
of the horror he has known.

Four are the watches of the night:
fill them now with gentle kindness
and no delay.
Lower his head first on a cool pillow and
bathe him in the dew of Lethe's waters.
His body, now cramped and rigid,
will gather strength as he relaxes and
rests to meet the new day.
Perform your fairest task as elves,
restore him to the sacred light.

CHORUS OF ELVES: *(Alternately solo, duo, and in chorus.)*

Serenade

When across the soft-green meadows
Warm and gentle breezes play,
Closing round in misty shadows
Softly falls the close of day;
Whispers gently peace to mortals,
Rocks the heart to childlike rest,
Closes up the daylight's portals
To those wearied eyes unblessed.

Notturno

Now the night is deeply darkling,
Hallowed star joins hallowed star,
Lights of power, or faintly sparkling,
Glimmer near, and gleam afar;
Glimmer in the lake so tender,
Gleam in heaven's vault profound,
The bright moon reigns in full-orbed splendor,
Making perfect peace abound.

Mattutino

The hours of the night have vanished,
Joy and grief are passed away.
Feel the promise! Pain is banished!
Trust the new and hopeful day.
Vales grow green, hills steep and steeper,
Shadows deepen thick with leaves,
And the harvest to the reaper
In long silvery billows heaves.

Réveille

Wishes, win them, without number,
Turn and face the dawning day,
You are wrapped in sleep's light slumber,
Cast it off and greet the day!
Be bold where others fear to tread,
Seize the day for all its worth,

Noble hearts are never worsted,
Forge onward to a grand new birth!

(A tremendous clangor heralds the approach of the sun.)

ARIEL:

Harken! Hark! The storm of hours!
Pealing out to spirit ears,
Rejoice! Another day is ours!
Rejoice! Another dawn appears!
Granite gates are crashing, crashing,
Phoebus's car wheels rattling, clashing—
What clangor announces the rising sun!
Drums and trumpets pealing clear,
Dazzling eye and stunning ear!
Away! Our elfin reign is done.
Into flowery chalice creep,
Rest in quiet, deep in sleep,
Or under rock, or under cleft;
If you hear it, you are deaf.

FAUST:

Life's pulses beat in me now with fresh vitality,
ready to greet the dawn's ethereal day.
Earth, great earth,
you were loyal to me in the night,
and now you, too,
revived anew,
already infuse me with a grand desire,
rousing in me a powerful resolve:
to strive and ever to strive to the pinnacle of Being.

The world is unlocked to view
in the dawn's first dim light;
the woods are alive and ring with a thousand voices;
and valleys high and low are shrouded in mist
till the clear light of heaven descends to their depths.
And from the misty haze
boughs and branches waken

and burst from the fragrant abyss where they rest.
Colors, too, colors upon colors,
emerge clear as day from the fertile ground
where every flower and leaf
is wet with pearls of dew.
The world about me has become a Paradise!

Look up!
Up there!
Already mighty peaks announce
that most solemn of hours!
They are the first to enjoy the eternal light
that later makes its way down to us.
And now the upper meadows are agleam
with brilliant clarity in all their greenness,
and step by step the slow descent is concluded—
and out comes the sun!
Ah, and dazed already by its radiance,
I turn aside my eyes from his painful glare.

Is it ever otherwise?
When with a keen desire
we have struggled our way up to the supreme moment,
and find the gates of fulfillment flung wide,
we are met by a burst of flame from eternal depths
that leaves us standing confounded.
Our aim was to light life's torch,
and an ocean surge of fire engulfs us.
And what a fire it is!
Is it love,
is it hate,
this fire that swirls around us,
alternating pain and joy beyond endurance,
driving us back to earth again
to hide in the misty veils of early youth?

Well—
then let the sun remain at my back.
I look and I see with greater and greater delight

this roaring waterfall gushing from its rocky crag.
Plunging from level to level,
it shatters into a thousand streams,
and then into thousands more, sending up clouds
of spray heaven high. And then,
gloriously rising from this storm of commotion,
the tinted arch of the rainbow's changing permanence—
now sharply etched,
now melting into air—
scatters fragrant showers all around.
In this I see a mirror of human striving.
Consider, and it's easily understood:
Life is not light, but the refracted color.

XXIX ᵏ IMPERIAL PALACE

The throne room. STATE COUNCIL awaiting the EMPEROR.
Trumpets. Splendidly dressed COURTIERS of every sort step forward.
The EMPEROR ascends the throne, the ASTROLOGER at his right hand.

EMPEROR:
　　Most dear and loyal subjects,
　　I greet you assembled here from near and far.
　　I see my philosopher at my side,
　　but what has happened to my Fool?

SQUIRE:
　　As you mounted the stairs, Sire,
　　he collapsed just behind your trailing robe.
　　Dead or drunk, who knows?
　　They lugged that tub of lard away.

SECOND SQUIRE:
　　In the blink of an eye, Sire,
　　another presented himself on the spot.
　　Exquisitely dressed he may be,
　　but he's so grotesque he frightens everyone.
　　He's being held at the door by guards

with crossed halberds.
Ah, but here he is, the brazen fool!

MEPHISTOPHELES: *(Kneeling at the throne.)*
What is accursed yet always welcome?
What is desired yet always rejected?
What is forever being protected?
What is harshly censured and accused?
Who is it you may not summon?
Whose name is a delight to all?
What approaches the steps to your throne?
What self-banishes itself from you?

EMPEROR:
Spare us your words for now!
This is no place for riddles;
that's these gentlemen's affair.
Ah, but I have it!
Let them pose theirs,
and you do the solving.
Now, that I'd be curious to hear!
I fear my former Fool has gone for good.
Come! Take his place beside me!

(MEPHISTOPHELES mounts the steps and stands at his left.)

MURMURS FROM THE CROWD:
—A new Fool.
—New troubles for us.
—Where's he from?
—How did he get in?
—The old Fool fell.
—He's done for.
—That one was a tub.
—This one's a twig.

EMPEROR:
So, most dear and loyal subjects,
I welcome you from near and far!

You are gathered here together
under an auspicious star that promises
prosperity and happiness.
But why, I ask you, why at just this time,
when we would free ourselves of cares and troubles,
when we long to pull on mummers' masks for Carnival
and do nothing so much as enjoy ourselves—
why, then, are we met,
why do we torment ourselves
with affairs of state?
But since you said it had to be,
well, then, let it be!

CHANCELLOR:
Justice,
that highest of virtues,
rests on the Emperor's head like a halo.
He alone has the power to exercise it.
What all men love, demand, desire,
what they desperately need,
it is his prerogative to give them,
his subjects, his people.

Ah, but what good is intelligence to the mind,
goodness to the heart,
readiness to the hand,
when the body politic rages with fever,
and one single evil spawns a whole host of evils?
One glance from this height across your vast empire, Sire,
will reveal a nightmare
in which Deformity reigns among deformities,
where Lawlessness rules in place of law,
and Error multiplies and populates the earth.

One man steals cattle, another a neighbor's wife,
and a third runs off with the altar's
chalice, candlestick, and crucifix,
and they end up boasting about it for years
without a scratch to limb or reputation.

Plaintiffs crowd into courtrooms
where the judge sits in state on his well-stuffed pillow,
while in the streets seething angry mobs
threaten rebellion.
A man supported by accomplices worse than he
has the audacity to brag of his heinous crime,
his infamy, whereas when innocence
has only itself to defend it
you will always hear the verdict "Guilty!"

And what happens in consequence?
The world falls apart,
decency is outraged,
and how is a spirit to develop
that will lead us to what is right and proper?
In the end, the worthy man has no choice
but to bow to flattery and bribery,
and the judge in his inability to punish
must join forces with the criminal.
For all the blackness of the picture I've painted,
I would prefer to have painted it even darker.

(Pause.)

Decisions cannot be avoided.
When all who injure are injured in turn,
then Majesty itself is threatened.

COMMANDER-IN-CHIEF:
What wild, chaotic days we live in!
Everyone kills and is killed in turn.
No matter our commands, they fall on deaf ears.
The burger behind his city's walls,
the knight atop his rock-bound eyrie,
have sworn themselves to outlast us
even to the fall of the empire,
and they maintain their forces intact.
Our mercenaries grow restless,
loudly demanding their pay;

and except for the fact that we owe them wages,
they'd long ago have deserted us.
Forbid them what they all demand
and you might as well stick your head in a hornet's nest.
The empire they swore to defend to the last man,
they themselves plunder and lay waste
from end to end, and their savage rioting
proceeds unchecked.
Already half our world lies in ruin,
and surrounding kingdoms say it's no concern of theirs.

TREASURER:
So much for allies!
The subsidies they pledged
come through like water from a well run dry.
Besides, Sire,
in the vastness of your empire
whose hands has property fallen into?
Go anywhere and you find
a new proprietor has moved in
who is very protective of his independence.
And what do we do? All we can:
stand passively by and watch him getting on.
We've given away so many rights,
we've no right left for ourselves.

And as for parties, as they're called,
there's no relying on them. Whether they
love you, hate you, praise you, chide you,
it means nothing anymore.
The Guelfs and the Ghibellines are laying low right now,
resting up from their latest encounter.
Who today cares about helping his neighbor?
Me and mine is their only concern.
Where's the gold?
The gates to it are barricaded.
Everyone scratching and scraping for anything they can get.
And still our treasury is empty.

STEWARD:

> Ah, and the things *I* have to contend with!
> Day after day we do all we can to save,
> but day after day our needs increase,
> along with my troubles.
> The cooks, of course, lack for nothing.
> Wild boar, venison, rabbit, turkey, chicken,
> geese and ducks, payment in kind as
> secured revenue,
> these still come in fairly regularly.
> But we *are* short on wine.
> There was a time when cask on cask
> was piled high in the cellar,
> the best vineyards, the best vintages,
> but the endless guzzling of the nobles
> has drained us to the last drops.
> The City Council, too, has had to
> tap its stocks. They grab any mug or bowl
> to swill it down, and the next thing you know
> they're under the table.
>
> So now I pay bills and wages with money from loans
> that eat up the future before it's arrived.
> Our pigs haven't time to fatten,
> the pillow's been pawned that we lay our heads on,
> and even the bread on the table is mortgaged.

EMPEROR: *(To MEPHISTOPHELES, after a moment's reflection.)*

> And you, Fool,
> what complaint do you have?

MEPHISTOPHELES:

> I? Why, none! None at all!
> I only look around and see the splendor
> of you and your court! Can confidence
> be lacking where Your Majesty wields absolute power
> and has forces to rout all opposition?
> Where goodwill is strengthened by ready intelligence,
> and energy of many kinds is at his disposal?

Given the circumstances,
how could evil prevail
where the stars shine so brightly?

MURMURS FROM THE CROWD:
—He's a rogue.
—He knows what's what.
—Clever with words.
—At least for now.
—I see
—what's behind all this.
—Well?
—Some scheme.

MEPHISTOPHELES:
Go where you like, there's always lack to be found.
Sometimes this, sometimes that.
Here it happens to be money.
Of course, you can't just pick it up off the floor;
but wisdom is clever in raising what lies most deep.
It's buried beneath ancient walls and in mountain veins,
coined and uncoined alike, and if you ask me
who's to bring it to light, I'd tell you:
a man blest with the mind that Nature gave him.

CHANCELLOR:
Nature! Mind!
How dare you talk that way to Christians!
We burn people for that!
Dangerous words!
Nature is sin, Mind is the devil's work!
Together they breed Doubt,
their misshapen bastard.

No more of that!
In our Emperor's ancient lands
time has brought forth only two estates,
the clergy and the knights.
It's they who guard the throne

against storms of violence,
and they take Church and State as their reward.

Rebellion, sedition, is the product of the
confused mind of the mob!
And who's behind it?
Heretics! Sorcerers!
They undermine us!
In town! In country!

(To MEPHISTOPHELES.)

And now you with your impudent trickery
are trying to smuggle them into our exalted circles.

(To the Court.)

Don't trust them!
They are kin to fools.
Their hearts are depraved.

MEPHISTOPHELES:
Aha!
Now I know you for what you are!
Men of learning.
What you don't touch is miles away;
what you don't grasp doesn't exist;
what you don't figure you take to be false;
what you don't weigh you take to be weightless;
what you don't mint you think is worthless.

EMPEROR:
This isn't solving our problem.
We still have needs.
What are you getting at with your Lenten sermon?
I'm sick and tired of the ifs, whens, and buts!
What we need is money!
All right, so get it for us!

MEPHISTOPHELES:

    I'll get you what you want.

    I'll get you more.

    Oh, it's easy, to be sure;

    but what's easy is always difficult.

    It's there, down there, lying there.

    The trick is how to get it—

    and who knows that?

    Think about it.

    In those days when hordes of migrating humanity

    flooded the land,

    those times of terror,

    this man, that man, many men,

    in fear hid away in the earth,

    here and there,

    their most precious possessions.

    It's been that way always,

    from the times of the mighty Romans to yesterday—

    even to today.

    And it's all still there,

    buried in the earth,

    lying in silence.

    And since the earth is the Emperor's,

    it's the Emperor who should have it.

TREASURER:

    For a Fool he's not doing badly.

    It's an ancient Imperial law.

CHANCELLOR:

    There's something not right here.

    It's Satan laying snares of wrought gold.

STEWARD:

    Let him bring what we need

    and I can deal with a bit of chicanery

COMMANDER-IN-CHIEF:

    Wise Fool, this!

What he promises will benefit all.
Where it comes from the military man
isn't prone to question.

MEPHISTOPHELES:
And if you think I've been less than truthful,
here's another, the Astrologer!
Question him!
If anyone knows the heavens, he does,
every sphere, every circle, the mansions, the hours.
Tell us, then, sir, how it looks up there.

MURMURS FROM THE CROWD:
—What a pair of rogues.
—It's a conspiracy.
—A fool and a dreamer.
—And so near the throne.
—The same old song.
—The Fool prompts.
—The Sage speaks.

ASTROLOGER: (Speaks, MEPHISTOPHELES prompts.)
The Sun himself is purest gold;
Mercury, his messenger,
run errands if well paid;
Lady Venus has bewitched you
in youth and age, smiling kindly
down upon you; chaste Luna is
changeable and full of caprice;
if Mars doesn't fail to strike,
he threatens with bluster.
Jupiter's shine is still the brightest,
while Saturn so far away seems small;
as metal we don't honor him much,
but for his weight,
a weight very great.
Ah, but when Luna and Sol accord,
gold with silver,
all's well with the world!

Everything is then at hand:
palaces, gardens,
lovely breasts, rosy cheeks.
All this may be had
from a highly learned man,
for no man here can do it for himself.

EMPEROR:
Everything he says I hear twice,
and still I'm not convinced.

MURMURS FROM THE CROWD:
—What is all this?
—A tired joke.
—Astrological nonsense.
—Alchemistic drivel.
—I've heard it all before.
—Had my leg pulled once too often.
—Just let him come.
—He's a fake, a quack.

MEPHISTOPHELES:
There they stand, wide-eyed and gaping,
refusing to honor my great find.
One of them babbles of mandrake root,
another claims he's seen the black hound.
Let them sneer all they like,
crack jokes, cry sorcery,
the time will come when their soles will itch
and their steady tread take a tumble.

It's then you will feel
the eternal hidden power of Nature.
From deep in subterranean depths
a trace of life works its way to the surface.
When your every limb is a-tremble,
when a certain place has an uncanny air,
don't hesitate then, but take up shovel and pick
and dig, for that's the spot, that's where it is,
that's where your treasure lies hidden!

MURMURS FROM THE CROWD:
—My foot feels like lead.
—There a cramp in my arm.
—That's gout.
—My big toe tickles.
—My whole back aches.
—This must be the biggest treasure trove ever.

EMPEROR:
Then hurry!
You won't slip away this time!
Prove your blathering lies are true!
Show us these noble chambers, now!
I'll lay down my sword and scepter and dig
with my own imperial hands and finish the job.
And if it's a lie, I'll send you to Hell.

MEPHISTOPHELES: *(Aside.)*
I dare say I could find my way there, all right.

(Aloud.)

But I can't stress enough the unclaimed wealth
waiting to be discovered everywhere.

The farmer plowing his field
turns up a pot of gold; scraping saltpeter
from its clay sides, trembling with joy,
he finds in his destitute hand
a roll of the purest gold.
As for that man with a nose for treasure,
what vaults there are to be blown open,
what clefts and passages must be passed through
to arrive at the region bordering the underworld!

There in spacious cellars long sealed off,
he will see row upon ordered row
of tankards of gold, bowls, plates,
goblets in abundance made of rubies,

and if he likes, he can use them,
for ancient wines stand nearby. But—
and you can take my word for it—
the wooden staves rotted long ago,
and tartar forms the cask that holds the wine.
Not only gold and jewels seek out the night,
but also the essences of such wines.

The wise man works here undismayed.
To search for treasure in daylight is child's play;
mysteries are at home in darkness.

EMPEROR:

I leave the mysteries to you!
What good is gloom?
Things worth having must be seen.
And who can tell a thief in the dark?
At night all cats are gray and cows black,
and as for those gold-heaped pots of yours,
plow them up and let us see them.

MEPHISTOPHELES:

Take hoe and spade and dig for yourself.
The work of a peasant will make you strong,
and a herd of golden calves will rise from the earth.
With no hesitation then,
and with full delight,
you can adorn yourself and your belovèd,
for jewels, colorful and sparkling,
will be yours to enhance both majesty and beauty.

EMPEROR:

Yes! Just hurry!
How long must we wait?

ASTROLOGER: *(Prompted again by MEPHISTOPHELES.)*
Sire, you must moderate
your too great eagerness.

First let us celebrate
Carnival and its merriment.
Distractions won't help,
but only keep us from our goal.
We must compose ourselves first,
do so in penitence,
and having done so,
earn the lower
by means of the higher.
Who wants the good
must first be good;
who seeks pleasure
must tame his blood;
who insists on wine
must press ripe grapes;
who longs for miracles
must strengthen his faith.

EMPEROR:

    Very well!
We'll pass our time in merriment,
and when Ash Wednesday comes
it will be all the more welcome.
So let's celebrate Carnival all the more wildly.

    (Trumpets. Exeunt all but MEPHISTOPHELES.)

MEPHISTOPHELES:

    Luck and merit
come as a pair
in the human design;
but little these fools
know of that.
If they held in hand
the Philosopher's Stone,
what good would it do them
without a philosopher?

XXX ⤴ A SPACIOUS HALL

With adjoining rooms decorated for the Carnival Masquerade.

HERALD:
> Forget for once you're in German lands,
> where Devils and Dunces and Death dance wildly.
> Today we're to have a bright and lusty revelry!
>
> On his journey to Rome,
> our great and Holy Emperor
> saw to his own profit, yes,
> but us he didn't forget,
> he saw to us, too,
> to our pleasure, too.
>
> Crossing the lofty Alps,
> he saw a land of infinite cheer,
> of unspeakable and eternal brightness,
> and, seeing, he conquered it.
>
> Then kneeling humbly to the Holy Father,
> he bent low to receive the right to rule;
> and though he went to fetch a golden crown,
> he fetched for us, too,
> in his infinite wisdom,
> the Fool's Cap and Carnival Mask.
>
> Now born anew in a festive mood,
> every man of us,
> worldly wise,
> pulls it down snugly
> over head and ears,
> and though he plays the Fool
> with wild and rowdy abandon,
> he remains as wise as ever he was.
>
> I see them there already,
> thronging and swaying this way and that,

in groups and pairs,
fondly mingling,
groups forming and groups dissolving,
in and out,
no fear of propriety.
The world with its untold fund of follies
remains unchanged:
one great, grand Fool!

FLOWER GIRLS: *(Singing to mandolins.)*

Drawn here by your courtly splendor
Decked out in all our best are we,
Maids of Florence, come to render
Tribute to your courtesy.

In our curly nut-brown hair
We have woven bright spring flowers,
Silken threads, and streamers fair,
As if plucked from nature's bowers.

We truly hope to win your praises
For our very special art;
Our flowers bloom all year in glazes,
Artificial and very smart.

Scraps of every color mingle,
Ordered to content your taste;
You may scoff at them in single,
But not *en masse* in order placed.

Charming are we to the sight,
Darlings to the eye and heart,
For woman's nature is bound tight
To the very soul of art.

HERALD:

Lovely ladies, show us now
the brimming baskets you bear on your heads,
and your bulging armloads of colorful flowers.

Let everyone choose what he likes best!
And be swift about it,
so every arbor and corridor becomes a garden!
Draw round,
for both the girls and their goods
are worthy closer inspection.

FLOWER GIRLS:

We make our sales, delightfully playing,
So let there be no haggling here;
Let each one know just what you're saying,
And make a purchase without fear.

(The FLOWER GIRLS daintily lay out their wares under the green arbors.)

GARDENERS: *(Singing to bass lutes.)*

Flowers, there, where you have placed them,
Charmingly your heads adorn,
So our fruits you will not scorn;
They'll delight you, if you taste them.

King plums, cherries, ripened peaches,
We sun-bronzed workers bid you buy!
The worst of judges is the eye,
So trust what tongue or palate teaches.

Come, come all with gladdening eyes,
To a feast we you invite;
A rose you can always poetize,
But an apple you must bite.

You, now in the bloom of youth,
Let us join you in your labors,
Let us build our booth by your booth,
As is only right for neighbors.

Beneath these arbors with festoons wound,
In the shade of peach-hung bowers,
Everything you want is found,
Buds and petals, fruit and flowers.

(Singing in turns and accompanied by guitars and bass lutes, the FLOWER GIRLS and GARDENERS continue to lay out their wares in tiers that gradually mount upward and offer them for sale.)

(Enter MOTHER and DAUGHTER.)

MOTHER:
> Dear girl, dear child,
> when you were born
> what a darling face you had,
> and so dainty of figure!
> I dressed you in a lovely bonnet,
> seeing you wed to the wealthiest of men,
> a bride already, his wife, a lady.
>
> But how many years have passed since then,
> unused, and nothing.
> Beaux have come and beaux have gone,
> beaux of all kinds, fled on by.
> Oh, yes, you danced sprightly with one,
> and with another you gave him a nudge,
> a subtle hint.
>
> Parties we planned all went wrong;
> Forfeit games and Odd-Man-Out,
> all, all a waste.
> But tonight be wise, love, bait your hook,
> spread your legs,
> fools are out in force, my dear!
> Catch one.

(Other beautiful young GIRLS join the others and intimate chatter ensues. FISHERMEN and BIRDCATCHERS with nets, fishing poles, limed sticks, and other gear, enter and fraternize with the GIRLS. Mutual attempts to attract, catch, evade, and hold fast lead to opportunities for pleasant banter.)

WOODCUTTERS: *(Enter boisterous and boorish.)*
> Room! Make room!

Give place! Make space!
Trees we fell,
They fall pell-mell,
Down as we tear them,
Down to the dell!
Crunching, crashing,
Straining and lashing,
They crash in the dust,
Fall, for they must!
Down to the dust!
And off as we bear them
They push and they thrust.
Say this in our praise
To the end of our days,
Were there no rough men
To work in the land,
Where, tell me, then,
Would you fine folks stand?
This is the truth,
Never forget it,
If we didn't sweat it,
How would you stretch
At your ease,
if you please?
You would all freeze!

PULCINELLI: *(Clumsy, almost silly.)*

Fools, you are hacks,
Born with bent backs!
We are the wise, who
Work never knew!
See here, our caps,
Our jackets and flaps,
We wear them so lightly,
So gaily, so sprightly—
We who are idle,
We saunter, we sidle,
In slippered feet,
Through market and street,

There to stand gaping,
Crowing and japing;
Under hubbub loud,
Through thronging crowd,
Eel-like we slip off,
All *en masse* trip off,
A rumpus to raise.
Whether you praise,
Or whether you blame,
To us it's the same!

PARASITES: *(Fawning greedily.)*
Woodcutters lusty,
You and your trusty
Coal-burning kin,
You are our men!
For bowing, for scraping,
Assenting and smiling,
Grand phrases shaping,
Obscure and beguiling,
Meant to blow hot
Or cold, or what not,
The moment to please—
What profit all these?
Let fire be given
In volume enormous,
Straight out of heaven,
If we had no billet,
No charcoal to fill it,
Our fireplace gaping,
Pray, how would it warm us
With heartening glow,
With no coal clumps to throw?
Steaming and roasting,
Stewing and toasting!
The grand gourmet
Is the licker of dishes
Who scents roast on the way,
And has visions of fishes

That render him able
To sit down at table.

DRUNKARD: *(Oblivious.)*
If nothing unpleasant gets in my way,
I'm bound to have a jolly day!
Look what I've brought you here without measure,
Songs to delight you, and holiday leisure!
And that's why I drink now! Drink-adrink-drink!
Clink glasses now, boys! Clinkety-clink!
You boys back there! Come, join in our fun!
When glasses clink, what's done is done!

My wife she jeered when she saw my clothes,
"You look like a clown!" she said, and rose,
And said she thinks I look like a joke,
And for all she cares I can lay down and croak!
But I drink for all that! Drink-adrink-drink!
Clink glasses now, boys! Clinkety-clink!
You boys are jokes, too! So join in the fun!
Clink your glasses, and done is done!

Never tell me I've lost my way!
For I know where I am, and I am where I say.
And I know where I am I will get my fill,
Credit lacking, I'll get credit still.
So I'll keep on drinking! Drink-adrink-drink!
Come on, boys! Now! Clinkety-clink!
To each his own, and join in the fun!
Clink your glasses, you've not yet done!

I take my pleasure where I can,
I do as well as any man;
And if I can no longer stand,
I'll lay me down and feel so grand.

CHORUS:
And so, good brothers, drink-adrink-drink!
Raise your glasses, clinkety-clink!

One of us ended under the table,
So keep your seat as long as you're able!

(Enter the GRACES.)

AGLAIA:

Into living we bring grace!
In your giving give it place!

HEGEMONE:

In receiving grace retain!
Sweet it is a wish to gain.

EUPHROSYNE:

And in days of thoughtful mood,
Let grace sweeten gratitude.

HERALD:

Everyone! Please! To one side!
What approaches now is not of your kind!
Behold a mountainous beast,
hung with rich, bright tapestries,
two tusks in its head and a snakelike trunk.
What a mystery!

Ah, but I have it!
I have the key!
On his neck a delicate woman
guides him with a slender staff.
And on his back in a towering structure
another one, glorious, exalted,
whose dazzling radiance all but blinds me.
Beside the beast are two women in chains;
one of them fearful, the other glad;
one of them hoping to be free,
the other believing herself free.
Let each now tell us who she is.

(Enter ZOÏLO-THERSITES.)

ZOÏLO-THERSITES:

    Hooo! Hooo!
    I see I've come in the nick of time and
    name the lot of you a tawdry mess!
    But my special target is Lady Victory up there.
    With her white wings spread
    she thinks she's an eagle, no doubt, and
    everything she sees she thinks is hers,
    people and lands alike.
    But bring me face to face
    with what is praiseworthy,
    and my anger rages.
    I bring the high low,
    and the low high,
    make crooked the straight,
    and the straight crooked.
    That alone is the source of my health.
    That is how I want it on earth.

HERALD:

    Evil cur! Take this!
    This commanding stroke of my pious staff!
    Cringe now, writhe and twist!
    But what's this?
    The double-masked dwarf crumples
    to a hideous shapeless mass!
    What is this miracle?
    The mass becomes an egg that swells and bursts,
    and out of it a pair of twins,
    an adder and a bat!
    The one crawls off in the dust,
    the other flies to the rafters!
    They hurry off to meet outside.
    I think wouldn't care to join them.

MURMURS FROM THE CROWD:

    —Hurry! There's dancing over there!
    —No! I wish I was out of here!
    —Do you feel the spells they're weaving, that crew?

—It whizzed past my hair!
—I felt it on my feet!
—None of us are hurt.
—But we've all had a fright.
—The fun's over.
—It's what they wanted, the beasts!

HERALD:

> Long the herald of your masquerades,
> I've stood at the gate and never failed
> to keep from the hall any evil
> to disturb your revels.
> But now, I fear, airborne spirits
> are surging through every window,
> and I know nothing to save you from ghosts or sorcery.
> The dwarf was suspicious enough,
> but now at the back there's a mighty onrush of figures
> whose meaning I'd like to expound,
> except I know nothing about them,
> and I ask your help.

> There! Look!
> Swerving through the crowd
> a glorious four-spanned coach,
> though it clears no path,
> no one makes way,
> no one pushes or shoves to get back.
> And there, far off,
> stars, glittering, rising, many-colored,
> shining, shifting,
> like a magic-lantern aglow,
> and on it comes snorting like a mighty storm.

> Make way!
> I shudder to see it!

BOY CHARIOTEER:

> Halt, my coursers!
> Slow, there, slow down!

Tame your wings,
mind the accustomed reins!
Master yourselves as I master you.
When I urge you onward, surge away.
But now we must honor these halls!

Look around you,
see the admiring crowd
thronging forward,
circle round circle!

But come, Herald, do your duty.
Describe us in your fashion,
name us, before we take off.
Being allegories,
I suspect you should recognize us.

HERALD:
Name you?
I couldn't possibly.
I'd do better
describing you.

BOY CHARIOTEER:
Then do so.

HERALD:
I must confess, first,
that you're young
and you're handsome.
A half-grown boy
that the ladies will happily
see fully grown one day.
You appear a future ladies' man,
a born seducer.

BOY CHARIOTEER:
Not bad!
But continue.

Let's see you find
the riddle's happy solution.

HERALD:
There's the lightning's flash
in the black of your eyes,
and night in the pitch-black
dark of your hair,
brightened by the jeweled
ribbon that circles it.
And what a delicate garment
flows from shoulder to foot,
hemmed in purple and
glittering tinsel.
You could almost
be taken for a girl,
except that, for good or ill,
even now you'd
rate with the girls
who'd put you through
love's ABCs.

BOY CHARIOTEER:
And what of him
seated here in such splendor
on my chariot's throne?

HERALD:
He appears a king,
rich and kind,
and the man who wins
his favor is fortunate!
Nothing further to
strive for himself,
he looks out only
for the needy,
and his pure pleasure in
giving is greater than the
happiness he takes in
possessions.

BOY CHARIOTEER:
   Good, but don't stop there;
   describe him precisely.

HERALD:
   How does one describe dignity?
   That healthy moon of a face
   and full mouth,
   the full-blown cheeks
   beneath a handsome turban,
   and luxuriously comfortable
   in his pleated robe!
   And what's to be said
   of his noble bearing!
   He looks every inch the ruler!

BOY CHARIOTEER:
   He's Plutus,
   god of Wealth,
   come in splendor
   to your Emperor
   who desires mightily
   to see him.

HERALD:
   And you?
   Tell us of yourself.
   Who are you?

BOY DRIVER:
   I am Prodigality.
   I am Poetry.
   The spendthrift who achieves fulfillment
   by squandering what is most personal to him.
   Like Plutus, I am immeasurably rich;
   I enliven his dances,
   his feasts and festivals,
   and what he lacks I supply.

HERALD:

> Boasting becomes you;
> but now let's see some of your arts.

BOY CHARIOTEER:

> Watch! I snap my fingers
> and already the chariot glitters brightly!
> Look!
> A string of pearls leaps out!

(He continues snapping his fingers all about.)

> You see?
> Golden clasps for neck or ear!
> Combs, coronets, rings set with priceless jewels!
> Now and again I dispense a spark of flame,
> hoping to see it catch somewhere.

HERALD:

> Look at them!
> Snatching and grabbing for treasure!
> The poor boy's nearly in danger of them!
> The way he throws gems,
> you'd think it was a dream,
> and everyone in the whole hall snatching!

> Ah, but here come new tricks!
> No matter what one seizes,
> it's a pale reward:
> it flutters off and he's
> empty handed
> Strings of pearls
> dissolve into so many beetles;
> they throw them off and they
> buzz around their heads,
> the poor dunces!
> Others, instead of a solid handful,
> find all they've grasped is
> frivolous butterflies.

The scoundrel!
How much he promises,
how little he delivers!

BOY CHARIOTEER:
It's clear, Herald,
you're good at announcing masks,
but it's not a herald's courtly duty
to delve beneath the surface.
That requires a sharper vision.
But I have no quarrel with you.
It is to you, my lord,
I will address my questions.

(He turns to PLUTUS.)

Wasn't it to me you entrusted
the whirlwind speed of your chariot?
And have I not successfully guided it for you?
Driven it well?
To where you've directed?
Have I not in bold flight soared aloft
to win for you the palm of victory?
Have I ever fought for you and failed?
And if a laurel wreath adorns your brow,
wasn't it I who wove it with wit and dedication?

PLUTUS:
If it is for me to bear witness
to your good character,
then I happily acknowledge
that you are spirit of my spirit.
Your every deed mirrors my will,
and you are far richer than I.
I prize above all my crowns
the laurel I now reward you with,
and I declare freely to all:
You are my belovèd son;
in you I am well pleased.

BOY CHARIOTEER: *(To the CROWD.)*
  I have strewn among you
  my finest gifts.
  On this head and that I see
  glowing a tiny flame
  I sparked into life.
  It leaps lightly
  from one to another;
  on this head it lingers,
  on others not,
  and only rarely
  does it flare up
  and in a brief flowering
  illuminate all around it.
  Sadly, on most,
  it dies out, unrecognized.

WOMEN GOSSIPS:
  —Do you see?
  —Up there?
  —On the chariot?
  —A charlatan!
  —And behind him a clown!
  —I've never seen him so thin!
  —Skin and bones!
  —Pinch him, he'd never feel it!

STARVELING:
  Women!
  Ah! They disgust me!
  Keep them away!
  I know I'll never suit them!
  In days when women ran the house,
  my name was Madam Avarice.
  Things were well run then,
  house in good order,
  much coming in,
  nothing going out!
  I kept a sharp eye on chests and cupboards

to see they didn't leak gold,
and they called it a mortal sin.

Ah, but what do women today
know about penny-pinching?
Like every miserable debtor
they have more desires than dollars.
And what's the husband to do?
Endure! Endure!
You turn around, a debt stares you in the face!
And then, let's say, she spins and earns some cash,
what does she do?
Spends it on herself, on her beau!
Ah, and that's not all!
Off she flies with her stable of lovers
to eat and drink better than ever her husband did!

As for me, her every move
makes me lust more for gold.
No more Madam Avarice for me!
I'm a man now, not a woman!
Call me Mr. Miser.

LEADER OF THE WOMEN:
  Ignore the old dragon!
  It's all lies and deception!
  He's come to make trouble with the men,
  and they're in enough trouble as it is.

CROWD OF WOMEN: *(En masse.)*
  —The scarecrow!
  —Give it to him!
  —Him? Threaten us?
  —Old skin-and-bones?
  —Let him try, the ugly banshee!
  —Paper dragons!
  —Wood and paper!
  —Let's get him!

HERALD:

    I order you by my staff, stay calm!
    Ah, but my help's not needed now.
    They've come to life, these fearsome monsters!
    I see them spread their double pairs of wings!
    How quickly they've won the space!
    They shake their scaly jaws and fire spews forth!
    The crowd flies in every direction!

    Now there's room.

    (PLUTUS descends from the chariot.)

    How regally he steps from the chariot!
    He signals;
    the dragons lift down the chest of gold
    with Avarice seated upon it.
    It rests now at his feet.
    A miracle has happened.

PLUTUS: *(To the BOY CHARIOTEER.)*

    Rid of this all-too-heavy burden,
    I set you free.
    Hurry off, now,
    to that realm
    that is uniquely yours.
    It is not here.
    Here we are surrounded by the
    confused, the ugly,
    the turbulent, the wild.
    Yours is a place where
    you can see with clarity,
    where you are yours alone,
    dependent only on yourself.
    There where beauty and goodness
    alone give delight—
    in solitude.
    Create your own world there!

BOY CHARIOTEER:

    As for me,
    I regard myself
    as your most honored ambassador,
    and will love you as next of kin.
    Where you are,
    is abundance;
    where I am,
    each feels himself
    gloriously blest.
    And yet,
    confused by this contrary life,
    man often hesitates:
    whether to follow you
    and live a life of ease,
    or me,
    and never cease
    to strive for the new.
    I never act in secret.
    Even with only a breath
    I give myself away.

    Farewell, now!
    I know you wish me happiness,
    but if ever you want me back,
    just whisper, and I'll be here.

    (Exit the BOY CHARIOTEER in the chariot.)

PLUTUS:

    It is time to release
    our treasures from captivity.
    I strike the locks
    with the herald's staff,
    and open it flies!
    See there!
    Molten gold,
    red as blood,
    bubbling up in brazen kettles

to threaten the treasure
of crowns, chains and rings.

CRIES FROM THE CROWD:
 —Look there, look!
 —Look at it well up!
 —Filled to the brim!
 —Golden vessels melting!
 —Rolls of gold coins tumbling!
 —Ducats dance as if being minted!
 —Oh, how my heart leaps!
 —All my desires!
 —Roll and spin across the floor!
 —It's offered!
 —Take it!
 —Bend and scoop it up!
 —We'll be rich!
 —The rest of us take the chest!

HERALD:
 What's this? Idiots!
 You think it's real?
 You think it's gold?
 It's a joke, a masquerade prank!
 Enough greed for one night!
 Counter chips would be too good for you!
 Fools!
 Taking a pretty effect
 for crude truth!
 What good is truth to you?
 Snatchers at illusion!
 Plutus, masked hero,
 master of mummery,
 drive them away for me!

PLUTUS:
 I dare say your staff will do.
 Lend it to me.
 I'll dip it deep

in this fiery brew.
There!
Now, masks, take care!
See how it sparkles and spits,
how it crackles!
The staff is beginning to glow!
Crowd too close and you'll
end up a cinder!
I'll begin my circuit now.

THE CROWD: *(Shouting and jostling.)*
—Oh, we're done for!
—Escape if you can!
—Back, get back, you in the rear!
—Hot sparks in my face!
—The red-hot staff is coming at me!
—We're lost, all of us!
—Back, get back, you masked fools!
—Idiots!
—If I had wings, I'd fly!

PLUTUS:
The crowd's scattered,
pushed back,
and no one burned,
only frightened.
Still, for safety's sake,
I'll draw an invisible line.

HERALD:
What a magnificent feat!
I'm grateful to your
wisdom and power!

PLUTUS:
Be patient, my noble friend;
there's more violence to come.

MISER:
Well, now, what do you say we amuse ourselves

with a look around at this charming assembly.
Ah, and wouldn't you know,
there, there she is,
woman,
always out front,
always when there's something tasty to be nibbled
or some sight to be stared at.
But let me assure you,
not being a shriveled prune as yet,
I still know a beautiful woman when I see one!
And since today it's to be had for the asking,
I think I just might go a-wooing.

Ah, but with all this noise, this crowd,
who can make himself heard?
I'll have to resort to a bit of pantomime.
There are some things hands, feet, and gestures
just can't say, and so I'll fall back on my arts
for a ruder prank.
This gold is a metal can be molded into any shape.
I'll treat it like wet clay and see what I get.

HERALD:
What's that skinny fool up to?
How can a walking skeleton be funny?
Look at him there,
kneading that gold like dough,
soft and pliable,
squeezing, pulling,
pummeling, pounding—
and still it's shapeless.
But there, look,
he's turning to those women,
and they scream and screech in disgust,
trying to escape.
I fear this rogue
is well versed in evil.
He appears to delight
the more he offends decency.
I can't just stand here

and watch this happen!
Where's my staff?
I'll drive him out!

PLUTUS:

He has no idea what's about to descend.
Soon there'll be no room for his foolish antics.
Law is a powerful weapon, but necessity more so.

TUMULT AND SINGING:

We, the Wild Men, shout and yell,
Sweeping from mountain height and dell,
We come, and stop us no one can,
We celebrate the mighty Pan.
We know what none else know, and fling
Ourselves into the vacant ring.

PLUTUS:

I know you well, and I know your great god Pan.
This is a bold plan you've entered into.
I also know what not everyone knows,
and so I dutifully open this circle's narrow boundary.

(Aside.)

I pray a fortuitous fate attend them!
Wondrous things are possible,
but little do they know where their steps lead them.
They're unprepared for what might happen.

WILD MEN SINGING:

All decked out, you gawk and stare!
But here we come, rough and rare,
Leaping, bounding, a frenzied pace,
A sturdy and a vigorous race.

FAUNS:

We fauns come dancing a jolly dance,
oak leaves crowning our curly hair,

pointy ears peeping out.
Our nose is snub,
our face is wide,
but women like us all the same.

SATYR:

A satyr, I hop behind him on goat's feet
and scrawny legs that suit me just fine.
For chamoislike, to amuse myself,
I climb high peaks to survey the world.

GNOMES:

Here we little gnomes come tripping,
not in pairs, but one by one,
crissing and crossing as we foot it.

NYMPHS IN CHORUS: *(Surrounding great PAN.)*

Great Pan is here!
Great Pan is come!
Great Pan who is All!
Surround him, nymphs, with happy dance,
float about him, circle him round!
He may be earnest, but he's kindly, too,
and he wishes us all to be merry.
He would be watchful,
would be ever attentive,
beneath the blue of heaven's arch,
except that brooklets ripple past,
and gentle, soft breezes caress him to drowse.
And when at noon he sleeps,
no leaf stirs,
and in the silent, motionless air
the healthy scent of Nature hovers,
and no nymph dare stay awake,
but falls asleep just where she stands.
Suddenly then his voice cries out
like lightning's crash, like the roaring sea,
and panic descends on even the mightiest,
armies scatter and heroes tremble.

So honor him to whom honor is due,
and praise him who brought us to this!

DEPUTATION OF GNOMES TO GREAT PAN:
Where rich and brightly shining ore
Threads its way through mountain core,
Only the divining rod can
Open the maze to the eyes of man.

We live in dark caves underground,
Like troglodytes, where no sun's found,
While up above in day's pure light
You give to man your treasures bright.

But now, nearby, we've found a treasure
Of so great wealth it's beyond measure;
A source so grand we never thought
To see its like from deep earth brought.

It's yours to bring this to fulfillment,
Lord, to save it from concealment;
Treasure in the Great Pan's hand
Brings benefit to every land.

PLUTUS: *(To the HERALD.)*
Let us compose ourselves now
with great solemnity
and allow to happen what will happen,
for you have proven yourself
a man supremely valiant.
A thing of such calamity is about to occur
that the world and the world's posterity will deny it
even to the end of time.
And so, it's for you to record it in your chronicle.

HERALD: *(Grasping the staff which PLUTUS continues to hold.)*
The dwarfs now, with enormous care,
lead Great Pan to the fiery spring
that seethes up from its gaping abyss,

then sinks again to its deepest depths,
leaving its gloomy mouth agape.
Then up again it wells, seething,
glowing, boiling fire,
while Great Pan looks on unperturbed,
enjoying the sight of this wonder
as pearls of foam spray out right and left.
How can he be so unsuspecting?
He's stooping low to look down in.
But his beard falls off and plunges downward!
Whose beard was it?
And whose smooth-shaved chin?
His hand hides it so none can see.

Ah, but what a calamity now!
The beard aflame flies back up
and sets afire his wreath, his head,
his breast! All our pleasure
is turned to grief! Running toward him
to put out the blaze, not one of his throng
of followers escapes!
Even as they slap and beat at the flames,
new flames are fanned,
a new blaze begun! Engulfed in fire,
a group of maskers burns to death!

But what's this I hear
spread by word of mouth from ear to ear?
O night, unhappy night,
cursed night,
what grief have you brought us!
Tomorrow will bring what no one wants to hear!
And I hear it shouted from every side.
"It was the Emperor who was burned!"
O God, if only it weren't true!
The Emperor burned and all those with him!

Curse them,
curse all those who misled him,

who dressed themselves in pine branches,
and bellowed riotous songs to all our doom!

O youth, youth,
when will you learn to moderate pleasure?
O Majesty, Majesty,
when will you learn to govern with sense
as great as your power?

Our forest is already afire,
tongues of flame licking upward
to the timbered ceiling, threatening
all the palace with ruin.
Our measure of woe is overfull.
Who is to save us?
All the splendor of Empire
reduced to ashes in a single night.

PLUTUS: *(Removes his mask to reveal himself as FAUST.)*
　　　　　　　　Now we've had enough of terror,
　　　　　　　　Let rescue come and banish error!
　　　　　　　　Let our staff make earth resound,
　　　　　　　　Setting it loudly on the ground!
　　　　　　　　And you, great, spacious circling air,
　　　　　　　　Breathe cooling breezes everywhere!
　　　　　　　　Come, mist and fog and pregnant cloud,
　　　　　　　　Engulf us in your vaporous shroud!
　　　　　　　　Drizzling cloudlets, dropping, drenching,
　　　　　　　　Everywhere fire's danger quenching,
　　　　　　　　Turn by your so soothing might
　　　　　　　　Flames that threaten us with fright
　　　　　　　　Into summer lightning's glow,
　　　　　　　　And put an end to this mocking show!
　　　　　　　　When spirits threaten us with ill,
　　　　　　　　It's time to use our magic skill.

XXXI ~ PLEASURE GARDEN

Morning sun.
The EMPEROR, COURTIERS. FAUST, and MEPHISTOPHELES,
respectably dressed according to the fashion, kneel before the EMPEROR.

FAUST:
Sire, do you forgive us last night's fireworks?

EMPEROR: *(Beckoning them to rise.)*
I could wish for many such entertainments.
Suddenly, like Pluto,
I saw myself in a glowing sphere
that burned all about me.
Before me out of a night black as coal,
appeared a rocky valley
aglow with tiny flares.
Out of many a pit surrounding me
swirled thousands of savage flames that soared on high
and, joining, formed a flickering vault of fire
that forever changed its shape.
And far in the distance,
I saw through its twisted columns of fire,
long processions of nations in motion,
converging on me in a wide circle,
to pay me homage as always.
I recognized one and another of my courtiers.
I appeared to myself a prince of a thousand salamanders.

MEPHISTOPHELES:
And so you are, Sire, for each element
recognizes your Majesty's supremacy.
You've tested fire and proven it obedient,
now cast yourself into the sea at its roughest,
and scarcely will you have trod the pearl-strewn floor,
than pale green heaving waves edged with purple
will form about you a glorious round,
a lovely place to dwell,
with you its central point.

And every step you take, these halls will follow,
for they are alive,
their very walls teem with life,
darting every which way.

Monsters of the sea
will throng and surge toward the strange, soft glow,
but none will be allowed to enter.
Dragons will sport in your sight,
richly colored, with scales of gold,
and sharks show you their lethal jaws,
and you will laugh in their teeth.

However much your court here may delight you,
you will never have witnessed such grand company.
Nor will you be long parted from what is loveliest.
Nereids will come,
curious to see the splendid new dwelling
in the sea's eternal freshness.
The young will be like fishes,
timid but no less wanton;
the older ones rather more prudent.
Thetis will hear the news and come,
proffering her hand and lips to the new Proteus.
And next there's the seat on the heights of Olympus—

EMPEROR:
Thank you, but no.
We ascend that throne soon enough.

MEPHISTOPHELES:
And as for the earth, Majesty,
you already own that.

EMPEROR:
What stroke of luck brought you here
straight out of the Arabian Nights?
Be as resourceful as Scheherazade
and I assure you the highest of favors.

Stand by me, for I will need you often
when the routine of your daily world distresses me.

STEWARD: *(Enters in haste.)*
Serene Highness, I never thought
that one day I would bring to you news
of such great good fortune!
I am blessed in your presence, Majesty,
with supreme happiness!
Our accounts are settled, every bill paid,
we have escaped the usurer's clutches,
and I am relieved of the torments of Hell!
Heaven could not be more joyous!

COMMANDER-IN-CHIEF: *(Following in haste.)*
Sire, we've begun to pay off the mercenaries,
and the whole army's reenlisted!
The troops are in fine fettle, and tapster and tart
are about their trades!

EMPEROR:
How freely you're all breathing for a change!
Your faces have lost their folds and are smiling again!
And to think you ran to tell me!

TREASURER: *(Who has already entered.)*
These are the men you should ask, Sire.
It was they who did it.

FAUST:
By right,
I think the Chancellor should explain it

CHANCELLOR: *(Approaching slowly.)*
Yes, whose old age is finally blest.
Hear now and behold this fateful paper
that has turned all woe to weal.

(He reads.)

"To whom it may concern,
hereby be advised that this note is worth
one thousand crowns, its collateral guaranteed
by countless treasures lying buried in Imperial Lands.
Plans are presently in motion to raise said treasure
and with it redeem this note."

EMPEROR:

What is this I suspect?
Fraud?
Some monstrous deception?

TREASURER:

Consider, Sire! Remember!
You signed it yourself, last night.
There you were, dressed as Great Pan,
and the Chancellor, in company with us,
approached you and said:

"Sign this note, Majesty,
and with a few strokes of the pen
crown this grand festivity
with salvation for your people!"

And sign it you did, Sire, and in the night
our nimble conjurors ran off thousands.
And to allow everyone without delay
to share in the benefit,
we at once stamped the whole series

Tens, thirties, fifties, hundreds
are now ready to hand.
You can't imagine the pleasure your subjects feel!
Take a look at your city.
It was dead and rotting before,
but now it's alive and teeming with pleasure seekers!
Your name has always meant happiness,
but never has it been regarded with such devotion.
The alphabet lost its value last night,
for in this signature all men find happiness!

EMPEROR:

    What are you saying?
    To the people it counts as gold?
    The court, the army, you say, treat it as money?
    I must confess, I don't understand it,
    but what a fool I'd be not to give it a try!.

STEWARD:

    We could never, even if we wanted,
    recover those notes.
    They took off like a bolt of lightning.
    There's not a money changer
    whose doors aren't thrown wide,
    and every note honored
    with gold and silver coin—
    at a discount, to be sure.
    From there it's off to the butcher, the baker, the bar.
    Half the world has only eating on its mind;
    the other half's strutting about in new finery.
    Clothiers cut their cloth and tailors sew.
    Wine flows like water in taverns
    toasting the Emperor.
    Food's a-frying and baking,
    and everywhere
    there's the clatter of dishes.

MEPHISTOPHELES:

    Walk alone some evening along the terraces,
    you'll spy the most beautiful of women
    dressed to kill. One eye, you'll notice,
    is concealed behind a peacock fan,
    while the other sizes you up and smiles,
    wondering if you have one of those special notes
    that leads to love faster than wit or eloquence.
    Why bother with a purse,
    when a banknote's place is snug in a lover's breast,
    close beside an amorous billet-doux?
    The priest will carry it piously in his breviary,
    and the soldier with a lighter money belt
    will swerve more swiftly.

I trust Your Majesty will pardon me
for treating this great achievement so lightly
by reciting such petty details.

FAUST:

The abundance of treasure buried deep in your lands
lies there useless, unused. No mind is so vast
as to grasp its extent; even fantasy
at its height is doomed to failure.
And yet there are spirits gifted with profound insight
who trust the infinite with infinite confidence.

MEPHISTOPHELES:

In place of gold and pearls,
paper money is really most convenient.
You know exactly what you've got.
No haggling, no bargaining.
No having to wait to steep yourself
in love or wine.
If it's coin you want, you go to a money changer;
and if that comes to no good,
you go out and you dig for a while.
You auction off a golden chain or goblet,
and the paper money, promptly amortized,
will put to shame all the doubters who called us fools.
Once used to this, no one will want it otherwise.
As a result, the Empire will never be anything
but well supplied with jewels, gold, and paper.

EMPEROR:

The Empire thanks you for this great benefice,
and the reward will as nearly as possible
equal the service. I entrust to you, therefore,
custodianship of our subterranean treasures,
for you are worthy of that great charge.
Who knows better than you
the full extent of the hoard?
And all digging will be under your direction.
Join forces, then, you masters of our treasures,

take pleasure in your honorable duties in which
the upper and the lower worlds are united in concord.

TREASURER:
Sire!
There will be not the remotest strife between us.
I welcome the sorcerer as a colleague.

(Exit with FAUST.)

EMPEROR:
I will now dispense gifts
to each man of my court,
but each of you must tell me how he will use it.

FIRST PAGE: *(Receiving some money.)*
I'll live a merry life,
lighthearted and content!

SECOND PAGE: *(Likewise.)*
I'll rush to buy rings
and a necklace for my darling.

FIRST CHAMBERLAIN: *(Receiving.)*
From now on I drink wine double the price.

SECOND CHAMBERLAIN: *(Likewise.)*
I already feel the dice itching in my pocket.

FIRST BANNERET: *(Thoughtfully.)*
I'll free my castle and land of debts.

SECOND BANNERET: *(Likewise.)*
It's a treasure I'll add to other treasures.

EMPEROR:
I was hoping to hear of great plans
and new endeavors, but knowing you,
one should have known better.

All this new wealth, and each of you is no different
from what you were.

FOOL: *(Entering.)*
    You're giving presents?
    Do I get one, too?

EMPEROR:
    Yes, and alive again
    you'll only spend it on drink.

FOOL:
    Magic money?
    I don't understand.

EMPEROR:
    I can believe that.
    You'll never learn.

FOOL:
    There's more falling on the floor!
    What do I do?

EMPEROR:
    They fell in your direction, pick them up.

    (Exit.)

FOOL:
    From what it says here,
    I must have five thousand crowns!

MEPHISTOPHELES:
    Ah, so you've been resurrected,
    you walking wineskin.

FOOL:

 I've done it often,
 but never with such luck!

MEPHISTOPHELES:

 You're breaking out in a sweat with all your rapture.

FOOL:

 Look at this!
 Is this real money?

MEPHISTOPHELES:

 With that you can eat till you're stuffed
 and drink till you're soused.

FOOL:

 And I can buy land and a house and cattle?

MEPHISTOPHELES:

 What else?
 Make an offer, it's yours.

FOOL:

 And a castle,
 and a forest for hunting,
 and a trout stream?

MEPHISTOPHELES:

 Trust me!
 I'd love to see you lord of a manor.

FOOL:

 Tonight I'll dream of real estate!

 (Exit.)

MEPHISTOPHELES:

 Who can doubt our fool's a mental paragon?

Enter FAUST and MEPHISTOPHELES.

MEPHISTOPHELES:
> What is it with these gloomy passageways?
> Why are you always dragging me off here?
> Isn't there pleasure enough in there?
> Do they bore you,
> that colorful crowd of courtiers?
> Not opportunity enough for your tricks and pranks?
> Is that it?

FAUST:
> Spare me your drivel!
> You ran out of tricks long ago,
> and now you chase around trying to avoid me.
> Look, I'm being pressured.
> The Emperor insists on seeing Paris and Helen—
> and he wants it here, now, without delay—
> clear images, there, in front of him,
> of the ideal man and the ideal woman.
> So get busy! Now!
> I gave my word, I can't break it!

MEPHISTOPHELES:
> What a thoughtless fool to make such a promise!

FAUST:
> No, old friend, you're the thoughtless fool.
> You failed to consider where your arts would lead us.
> First we made him rich,
> and now we're meant to amuse him.

MEPHISTOPHELES:
> It's not a matter of snapping your fingers and presto!
> This is alien territory you're invading,
> and the steps are steep and winding.
> You'll end up getting wickedly involved again,

if you think it's as easy conjuring up Helen
as that phantom paper money.

Well now, I'm at your service
when it comes to producing witchy witches
and ghostly ghosts,
not to mention goiter-deformed dwarves;
but the Devil's darlings,
while not to be dismissed lightly,
won't pass muster for classical heroines.

FAUST:

There you go again,
grinding out the same old tune!
There's never any certainty dealing with you.
You're the father of all hindrances,
and for every remedy you want a new reward.
I know how it works:
you mumble a few words, and presto, it's done,
even before I've turned around to look.

MEPHISTOPHELES:

Those pagans don't concern me.
They have their own sort of Hell.
But there is a means—

FAUST:

Tell me! Tell me *now!*

MEPHISTOPHELES:

These are higher mysteries.
I do so reluctantly.

Goddesses are enthroned in sublime solitude,
outside time,
outside space—
even to speak of them embarrasses me.
They are the Mothers!

FAUST: *(Startled.)*
The Mothers!

MEPHISTOPHELES:
What's that? Afraid?

FAUST:
The Mothers! The Mothers!
It sounds so strange.

MEPHISTOPHELES:
And so it is.
Goddesses unknown to you mortals,
and reluctantly named by us.
You'll need to dig deep to reach them.
It's your fault we're having to do this.

FAUST:
Which way?

MEPHISTOPHELES:
No way!
To the unvisited, never to be visited;
to the unsolicited, never to be solicited.

Are you ready?
You will find there neither lock nor bolt to constrain you;
you will be driven about by solitude.
Are desolation and solitude concepts you can grasp?

FAUST:
I dare say you might have spared me that!
It smells of the witch's kitchen of a long time past.
The world was with me then,
I had no choice;
what I learned was nothing,
and nothing is what I taught.
If I spoke reasonably what I saw to be reasonable,
the contradictions would have been twice as loud.

Malevolently wronged,
I escaped into the solitude of the wilderness;
then finally,
so as not to live wholly alone and neglected,
I resigned myself to the Devil.

MEPHISTOPHELES:
Yes, and if you'd swum clear across the ocean
and gazed on its infinitude,
you'd still have seen something,
wave following upon wave.
And even when death threatened,
there would still have been something to see:
dolphins darting sleekly through green waters,
a rack of clouds, the sun, the moon, and stars.

But you will see nothing
in the eternally empty distance,
will hear no step you take,
find nothing firm to rest upon.

FAUST:
You sound like the father of all mystagogues
deceiving his neophyte disciples.
Except in reverse.
You send me into emptiness
to perfect my art and my powers;
but you treat me like the cat in the fable,
to claw out your chestnuts from the fire.

So be it!
We'll fathom this mystery yet,
and in your Nothing I hope to find the All.

MEPHISTOPHELES:
I praise you before you part from me.
I see you know the Devil well.
Here. Take this key.

FAUST:
>   That little thing!

MEPHISTOPHELES:
>   Take hold of it first and don't underestimate it.

FAUST:
>   It's growing in my hand!
>   It shines, it flashes!

MEPHISTOPHELES:
>   Ah, you're beginning to see now what it's worth?
>   That key will seek out the right spot,
>   so follow it down.
>   It will lead you to the Mothers.

FAUST: *(Shuddering.)*
>   The Mothers!
>   Why does it always strike me like a blow?
>   What is this word I can't bear to hear?

MEPHISTOPHELES:
>   Why should a new word disturb you?
>   Are you so narrow-minded?
>   Only comfortable with what you've heard before?
>   Whatever comes, whatever its sound,
>   let nothing disturb you.
>   You're well accustomed now to strange happenings.

FAUST:
>   What do you want of me,
>   to turn to stone?
>   That's not where my salvation lies.
>   Shuddering awe is the greatest part of Man.
>   However fiercely the world may seek to stifle it,
>   once we're stirred profoundly,
>   we're open to the Infinite.

MEPHISTOPHELES:
>   Sink down!

Or, if you like, ascend!
It's all the same.
Leave behind the created world and
enter the unbound world of pure forms,
and find pleasure in what has long ceased to be.
They will swirl about you like drifting clouds;
but you have only to brandish the key
to keep them away.

FAUST: *(Enthusiastically.)*
Right!
Grasping it firmly now
I feel new strength!
My chest expands!
On to the Great Work!

MEPHISTOPHELES:
When you see a glowing tripod,
you'll know you have reached the deepest of all depths.
By its gleam you will see the Mothers.
Some will be seated, others standing or strolling—
as chance will have it.

Formation, transformation:
Eternal Mind's eternal conservation.

They're swarmed around by all of creation's creatures,
but all they see are empty forms:
you won't be seen.
Be bold, the danger is great.
Walk straight to the tripod and touch it with the key.

(FAUST, with the key, assumes a decidedly commanding attitude as MEPHISTOPHELES watches him.)

That's the way!
Like an honorable servant
it will connect and follow you.
Good fortune will raise you up,
and before they notice, you'll be back here with it.

And when you are, you will summon
hero and heroine out of the night,
the first one bold enough to do the deed.
It will be done,
and you will have done it.
From then on, assisted by magic means,
the cloud of incense will transform itself into gods.

FAUST:
What now?

MEPHISTOPHELES:
Strive downward with all of your being.
Stamp and you'll descend.
Stamp again and you'll rise.

(FAUST stamps his foot and sinks out of sight.)

MEPHISTOPHELES:
I really do hope the key works!
I'm curious to see if he returns.

XXXIII ✍ BRIGHTLY LIGHTED HALLS

EMPEROR and PRINCES.
The COURT in motion through the rooms.

CHAMBERLAIN: (To MEPHISTOPHELES.)
You still owe us the spectacle of the ghosts.
Get to work.
The Emperor is impatient.

STEWARD:
His Majesty has just now enquired!
Hurry!
You don't humiliate an emperor!

MEPHISTOPHELES:

> My colleague's left on that mission,
> so have no fear, he knows his business.
> He's off just now toiling in quiet seclusion.
> It takes great diligence, you see,
> to raise such a treasure—
> to raise Beauty—yes,
> the highest art of a skilled wizard.

STEWARD:

> What arts you use are quite immaterial!
> Just hurry!
> The Emperor demands results.

BLONDE: *(To MEPHISTOPHELES.)*

> Excuse me, sir, a word!
> As you see, I have a very clear complexion,
> but it's not always so.
> In summer I break out
> in the most unsightly freckles.
> By the hundreds,
> all reddish brown.
> On this clear white skin!
> Have you a remedy?

MEPHISTOPHELES:

> What a pity!
> And such a dazzling little darling, too,
> spotted in May like a panther cub!
> Take spawn of frog and tongue of toad,
> mix well together
> and distill with great care
> by the light of the full moon.
> Then, when the moon is on the wane,
> apply it cautiously. Come spring,
> your spots will be no more.

BRUNETTE:

> O this crowd!

Pressing round to seek your favors, sir!
Help me, I beg of you.
A remedy!
I have a frozen foot that prevents me from
walking or dancing—
even from curtsying properly.

MEPHISTOPHELES:

May I place my foot on yours?

BRUNETTE:

As lovers do, do you mean?

MEPHISTOPHELES:

When I do it, child, there's a higher significance.
Homeopathy will do the trick. Foot heals foot,
and so with other parts of the body.
Come here! Careful!
You needn't return it!

BRUNETTE: *(Shrieking.)*

Ow! That hurts!
It's like my foot's on fire!
That was some hard tread.
Like a horse's hoof.

MEPHISTOPHELES:

Yes, but you're cured, you see.
Now you can dance all you like—
and play footsies with your lover under the table.

LADY: *(Pressing forward.)*

Let me through!
O the pain, the pain!
The rage that burns in my heart!
Only yesterday he doted on me;
now he's babbling with *her* and
turned his back on me!

MEPHISTOPHELES:

A difficult case, I admit.
But listen to me.
You must take this piece of charcoal
and work your way up quite close to him.
With the charcoal then
you'll put a mark on him somewhere—
arm, coat, shoulder, wherever,
and at once he'll suffer the sweet pangs of remorse.
Immediately, then, you must swallow the charcoal
and let neither wine nor water touch your lips.
This very night he'll be sighing at your door.

LADY:

I trust it's not poisonous?

MEPHISTOPHELES: *(Indignant.)*

You will show respect where it's due, madam!
One must search far and wide
for charcoal like this.
It comes from a funeral pyre—
an auto-da-fè—an activity
we once engaged in more assiduously.

PAGE:

I'm in love,
but they say I'm too young.

MEPHISTOPHELES: *(Aside.)*

I'm at wit's end!
Whom do I listen to next!

(To the PAGE.)

Forget the sweet young things; older women
will know how to appreciate you more.

(Others crowd around him.)

And still they come!
How will I survive this?
I'll have to resort to telling the truth!
What a coward's way out for the Devil!
It's getting desperate!

O Mothers, Mothers! Let Faust go!

(Looking around.)

The candles are burning dimmer now,
and all at once the court begins to move,
winding its decorous procession
through long corridors and distant galleries.
Splendid!
They're now filing into the old Hall of the Knights,
which, for all its size, can scarcely contain them.
Tapestries cover its ancient wide walls,
every niche and corner
decorated with suits of armor.
No need of magic words here, I dare say.
The spirits will find the way by themselves.

XXXIV ↙ HALL OF THE KNIGHTS

Dim illumination.
The EMPEROR and the COURT have entered.

HERALD:
My accustomed office is to announce the play,
but not tonight; secret forces are at work here,
spirit antics causing such confusion
that reason cannot explain on rational grounds.
The chairs are arranged and in order,
the Emperor seated facing the wall,
enjoying scenes of great battles on the tapestries.

So here they sit,

lords and ladies of the court;
in the rear crowded benches for the lesser sort.
And lovers, undaunted by the uncanny twilight,
cuddle in the shadows.
I see all are seated properly now.
We may begin.
The spirits may enter!

(Trumpets.)

ASTROLOGER:
Let the play begin!
It is His Majesty's wish!

Walls, open!
No hindrance now,
magic is at hand!
Tapestries disappear as if furled by fire,
the wall splits, folds back,
and out of nowhere a deep stage appears,
bathing us in mysterious light.
I now will mount the proscenium.

MEPHISTOPHELES: *(His head popping out of the prompter's box.)*
I hope you all approve.
Prompting, after all,
is the Devil's rhetoric.

(To the ASTROLOGER.)

You understand the motions of the stars,
you'll have no trouble
understanding my whispers.

ASTROLOGER:
Prompted by magic,
a temple rises before us,
a mighty structure sustained by rows of columns,
like Atlas supporting the heavens.

Any two would suffice
for a monumental building.

ARCHITECT:
So that's what they call Classical!
I'm at a loss to know what to praise.
It's clumsy, ponderous is what it is!
What's crude is called noble,
and what's awkward, grand.
Give me slender pillars anytime,
pillars striving upward into infinity,
pointed arches that lift the spirit on high.
Now that's an edifying style!

ASTROLOGER:
Welcome and reverence these star-favored hours!
Let reason be held in abeyance by magic's power,
and audacious fantasy in glorious progress
come freely from afar.
Behold the scene you so boldly desired.
It is impossible, therefore worthy of belief.

(FAUST mounts to the proscenium on the other side.)

A wreath on his head and in priestly garments,
the man of miracles accomplishes now
what he so confidently began.

A tripod rises with him out of the depths,
and already I smell incense from its brazier.

He now prepares to bless the Great Work.
Only good fortune may attend him now.

FAUST: *(Grandly.)*
In your name, Mothers,
you who sit enthroned in the Boundless,
who dwell eternally in Solitude,
yet in company!

About your heads
hover the forms of all living things,
in motion, and yet dead.
What once was,
in all radiance and splendor,
moves there still,
seeking a place in Eternity.
And you, in your omnipotence,
divide it between the bright canopy of day
and the vault of night; some to be caught up
in life's blessèd course, others to be sought out
by the fearless magician, who alone,
intrepidly, reveals for all to see,
what is worthy of wonder.

ASTROLOGER:
His glowing key no sooner touches the censer
than at once a misty vapor engulfs the stage.
Stealing in, it billows in cloudlike fashion,
stretching, swelling, condensing,
twining about, parting, joining.

But now behold a spirit masterpiece.
As they approach they make music!
Airy tones create a mystery,
and as they move all things become melody.
Everything, columns, triglyph, rings;
I truly believe the entire temple is singing!
The mist is settling now, and through the haze,
with measured step,
a beautiful youth steps forth.

Here I end my task, for I needn't name him.
Who could fail to know the charming Paris.

(PARIS steps forward.)

FIRST LADY:
O what a sight of youth and vigor!

SECOND LADY:

> Ripe and fresh as a juicy peach!

THIRD LADY:

> The delicate, sweetly swelling lips!

FOURTH LADY:

> A cup, I'll wager, you long to sip at.

FIFTH LADY:

> He's very pretty, but lacks refinement.

SIXTH LADY:

> He could be a bit less awkward, too.

FIRST KNIGHT:

> Too much of the shepherd about him.
> Where's the prince, the courtly manners?

SECOND KNIGHT:

> Yes, well, half naked he's handsome enough;
> but first we'd have to see him in armor.

A LADY:

> Look at the graceful way he sits.

FIRST KNIGHT:

> A lap, I dare say, you wouldn't mind sitting on?

ANOTHER LADY:

> How prettily he rests his arm on his head.

CHAMBERLAIN:

> How vulgar!
> It isn't proper!

A LADY:

> You gentlemen find fault with everything.

CHAMBERLAIN:

Lolling in the Emperor's presence!

A LADY:

It's just his way.
He thinks he's alone.

CHAMBERLAIN:

Even court plays should follow decorum.

A LADY:

The little darling has fallen asleep.

CHAMBERLAIN:

He'll soon be snoring.
That's nature for you!

YOUNG LADY: *(Enraptured.)*

What fragrance is that mingling with the incense
that moves my heart so and brings refreshment?

OLDER LADY:

There's a breath blowing deep in my heart.
It comes from him.

OLDEST LADY:

It's ambrosia,
the scent of flowering youth,
filling the air around us.

(HELEN appears.)

MEPHISTOPHELES:

So there she is!
Well, I'd lose no sleep over her.
Pretty, yes, but not my cup of tea.

ASTROLOGER:

As a man of honor, I must confess I'm helpless.

If I had tongues of fire they would not serve!
When Beauty, forever the poet's inspiration,
comes, the singer is driven beyond himself,
and he who possesses her
has known too much of joy.

FAUST:
Do I still have eyes?
Or is it deep in my soul
I see Beauty's wellspring in full stream?
My quest of terror has brought me a blissful reward.
How without meaning,
how closed the world was to me!
But my priesthood has made it desirable,
well founded, enduring!
May the breath of life desert me
if I resign myself to living without you.

The fair form that bewitched me long ago
in a magic reflection
was a mere mocking counterfeit of this Beauty.

I pledge to you herewith, as tribute due,
the sum of my strength,
the quintessence of passion,
affection, love, adoration, madness!

MEPHISTOPHELES: *(From the prompter's box.)*
Control yourself!
Remember, you're acting!

OLDER LADY:
Tall, well built, only the head too small.

YOUNGER LADY:
Look at her feet.
How coarse they are.

DIPLOMAT:

>I've seen such princesses before.
>I'd say she's quite perfect from head to toe.

COURTIER:

>She's approaching the sleeper with gentle guile.

A LADY:

>How ugly beside his pure youthful image.

POET:

>Her beauty bathes him in her radiance.

A LADY:

>Just like the painting,
>*Endymion and Luna.*

POET:

>Quite right.
>She seems to be sinking now,
>bending to breathe in the breath of his lips.
>Enviable! A kiss!
>His cup runs over!

DUENNA:

>Imagine!
>In front of everyone!
>Too much!

FAUST:

>What right has that boy to such favors!

MEPHISTOPHELES:

>Quiet!
>Keep it down there!
>Let the spook do what it likes.

COURTIER:

>She's tiptoeing away as he wakens.

A LADY:

> She's looking back!
> I knew she would!

COURTIER:

> He's astonished.
> A miracle's happened to him.

A LADY:

> Not to her.
> She's seen it before.

COURTIER:

> She's turned with great dignity to face him.

A LADY:

> She'll be playing tutor to him now.
> Men are such fools in these matters.
> And he fancies himself the first.

A KNIGHT:

> Let's not argue.
> Majestically marvelous!

A LADY:

> The slut!
> How vulgar!

PAGE:

> I sure wouldn't mind trading places with him!

COURTIER:

> She can snare any man she wants.

A LADY:

> That trinket's been passed through too many hands;
> even the gilding's worn thin.

ANOTHER LADY:

> She's been at it since she was ten.

A KNIGHT:

> When opportunity offers the best, we take it.
> But I wouldn't turn down leftovers lovely as that.

PEDANT:

> I see her clearly enough, though I must confess
> to doubting that she's authentic.
> The evidence of eyes can be misleading.
> And so I prefer to stick to the books,
> where it says that Helen delighted mightily
> all the graybeards of Troy;
> a fact that fits quite well here.
> First, because I'm no longer young,
> and second, because I find her most attractive.

ASTROLOGER:

> A boy no longer,
> but a man heroic and daring,
> he embraces her who can scarcely defend herself.
> His arms now strong,
> he lifts her high!
> Will he abduct her, I wonder?

FAUST:

> Rash fool!
> How do you dare!
> You don't listen! Stop!
> This is too much!

MEPHISTOPHELES:

> But it's all your doing!
> It's all in your mind,
> this spook play!

ASTROLOGER:

> Just one word more.
> Considering all that's happened,
> I'll call this piece "The Rape of Helen."

FAUST:

Rape! And I?
Do I count for nothing?
The key is still in my hand!
The key that led me through frightful seas of solitude
here to secure ground!
Here I have a footing.
Here I face realities!
Here is where spirit dares to fight with spirits
to create the double kingdom wide as air!
How far she was then,
now she could not be nearer.
I'll rescue her, and she will be mine twice over.
I'll take the risk, I'll dare!
Mothers! You Mothers!
Grant that it be so!
He who has known her
can never live without her.

ASTROLOGER:

Faust, what are you doing?
Faust!
Look at him!
He seizes her by force,
and already her form has begun to fade.
He turns the key toward the boy now,
it touches him!
Aiiii! Aiiii!
Horrors!
Gone!
Gone!

(Explosion. FAUST lies on the floor. The spirits dissolve in vapor.)

MEPHISTOPHELES: (Throwing FAUST over his shoulder.)
Well, that's life for you!
Not even the Devil should bother himself with fools.

(Darkness. Tumult.)

ACT II

XXXV ✍ A HIGH-VAULTED NARROW GOTHIC CHAMBER

Formerly FAUST's study, unchanged. MEPHISTOPHELES steps from behind a curtain. Raising it, he looks back and FAUST is discovered prostrate on an old-fashioned bed.

MEPHISTOPHELES:
Lie there, luckless wretch,
misled into a love not easy to break.
A man paralyzed by Helen
will not so readily reclaim his senses.

(Looking about him.)

I look around, here, there,
wherever my eye lights, and see that
nothing is changed, nothing damaged.
The painted panes are dimmer,
or so it seems;
cobwebs everywhere;
ink dried, yellowed paper—
but nothing out of place;
even the pen still here, used by Faust
to sign himself over to the Devil.

(Picks up the pen.)

Ah, yes! Here it is!
A droplet of blood still lodged in the tube of the quill,
the very same blood I had to coax from him.
What a collector's piece!
A unique specimen!

And here's the old fur robe
hanging on its ancient peg,

reminding me of the joke I played
on that poor lad some years ago,
confusing his mind with my mock-serious nonsense.
I suspect he's still gnawing on that bone.

Well, old moth-eaten friend,
I must confess I feel the urge
to wrap myself again in your furry warmth
and play the professor once more,
utterly confident that only he is right.
Academics know how to carry off that farce,
but unfortunately the Devil lost it long ago.

*(He shakes the robe he has taken down, and crickets, beetles, and moths
fly out.)*

CHORUS OF INSECTS:
                We welcome your coming,
                Old patron and friend;
                With buzzing and humming
                On you we attend.
                Singly, in silence,
                You planted us here,
                Swarming by thousands,
                To you we appear!
                The rogue in the bosom
                Hides close in his lair;
                Our fur bed we gladly
                Forsake for the air.

MEPHISTOPHELES:
Ah! What a grand surprise!
My youthful creation!
Sow as you will and in time you'll reap.

But let me shake this ragtag robe once more
and see if there's any left.

(He shakes the robe.)

Ah! And there they are,
a stray one or two fluttering out!

Up with you now!
Up and away, you little darlings!
Hide, you hear?
Here and there!
Every dust-layered corner and niche!
There are thousands waiting for you
to call them home!

Old paper boxes standing about,
this crusty brown parchment,
dusty shards of age-old pottery,
or the empty sockets of those skulls on the shelf!
In a place as moldy and mangy as this,
strange things will breed in the mind as well as the dust.

(He slips into the robe.)

Come, cover my shoulders one more time!
I'll play the principal part in our little show
as well as act the boss.
But how can I be that
when there's no one here knows me?

(He pulls the bell cord, causing a shrill, piercing sound to make the walls tremble and the doors to burst open.)

FAMULUS: *(Enters, staggering out of a long, dark corridor.)*
What a clanging!
What a terror!
Stairs sway, walls quiver,
storm and lightning threaten through the painted panes!
The floor gives way, and rubble and mortar
rain down on my head! And this door,
locked and bolted to entry,
threw back its bolts
at the force of some magic power!

And there! Look!
Standing there! What horror!
A giant standing in Faust's old robe!
He sees me, staring, beckons me on!
Ah, my knees are about to betray me!
Do I run? Do I stay? Oh!
What will happen to me?

MEPHISTOPHELES: *(Beckoning.)*
Come, my friend!
Your name is Nicodemus?

FAMULUS:
Most Reverend Sir! It is.
Oremus!

MEPHISTOPHELES:
None of that, now.

FAMULUS:
I'm pleased you know me.

MEPHISTOPHELES:
Ah, indeed I know you.
No spring chicken, you,
my moss-grown chap,
and still in school.
Yes, well.
But even a man of learning goes on studying;
it appears he can't help it.
And so he builds himself a shabby little card house
that not even the greatest mind could finish.

Well, and then there's your master.
Who hasn't heard of the noble Dr. Wagner,
the foremost intellect now in the world of knowledge!
He alone holds it all together,
adding daily to the store of wisdom.
All the world, eager for knowledge,

throngs to the lectures of this semaphore of thinkers,
who, like St. Peter, wields the keys
that unlock the upper and lower worlds.
There's no one alive can hold a candle to him.
The brilliance and glow of his fame and glory
have even cast a shadow on the name of Faust.
Professor Wagner, yes,
the only true discoverer.

FAMULUS:

Pardon, Most Reverend Sir,
if I dare to contradict you,
but it's not that way at all.
He's a modest man, my master,
a man who never reconciled himself
to the mysterious disappearance
of that exalted man.
He hopes and prays daily for solace
and salvation from his return.
This room, just as in that great man's day,
is untouched, just as he left it,
awaiting its own master.
I scarcely dared to enter it, sir.
What is it must be written in the stars
to make the very walls shake with terror,
and the doorposts to tremble?
Even the bolts sprang back,
or you couldn't have entered.

MEPHISTOPHELES:

Where has your Master Wagner gone?
Take me to him or bring him here.

FAMULUS:

Oh, no, sir!
He's given strict orders.
I wouldn't dare interrupt him.
For months now he's been in total seclusion
toiling over his Great Work.

This gentlest of learned men
resembles a charcoal burner, his face
black from ears to nose, and his eyes
red from puffing at the flame.
He hangs on to every moment.
The clang of his tongs is music to his ears.

MEPHISTOPHELES:
But why should he reject me?
I'm the very one to hasten his success.

(Exit the FAMULUS. MEPHISTOPHELES seats himself solemnly.)

No sooner have I taken up my post
than I see a guest stirring back there,
familiar to me, to be sure,
except this time with a Bachelor's degree,
and cheekier than is good for him, I dare say.

BACCALAUREATE: *(Storming down the corridor.)*
What's this?
Doors and gates thrown wide open?
About time, too! Let in some air!
Let us breathe for a change,
rather than stifle in this decay,
living like corpses, rotting, wasting away
in this moldy heap of rubbish!

These walls are leaning and sagging,
about to collapse, and either I get out of here
fast or be buried by them.
I risk as much as the next,
but no one's dragging me farther into this house.

But wait.

Yes, I've been here before!
I have! Years ago.
I was a freshman.

Timid little mouse, scared of my own shadow.
God, and naïve! I trusted them—
those gray-bearded old fools and their eternal babble!
They lied is what they did,
lied to me,
lied right out of their crusty ancient books!
Teaching they called it!
Telling me what they knew, they said!
When what they knew they didn't themselves believe!
Wasting their lives and mine!

But what's that?
Someone back in that cell—
sitting in the gloom.
Coming closer, I can't believe what I'm seeing.
Still sitting there, just as I left him,
still wrapped in that shaggy fleece.
I thought at the time he was terribly wise;
that, of course, was because I wasn't.
This time that won't be a problem.

Let's have at him then!

Well, now, old gentleman
(if your bald, bowed head
is still unmoistened by Lethe's turgid stream),
you may recognize a former student,
who meanwhile has outgrown the master's rod.
I find you just as I left you.
As for myself,
I return quite another man.

MEPHISTOPHELES:
I'm glad the bell brought you.
I had no small opinion of you back then.
The caterpillar and chrysalis give fair warning
of the beautiful butterfly to come.
I remember your childish pleasure
in your curly head and lace collar.

I suspect you never wore a pigtail.
Ah, and today your hair is cut short.
A Swedish cut, as they say.
It makes you look quite manly and resolute;
just don't go home in the "absolute."

BACCALAUREATE:
Old man—
we may be in the same old place,
but times have changed, remember;
we can do without the double entendres.
I'm not as gullible as I once was.
You had your fun with me back then,
with no great effort; but, then,
I was naïve.
That won't happen again.

MEPHISTOPHELES:
Speak the unvarnished truth to the young
and they squirm in discomfort.
But when years later
they learn from bitter experience,
they flatter themselves
they discovered it on their own,
and there's no good word
for the poor old idiot of a teacher.

BACCALAUREATE:
Scoundrel, perhaps.
What teacher ever told the truth
straight to our faces?
By contrivance they overstate or understate,
gravely one time, beaming the next,
all very clever,
to their docile, trusting students.

MEPHISTOPHELES:
There is, of course, a time for learning;
but you, I see, are yourself ready to teach.

And I'm certain that in the months and years
you've stored up all kinds of experience.

BACCALAUREATE:
Experience!
Smoke in the wind is more like it!
Not equal to the mind of man.
Confess: what's known as knowledge
isn't worth the knowing.

MEPHISTOPHELES: *(After a pause.)*
Yes, I suspected it long ago.
I was a fool; and now I see how
shallow and silly I am.

BACCALAUREATE:
Glad to hear it. You're talking sense.
The first old-timer I've known to be reasonable!

MEPHISTOPHELES:
I've searched for buried golden treasures,
and come back with dust and ashes.

BACCALAUREATE:
Admit it,
that bald head of yours
is worth no more than those
skulls over there!

MEPHISTOPHELES: *(Genially.)*
I trust, my friend,
you don't know how rude you are.

BACCALAUREATE:
To be polite in German is to be a liar.

*(MEPHISTOPHELES has been inching closer to the proscenium in his
wheelchair.)*

MEPHISTOPHELES: *(To the audience.)*
>   I'm running out of light and air up here.
>   Do you think you might accommodate me down there?

BACCALAUREATE:
>   How presumptuous!
>   At a time of life when you're nothing,
>   when you don't count,
>   to go on pretending you're somebody!
>   Life and blood are one and the same,
>   everything in life depends on it, and
>   where is it fresher and more vital,
>   where does it surge with primal force more
>   vigorously than in the body of youth?
>   It's the source of all creativity:
>   new life out of life.
>   It's a time when everything is on the move;
>   things get done; when the weak falter,
>   they're pushed aside, and the fit,
>   the vigorous, take their place.
>
>   While we have conquered half the world with ideas,
>   what have you done
>   but nod, ponder, dream, deliberate?
>   Plans, always plans!
>   No doubt about it,
>   age is a cold fever,
>   an ague of whims and impotent fantasies.
>   You've left thirty behind, you say?
>   You're as good as dead.
>   The best advice would be to kill you all off.

MEPHISTOPHELES:
>   What could the Devil add to that?

BACCALAUREATE:
>   If I don't will it, the Devil doesn't exist.

MEPHISTOPHELES: *(Aside.)*
>   The Devil will get you yet before too long.

BACCALAUREATE:

This is the noblest mission of the young!
The world was not, until I gave it being.
I urged the sun to rise out of the sea.
It was I who set the moon on its changing course.
As I passed by the earth put on its finest,
grew green and blossomed to meet me.
At my sign, the stars in all their splendor
spread out in the heavens on that first night.
Who but I delivered you from the narrow,
literal-minded philistine?
But I'm free, free as the voice inside me,
and joyous to be so, to follow my inner light
and move as swiftly as thought can carry me,
day before me, and behind me night.

(Exit.)

MEPHISTOPHELES:

Off you go in your glory, then!
What an original!
How it would wound him to know
that nothing wise or foolish can be thought
that wasn't thought many ages ago.

But there's no harm in the boy.
Times change, things change;
a few years and all will be different.
However absurdly the grape juice foams and sputters,
in the end it turns into some sort of wine.

(To the younger members of the audience who fail to applaud.)

I see my words leave you cold, my dears,
but that's quite all right; just remember,
the Devil's old; when you're older,
you'll know what he's about.

XXXVI ⚘ LABORATORY

A medieval alchemist's workshop crammed with extensive, clumsy apparatus for fantastic purposes.

WAGNER: *(At the furnace.)*
That dreadful bell's ringing sends a shudder
through these sooty walls.
It can't be long now,
an end to the uncertainty of my most solemn hopes.

The darkness begins to brighten.
Something's glowing in the heart of the phial,
like a live coal, yes, the most glorious carbuncle,
radiating shafts of light into the darkness.
And now a bright white light!

Oh, don't let me lose it!
Not again!
Oh, God, what's that rattling the door?

MEPHISTOPHELES: *(Entering.)*
A very good greeting to you, friend!

WAGNER: *(Anxiously.)*
Welcome, rather, to this hour's great star!

(Softly.)

But not a word, not a breath;
a glorious work will soon be accomplished.

MEPHISTOPHELES: *(More softly.)*
What is it? Tell me.

WAGNER: *(More softly.)*
A man is in the making.

MEPHISTOPHELES:
A man?

And what pair of lovers
did you lock in your chimney?

WAGNER:
O God help me, no!
That's so out of fashion! A farce!
The tender point from which life sprang,
the subtle, thrusting inward force that
took and gave to make itself,
assimilating like and unlike,
is now discredited.

The beast will always find its pleasure there,
but man, whose gifts are greater,
greater! must find a higher, nobler origin.

(Turning to the furnace.)

Look there! How it gleams!
Let us now hope for the possible!
I make a mixture from many hundred substances—
it's always the mixture that counts—and, mixing,
leisurely compound the human substance,
seal it in an alembic and cohobate it thoroughly,
and the Work, the Great Work,
will in secret have been accomplished.

(Turning again to the furnace.)

It's happening!
The moving mass is clearing itself.
I'm surer now, more than ever!
What once was Nature's deepest mystery,
we now accomplish boldly with Intelligence.
What once Nature accomplished organically,
we will achieve by crystallization!

MEPHISTOPHELES:
Live long and learn a lot

and there will be nothing new under the sun.
In my worldly wanderings,
I've run into more than a few synthetic people.

WAGNER: *(Who has never removed his eyes from the phial.)*
It's rising, flashing, swelling!
Another moment and it's done!
Great ideas always seem insane at the start;
but the time will come when we'll laugh at haphazard chance,
and a brain capable of great thinking
will have been made by a thinking man!

(Rapturously observing the phial.)

The glass rings out with a grand harmonious power!
More opaque now,
now more clear.
It *will* come now,
it *must* come!
Look! You see? Inside!
A tiny shape!
A charming little man! Gesturing!
What more can we want,
what more can the world want?
The secret is out.
In the bright light of day.
Listen—
listen to the sound—
it's—it's becoming a voice—
it's speaking—

HOMUNCULUS: *(To WAGNER from inside the phial.)*
So, little father, how about that!
That was no joke, believe me!
Come on, give me a hug,
but careful you don't crack my glass,
not too tight.
That's the way it is. Not all of space
is big enough for what is natural,
whereas the artificial requires containment.

(To MEPHISTOPHELES.)

So, cousin, you here, too, you rascal?
And just in time, too.
Many thanks.
It's a lucky chance brings you.
Since I exist, I must be always active,
and I'd like to begin at once. You're just the one
to show me a shortcut when I need it.

WAGNER:

A word first, if you don't mind.
I've always found myself embarrassed by people,
old and young, who bombard me with their problems.
For example, they're always asking how
body and soul can fit so finely together,
cling so tightly, as if they'd never part,
and yet they're always at each other's throats,
making life miserable.
And then—

MEPHISTOPHELES:

Hold on there! Not so fast!
I'd ask, rather,
why husband and wife get along so miserably?
That's one thing, friend, you'll never be clear about.
There's work to be done,
and our little one here is eager.

HOMUNCULUS:

What needs doing?

MEPHISTOPHELES: *(Pointing to a side door.)*
Show your talents there.

WAGNER: *(Continues staring into the phial.)*
I swear, you're the loveliest little boy!

(The side door opens to reveal FAUST lying on a couch.)

HOMUNCULUS: *(Astonished.)*
  Remarkable!

  (The phial slips out of WAGNER's hands, hovers over FAUST, and sheds light down upon him.)

  The beauty of the place!
  Clear streams in a dense grove.
  Women, undressing.
  Delightful!
  But it gets better all the time.
  There's one, I see,
  the loveliest of them all,
  a splendid creature,
  born of a race of heroes,
  no, of the gods.
  She slips her foot into the transparent waters;
  her lovely body's life flame
  cools in the shimmering crystal of the water.
  But what is that rush of wings,
  that roar and plunge that startles the placid waters?
  The women scatter in fright,
  and only she, the queen, looks on calmly
  with a woman's confident pride.
  She beholds with pleasure as the prince of swans,
  importunately yet gently,
  presses against her knees.
  You would almost think he's at home there.

  Suddenly a mist arises,
  and with its closely woven veil
  conceals that loveliest of scenes.

MEPHISTOPHELES:
  What a tale, I must say!
  You may be small,
  but your fantasy certainly isn't.
  I see nothing—

HOMUNCULUS:

I believe you.
How could it be otherwise?
Born in the North,
raised in the romantic mist of medievalism,
in the chaos of monks and armor-plated chivalry,
how could you fail to see with blinkered eyes?
Your rightful home is in obscurity.

(Looking about.)

Look around you!
Stones discolored, blackened with age,
moldy, mildewed, pointed arches,
vulgarly ornate!
Horrible!
If this man wakens here there'll be more trouble,
for he'll die on the spot.
Forest springs, swans, naked beauties—
that was his prophetic dream.
How could he endure it here? Not even I
with my adaptable nature could do that.
Let's get him out of here fast.

MEPHISTOPHELES:

I like your solution.

HOMUNCULUS:

Order the warrior into battle,
take the girl to the dance,
and the rest will follow.
But it just occurs to me that
this is Classical Walpurgis Night.
It's the best that could happen to him.
We'll take him to his element.

MEPHISTOPHELES:

I've never heard of it.

HOMUNCULUS:

> Yes, how could you have?
> The only ghosts you know are romantic.
> And yet, to be genuine, a ghost must be classical, too.

MEPHISTOPHELES:

> Yes, well, how do we get there?
> I've already had too much of antique colleagues.

HOMUNCULUS:

> Your favorite pleasure ground, Satan,
> as I understand, is the Northwest.
> This time we sail southeastward.
> To a great plain where the Peneios flows freely
> through groves and thickets
> in cool and winding bends.
> And the plain stretches even to mountain gorges
> where the lowlands rise,
> and up above lies Pharsalos,
> the old and the new.

MEPHISTOPHELES:

> Spare me!
> I've had enough of your ancient history!
> Eternal battles between tyranny and slavery!
> They bore me.
> No sooner does the fighting end
> than it begins all over again.
> And neither side, neither, notices
> that it's Asmodeus back of it all,
> teasing them.
> They fight, it's said, for the rights of freedom;
> but more properly seen, it's slaves fighting slaves.

HOMUNCULUS:

> Allow men their contrariety.
> Staying intact is no easy task.
> From boyhood on he has to defend himself;
> it's what makes him a man.

The question is, how does this man recover?
If you have a remedy, test it here;
but if you can't, leave it to me.

MEPHISTOPHELES:
I could try out some of my Brocken tricks,
except for the heathenish bolts blocking the gate.
Those Greeks were never good for much.
They dazzle you with the free play of the senses,
luring men's hearts into a colorful kind of sinning;
and what is ours, our sinning, but a morass of gloom?
So what do we do now?

HOMUNCULUS:
Considering you were never shy,
if I say Thessalian witches you'd know what I mean.

MEPHISTOPHELES: *(Lecherously.)*
Thessalian witches!
Yes, well! That's a different story!
I've been curious about them for quite some time.
Night after night, of course, might be less than a pleasure.
But a visit?
What's there to lose?

HOMUNCULUS:
Bring your cloak and wrap it around our knight.
As before, it will carry the two of you.
I'll light the way.

WAGNER: *(Anxiously.)*
And what about me?

HOMUNCULUS:
You, Wagner?
Well, you'll be staying home;
you have important things to do.
Perusing your ancient parchments,
you must do as they instruct;

collect life's elements and cautiously fit them together.
Consider the What,
but even more the How.
As I wander the world, I may discover
the dot that completes your *i*.
Then the Great Purpose will have been achieved.
And such striving deserves a reward:
gold, honor, fame, a long healthy life,
and, who knows,
perhaps even knowledge and integrity.
Farewell!

WAGNER: *(Distressed.)*
Farewell!
This pains me terribly.
I already fear I'll never see you again.

MEPHISTOPHELES:
Quickly now! Off to the Peneios!
Our cousin is not to be scorned.

(To the audience.)

In the end we remain dependent on creatures we've created.

CLASSICAL WALPURGIS NIGHT
XXXVII ⚡ THE PHARSALIAN PLAIN. DARKNESS

ERICHTHO:
How often before have I come to this fearful festival,
I, Erichtho,
Erichtho the Dismal they call me,
but not so repulsive as the spiteful poets
exaggerate me to be with their slanderous tongues,
they who are never done with their praising and carping.

I begin to see stretched out before me in the valley

the pale gray surge of tents, an afterimage
of that most harrowing and cruel of nights.

How often it has recurred,
and how often to the end of time it will return!
Neither side yields the empire to the other.
Nor will anyone yield it to him
who got it by force and rules it by force.
The man who fails to master his inner self
will lust in his arrogance to master his neighbor's will.

It was here, on this field,
a great battle was fought;
an example of how a mighty power
pits itself against one mightier still,
rips to shreds the richly flowered garland
of Liberty, and coils the stiff laurel
around the conqueror's head.
Here Pompey dreamed the dream of youthful glories;
there Caesar, waking,
kept watch on fate's quivering balance.
They'll measure themselves against each other;
and all the world knows who prevailed.

Watch fires burn red,
spreading their glowing largess through the night;
the ground exhales the reflection of long-spilt blood;
and lured there by the night's miraculous splendor,
the assembling legion of Greek myth gathers.
Hovering uncertainly or sitting at ease
at each fire are the fabulous forms
of ancient days.
The moon, admittedly not full,
but shining brightly, is risen and
sheds its soft radiance everywhere.
The illusion of the tents has disappeared,
and the fires are burning blue.

But what's that above me?

A meteor?
Who'd have expected it?
Its shine reveals a rounded bodily thing.
I scent life.
I mustn't get too close, being harmful to life.
It would do my name no good and serve no purpose.
It's descending, I see.
I'll be prudent now and withdraw.

(Exit. The AERONAUTS appear from above.)

HOMUNCULUS:

> I'll take another spin around
> Above these flames and phantoms dreary;
> Down there upon that battleground
> Things look ghostly, wild, and eerie.

MEPHISTOPHELES:

> In the northland's waste I'd see
> Ghastly shapes and horrors rare,
> Here hideous ghosts appear to me,
> And I'm as much at home as there.

HOMUNCULUS:

> Look! That tall, gaunt figure there!
> Striding off, I'm sure, afraid.

MEPHISTOPHELES:

> She saw us riding through the air.
> Who can blame the frightened shade?

HOMUNCULUS:

> Let her go! Set down your knight;
> In this land of myth he will revive;
> Freed of horror and of fright,
> He will flourish, he will thrive.

FAUST: *(Touching the ground.)*
> Where is she?

HOMUNCULUS:

>Can't say exactly.
>But probably if you ask around you'll find her.
>Hurry, and before dawn
>you can check at all the fires.
>A man who has dared descend to the Mothers
>has nothing more to fear.

MEPHISTOPHELES:

>Since I have my own reasons for being here,
>I suggest each of us
>search out his own adventure among the fires.
>When it's time to reunite,
>our little friend here
>will let his glass shine out and sound.

HOMUNCULUS:

>This is how it will sound and flash.

(The glass sounds and shines powerfully.)

>Off we go now in search of new wonders.

(Exeunt MEPHISTOPHELES and HOMUNCULUS in opposite directions.)

FAUST: *(Alone.)*

>Where is she?
>But why ask!
>If this isn't the same soil
>her foot touched, or the wave that
>swirled at her feet, it's the air, at least,
>the air that spoke her speech.
>Here, by a miracle, here I am, in Greece!
>No sooner I touched the ground,
>I knew where I was:
>new life surged, warming me after sleep,
>like an Antaeus of the spirit.
>No matter how strange what I may encounter,
>I'll explore this labyrinth of flames in all earnestness.

(Exit.)

XXXVIII ❧ ON THE UPPER PENEIOS

MEPHISTOPHELES: *(Sniffing about.)*
>I must say,
>as I wander among these modest fires,
>I feel quite the foreigner. They're mostly
>naked as jaybirds, only here and there
>do I see a shift. The sphinxes are shameless,
>the griffins downright impudent, and all these
>winged and curly fleeced things
>that display themselves fore and aft!
>
>I have to admit, of course,
>that at heart we're as indecent as the next,
>but this antique style I find a bit too intense.
>It needs mastering, reforming,
>in the modern style,
>to reflect the new sensibility,
>a bit of plaster here and there,
>if you know what I mean.
>What a repulsive lot!
>
>But I mustn't let it get the better of me.
>I'll greet them courteously;
>after all, I'm a guest.
>
>Greetings, fair ladies!
>And greetings to you, wise old grayfins!

GRIFFIN: *(Snarling.)*
>Grayfins!
>Not grayfins!
>Griffins! Ah!
>How dare you call anyone gray!
>A word's sound tells you its origin.
>Gray, grouchy, grim, gruesome,
>grating, grave, groaning.
>Etymologically they all agree,
>it's just that we don't agree *with* them.

MEPHISTOPHELES:
>Yes, well, but not to digress—
>the *gr* in griffin is surely a sound that pleases you?
>An honorific title!

GRIFFIN: *(Snarling as before, and throughout.)*
>Of course! The affinity's proven;
>often condemned, to be sure,
>but more often praised.
>A griffin grips,
>a griffin grabs,
>whether girls or gold or coronets.
>Dame Fortune is gracious to him who grabs.

GIANT ANTS:
>You speak of gold.
>We'd gathered quite a hoard and stashed it
>in all kinds of secret caves and hollows.
>But they smelled it out, those Arimasps,
>and carried it off we don't know where.
>Look at them over there, laughing at us.

GRIFFINS:
>Rest easy, we'll make them confess.

ARIMASPS:
>Not tonight you won't!
>Tonight we celebrate carnival!
>And by tomorrow we'll have run through it all.
>This time we'll get away with it.

MEPHISTOPHELES: *(Has sat down between the SPHINXES.)*
>How easy I find it to be at home here!
>I understand every one of you!

SPHINXES:
>We whisper our ghostly sounds,
>which you then give body to.
>For now your name will do,
>until we know you better.

MEPHISTOPHELES:
     It's widely believed that I have many names.
     But tell me, are there any British around?
     They do a lot of traveling,
     seeking out battlefields, waterfalls,
     all kinds of ruins and musty classical sites.
     This would be quite an adventure for them.
     They know me, they can bear witness.
     There's a stage play where I'm known as Old Iniquity.

SPHINX:
     How did they hit on that?

MEPHISTOPHELES:
     I can't imagine.

SPHINX:
     I see.
     What do you know of the stars?
     What aspects prevail at this hour?

MEPHISTOPHELES: *(Looking upward.)*
     Shooting stars, one after another,
     a waning but bright-shining moon,
     and what's more, I feel very comfortable here,
     keeping warn beside your lion's skin.
     Why wander out of one's depth?
     Give us some riddles,
     or at least a charade or two.

SPHINX:
     Only say what you are,
     that's riddle enough. Try, for once,
     to unravel your innermost being:
     "Needed by both pious and wicked men.
     A padded vest for the first's aesthetic thrusts;
     a partner for the second's wild adventures;
     and both together merely to amuse the gods."

FIRST GRIFFIN: *(Snarling.)*
> I don't like him!

SECOND GRIFFIN: *(Snarling even worse.)*
> What does he want of us?

BOTH GRIFFINS:
> Nasty man!
> He doesn't belong here!

MEPHISTOPHELES: *(Brutally.)*
> Perhaps you think your visitor
> is short on nails to tear with,
> compared with your sharp claws?
> Try me! We'll see!

SPHINX: *(Gently.)*
> You may stay. You'll soon be wanting
> to leave by your own choice.
> Where you come from,
> you think you're somebody, but here,
> if I'm not mistaken, you're ill at ease.

MEPHISTOPHELES:
> Your upper half is really quite appetizing;
> it's the down-below I find disgusting.

SPHINX:
> False creature, you'll pay for your rudeness!
> Our claws are healthy, but you with your shriveled
> horse's hoof will find no pleasure in our company.

(SIRENS are heard tuning up in the poplar trees.)

MEPHISTOPHELES:
> What are those birds in the poplar trees by the river?

SPHINX:
> Be on your guard! Their sing-song
> has destroyed the very best of men.

SIRENS:

>   Why waste time, why linger long
>   By mingling there with what's unsightly?
>   Here we sirens come, so sprightly,
>   Singing our melodious song
>   As is right for a siren throng!

SPHINXES: *(Mocking them in the same melody.)*

>   Hurry, force them to the ground,
>   For hidden in those leaves are found
>   Talons long, hooked, and hideous,
>   Which will fall on you perfidious,
>   Should you lend ears to their sound.

SIRENS:

>   Away with hate, away with envy!
>   In the purest chalice pour we
>   All the brightest joys there be.
>   Best of water, best of earth,
>   Shapes of beauty, shapes of mirth,
>   Shall be one to welcome thee.

MEPHISTOPHELES:

>   What am I hearing?
>   The latest fashion?
>   Ah, neat novelties, to be sure!
>   Voice and string combine to sing,
>   all intertwining in their rhyming,
>   one about the other.
>   It's lost on me, this warbling.
>   It tickles my ear,
>   but fails to move my heart.

SPHINXES:

>   Ha! Your heart!
>   Don't flatter yourself!
>   A shriveled leather pouch is more like it,
>   to judge by your face.

FAUST: *(Entering.)*
>How wondrous!
>How grand this sight!
>That in the repellant there can be
>such strength and greatness!
>I seem to sense that all will be well.
>Where does this solemn sight transport me?

(Referring to the SPHINXES.)

Before these Oedipus once stood.

(Referring to the SIRENS.)

Odysseus writhed before these in bonds of hemp.

(Referring to the GIANT ANTS.)

These hoarded the greatest of treasures.

(Referring to the GRIFFINS.)

And these guarded it faithfully and without fail.

>I feel a refreshing spirit surging through me.
>How grand are these forms,
>how grand are the memories they bring!

MEPHISTOPHELES:
>Time was you'd have abominated their like,
>but now they seem to suit.
>When looking for the beloved
>even monsters are welcome.

FAUST: *(To the SPHINXES.)*
>Answer me, you in the shapes of women:
>has any of you seen Helen?

SPHINXES:

 We're not of her time.
 Herakles slew the last of us long before.
 But Chiron will know. Ask him.
 He's galloping about somewhere this ghostly night.
 If he stops and answers,
 you'll surely succeed.

SIRENS:

        Repel us now, you lose your glory!
        When wise Odysseus dwelt beside us,
        He neither mocked us, nor defied us,
        But told us many a thrilling story.
        Come with us, come, to the bright sea,
        Come, come dwell with us, and we
        Will tell you all he said. You'll see.

SPHINX:

 Scorn them, noble man,
 don't be deceived!
 Odysseus bound himself to his mast;
 rather let our good counsel bind you.
 And if you find Great Chiron,
 he'll tell you what I've promised.

 (Exit FAUST.)

MEPHISTOPHELES: *(Irritably.)*

 What endless file of cawing is that?
 Flying past so fast it can't be seen!
 And single file!
 They'd tire even a huntsman!

SPHINX:

 They're friendly.
 Don't let them frighten you.
 They're known as the swift Stymphalids,
 with vulture beaks and the feet of geese.
 They soar past like winter storm winds

that not even Herakles' arrows could harm.
Their cawing is meant well;
they'd like to join us as near relations.

MEPHISTOPHELES: *(As if intimidated.)*
What is that hissing I hear?

SPHINX:
You needn't be afraid of them.
They're the heads of the Lernaean Hydra.
Though missing a body,
they still think they're something.

But what's happening to you?
Why the gestures? So restless!
Where do you want to go?
Well, go then! Wherever you want!
Craning your head like that!
Ah, I see!
That group over there. So that's it.
Don't hold back. Go on!
Tell them what pretty faces they have;
they'll love you for it.
Those are the lamias,
clever, refined little tarts with smiling mouths
and seductive eyes—
favorites of the satyrs.
Your horse's hoof won't be a hindrance.
Give it a try!

MEPHISTOPHELES:
I trust you'll stay here, then, so I can find you?

SPHINXES:
Feel free! Go!
Mix with that airy rabble!
Being from Egypt, we're used to waiting millennia.
But never fail to respect our situation.
Enthroned before the pyramids,

we regulate the cycles of sun and moon,
witness the supreme fate of nations,
see war and peace, drought and flood—
with calm passivity.

XXXIX ✒ ON THE LOWER PENEIOS

*RIVER GOD PENEIOS surrounded by TRIBUTARY RIVER GODS
and NYMPHS.*

PENEIOS: *(Waking.)*
>Rustling rushes, stir, stir slowly!
>Tangled sister reeds breathe lowly!
>Willows waving, softly sighing,
>To the aspens' thrill replying,
>Soothe my interrupted dream!
>A dreadful premonition wakes me,
>Some mysterious tremor shakes me
>From my slumber-peaceful stream.

FAUST: *(Approaching the river's edge.)*
>Do my ears deceive me? Are there voices
>behind these twining leaves and branches?
>How human they sound.
>The rippling waters chatter on,
>and breezes titter away in jest.

NYMPHS: *(To FAUST.)*
>Come to our streams,
>Here you'll find rest,
>Here let your dreams
>Answer your quest.
>Here in the cool
>Your limbs will be dressed,
>By our soft rustling pool
>We'll sing you to rest.

FAUST:

> Dream? No!
> *Now, now* I'm awake!
> O let them be, those unspeakably lovely figures!
> How deeply the dear sight moves me!
> Are they dream?
> Are they memory?
> Once before I felt myself so blest.
> Waters idle through cool, dense, swaying thickets,
> no rushing sound, no rustle, scarcely a ripple;
> and from every side numberless springs flow together
> to form this clear, clean, shallow pool for bathing.
>
> And there they play,
> young, healthy limbs of lovely women,
> seen twice over, to my eye's delight,
> in the liquid mirror of the waters.
> Some swim boldly,
> others wade timidly,
> till at last all join in a great white splash
> and shrieks and shouts and laughter.
>
> These should content me,
> my eyes should feast their fill,
> but my senses urge me on, and I turn my gaze
> toward that screen of thick foliage, that green veil
> that conceals the exalted queen.
>
> What a marvelous sight!
> Swans from hidden bays and inlets,
> swimming with simple but majestic dignity,
> floating silently,
> tenderly sociable,
> but nonetheless proud and self-assured:
> see how each moves his head and beak.
>
> But one of them seems more proud,
> more bold than the rest.
> Chest thrust forward,

feathers puffing,
he sails swiftly on through the flock,
a cresting wave himself, he rides the waves,
invading that sacred place.

The others, sailing calmly in their shells
of bright feathers, suddenly, quite unexpected,
in mock attack, tease the timid young beauties
to forget their duty and think only of their own safety.

NYMPHS:

> Sisters, hurry, lay your ear
> To the bank's cool grassy mound;
> Tell me, quickly, do you hear
> The thud of horses on the ground?
> Who, I wonder, rides so fast,
> Bringing news or riding past?

FAUST:

> What is that sound!
> The earth pounding!
> As though a horse's hooves resounding!
> Faster! Faster! What is it I see?
> There! There!
> Can good fortune come so soon?
> O unspeakable wonder! A horseman approaching
> at a rapid trot, his mount a dazzling radiance!
> He appears a man blest with spirit and courage.
> I know him! I know him, yes, yes!
> Philyra's son, her famous son!
> Chiron!
> Stop! O stop!
> I've something to tell you—

CHIRON:

> What? What is it?

FAUST:

> Slow down! Not so fast!

CHIRON:

> I never rest.

FAUST:

> Then take me with you! Please!

CHIRON:

> Jump on up!
> Once you're in place on my back,
> I can ask you where you're headed?
> If it's ferrying across the river you need,
> I'm at your service.

FAUST: *(Mounting.)*

> Wherever you like.
> I'm eternally grateful to you—
> you, the great one, the noble tutor,
> who to his glory mentored a race of heroes,
> that splendid brotherhood of Argonauts,
> and others who created a world for poets to sing of.

CHIRON:

> Let's forget that, shall we?
> Not even Athena rates very high as a mentor.
> In the end they go off, these heroes,
> and carry on as if we'd taught them nothing.

FAUST:

> Here I sit and in my arms embrace,
> in body and spirit,
> the great physician who knows every herb and root,
> healer of the sick and reliever of human pain.

CHIRON:

> If beside me some hero was wounded,
> I knew what to do,
> where to get help and advice;
> but I gave it up in the end, my skills,
> and monks and witches' quackery took it over.

FAUST:

   Like all the truly great you're
   embarrassed by praise. Modesty makes you
   avoid it, and you act as if all were like you.

CHIRON:

   And you, I'd say, are an adept dissembler.
   You flatter both ruler and ruled in the same breath.

FAUST:

   Admit at least you saw the greatest of your time,
   emulated what was noblest in your actions,
   and lived a life worthy of a demigod.
   But tell me,
   which of them all did you honor the most?

CHIRON:

   In that sublime assembly of the Argonauts,
   each was splendid in his own way;
   and considering what virtue it was that informed him,
   each could step in where others were lacking.
   The Dioskouroi where youth and beauty counted;
   the Boreads where decisive swift action was called for.
   As for Jason, he was strong, thoughtful, clever
   and accommodating in counsel, not to mention
   attractive to women.

   And then there was Orpheus,
   a thoughtful, delicate sort,
   who when he struck his lyre surpassed them all.
   And keen-eyed Lynceus who night and day
   steered that sacred ship through every peril.
   Comradeship is the only test for courage:
   when one man acts he's praised by all the others.

FAUST:

   Have you nothing to say of Herakles?

CHIRON:

   Oh, no! Don't break my heart!

I'd never laid eyes on Phoebus, or Ares, or Hermes
and all the others—and then,
there before me, I saw him,
and in seeing I saw what men can only
praise as divine.
Born to be a king, in youth
he was glorious to see,
subject to his elder brother,
though also, no less, to the loveliest of women.
Earth will never see his like again,
nor Hebe lead him into heaven.
Poets will labor in vain to sing his praises,
and sculptors torture stone to make his image.

FAUST:

Let sculptors boast all they like,
no one has ever portrayed him as well as your words.
Having spoken now of the most splendid of men,
tell me of the loveliest of women.

CHIRON:

What! Female beauty!
Female beauty is nothing,
a rigid, lifeless image!
I reserve my praise for those
whose being is a fountain of joy in life.
Beauty is its own obsession, its own bliss.
Ah, but add to it Grace,
and it becomes irresistible,
charm that escapes the contemplative and
surges to active devotion.
Like Helen when I carried her.

FAUST:

Carried her?

CHIRON:

Yes, on this back.

FAUST:

My mind is already reeling, and now this!

CHIRON:

She held me by the mane, just as you are.

FAUST:

O God, I'm about to lose my senses!
Tell me, tell me about it?
She's everything I desire!
Everything!
Where, where did you take her? Tell me!

CHIRON:

The telling is easy.
Her brothers the Dioskouroi had
freed their little sister
from the hands of highwaymen.
But they weren't the sort to take a beating lightly,
and after they'd rallied soon were in pursuit.
The brothers and their sister, however,
were slowed down by the swamps near Eleusis.
While her brothers waded,
I paddled my way across.
Once there, she dismounted, and
stroking my dripping mane, thanked me with
sweet compliments.
How gentle she was,
but serious, too, and gracious,
so self-assured, and so young—
an old man's joy!

FAUST:

A girl of only ten!

CHIRON:

Ah, poor man, deceived by the philologists!
You'd think their self-deception were enough for them.
The mythological woman is an odd sort.

The poet makes use of her however he likes.
She never grows up, never grows old,
is forever appetizing;
abducted as a girl, she's courted in her senility.
Poets aren't bound by time.

FAUST:

Then neither will she be bound by time!
Achilles, himself outside of time,
found and made her his own on Pherae.
What rare fortune, to wrest from fate
one's own true love!
Why, then, shouldn't I, with my fierce longing,
bring back to life this one and only form?
This deathless being,
the equal of gods by her birth,
as great as she is tender,
sublime as she is lovable?
You saw her once long ago,
but I saw her today:
a vision of loveliness, charm and desire.
My mind and soul are possessed, my entire being!
Without her, life is not possible.

CHIRON:

My poor man, what an odd case you present!
Humans would say you're in a state of rapture.
We spirits find you really quite deranged.

But you're in luck, I'm happy to say.
Once each year, very briefly,
I visit Manto, Aesculapius' daughter.
In silent prayer she beseeches her father,
for his own honor's sake,
at last to shed some light on physicians' minds,
and convert them from their reckless slaughter.

She's a favorite of mine of all the Sibyls' guild.
Nothing grotesque here, only kindness,
concern and gentle good works.

Stay with her awhile; she'll cure you
with her knowledge of herbs, I assure you.

FAUST:

Cure? I don't want to be cured!
My mind is sound!
I will *not* be one of the common herd!

CHIRON:

Don't fail to drink at the healing spring.
Hurry! Dismount! We're at the site!

FAUST:

Where have you brought me in this
dreadful night through gravelly waters?

CHIRON:

This is where Rome and Greece met in battle.
Peneios on the right,
Olympus on the left,
and the greatest empire sunk into the sand.
The king fled, the citizens won.

Look up!
Behold the eternal temple
bathed in moonlight!

MANTO: *(Dreaming within.)*

The sacred threshold
resounds with horse's hoofs;
demigods draw near.

CHIRON:

How true!
Only open your eyes.

MANTO: *(Awaking.)*

Welcome!
I see you haven't failed me.

CHIRON:
    Failed you?
    Not while your temple stands.

MANTO:
    Are you still the tireless rover?

CHIRON:
    While you dwell here in quiet contentment,
    my will is to wander.

MANTO:
    While I abide,
    Time circles round me.
    Who is this?

CHIRON:
    The turmoil of this infamous night
    has swept him here.
    He's mad.
    He's out to win Helen,
    but doesn't know how or where to begin.
    If anyone needs a cure, it's he.

MANTO:
    I love the man who desires the impossible.

    (CHIRON is far away by now.)

    Enter here, bold youth, and rejoice!
    This dark passage leads to the core of Olympus
    where Persephone secretly listens for forbidden greetings.
    I once smuggled Oedipus into this passage.
    Make better use of it than he.
    Quick! Take heart!

    (They descend.)

XL ✒ ON THE UPPER PENEIOS AS BEFORE

SIRENS:

> Plunge into Peneios! There!
> Oh, what joy it is to swim,
> Splashing, singing hymn on hymn,
> For these poor mortals in despair!
> Without water naught will thrive!
> Hurry, then, and when we gain
> The vast Aegean's azure main
> Every pleasure shall revive!

(Earthquake.)

> The wildly foaming wave sweeps back,
> No longer in its ancient track;
> All earth quakes, the waters shiver,
> Bank and gravel smoke and quiver.
> Let us flee this, one and all,
> Before a worse disaster fall!
>
> Away, and let our joys abound
> In bright ocean's festive round,
> Where gentle billows lap the shore,
> Rippling, sparkling at Neptune's door;
> where the fair moon floats on high,
> shedding light in a glistening sky,
> And, mirrored in the ocean's blue,
> Wets us with her sacred dew.
> Life is freedom in the ocean,
> Here we suffer dread commotion.

SEISMOS: *(Growling and grumbling deep in the earth.)*

> One more thrust with might and main,
> Let the shoulders heave and strain,
> And we earth's upper crust will gain,
> Where all life gives way before us!

SPHINXES:

> What a tremor, what a rumble,
> What a gruesome grating, grumble,
> What a reeling, what a quaking!
> This way first, then that way shaking!
> But you'll not see us budge an inch,
> However close the dreadful pinch,
> Even though all Hell broke loose!
>
> Now a mound out of the ground
> Rises up with a dreadful sound.
> We know him well, for who but he
> Raised fair Delos from the sea,
> Grizzled old codger, from ocean's floor,
> To give mother Leto a shore to bear
> Bright Phoebus and his sister there.
>
> Now thrusting, squeezing, straining, prying,
> Arms stretched taut and shoulders plying,
> Atlas-like he lifts his shoulders,
> Heaves up soil and massive boulders,
> Sand and gravel, shale and clay,
> Where once our tranquil river lay.
> Across our peaceful valley floor
> He cuts a gap and then no more.
> For like a massive caryatid,
> Waist-deep in the bare earth squatted,
> He stops, unmoving, without a groan,
> Bearing a monstrous weight of stone,
> Nearer he will not approach,
> Nor upon our haunt encroach.

SEISMOS:

> All this is my doing, mine alone,
> as the world will one day concede.
> What would your earth have been without
> the beauty my jostling and jolting gave it?
> And your mountains,
> soaring splendidly into the sky,

had I not thrust them upward
to enchant your senses
with a grand spectacle?
In the days when my parents,
Night and Chaos, prevailed,
I was strong and made no secret of it.
Playing boyhood games with the Titans,
we tossed around Pelion and Ossa
like so many balls; until finally,
tired of our youthful exuberance,
as a prank,
we wickedly tossed the two mountains
on top of Parnassus,
giving it a twin-peaked cap.

Apollo, now, likes nothing so much as
dwelling there with the choir of blessèd Muses.
And who but I fashioned and thrust on high
the throne for Zeus and his thunderbolts?
So here I am again, thrusting
with unspeakable strength out of the abyss,
welcoming all who will to begin a new life
and settle on the new land that is me!

SPHINXES:

Had we not seen with our own eyes
this mountain squeezed from the earth,
we'd say it was old as time.
It's rocks are still on the rise,
pushing into place,
and a forest is growing its way up the slope.
But that means nothing to us sphinxes.
We sit enthroned on our sacred site,
and nothing disturbs us.

GRIFFINS:

We see golden foil and nuggets quivering,
gleaming through a million crannies.
Emmets, this is no treasure to lose!
Get busy there and dig out your hoard!

CHORUS OF GIANT ANTS:

> Fast as the giant ones
> Up there upheave it,
> Seize it, you pliant ones,
> Never to leave it.
> Search every cranny in
> Ranging and rifling;
> None that there's any in
> Can be too trifling.
> The murkiest, shiniest,
> Fail not to explore it;
> Each speck, the tiniest,
> Seize it and store it.
> Work with a will,
> Till all is rolled out:
> Move the hill as it will,
> Just get the gold out!

GRIFFINS: *(To the ANTS returning with the gold.)*

> Bring it in here!
> Bring it! Bring it!
> Pile it high!
> Our claws will grasp it
> better than any bolt!
> No treasure's too
> great for us to guard!

PYGMIES:

> Surprise! Here we are!
> And already in place!
> Better not to ask how or where from,
> because we don't have a clue.
> Really, all we can say is that we're here.
> We figure there's nowhere not worth living;
> that it can be cheerful anywhere.
> And wherever a chink in a rock appears,
> a dwarf is sure to turn up soon.
> In pairs, of course, man and wife,
> industrious couple, too,
> a model pair, to be sure.

Who knows, maybe Paradise was like this.
We're just glad to be here, and
thank our lucky stars for it. East or west,
Mother Earth is forever fruitful.

DACTYLS:

If Earth Mother in a single night
Could bring these little ones to light,
Then She the littlest can create,
And each of us will find a mate.

PYGMY ELDERS:

Hurry! Make haste!
See you're properly placed!
With speed as our muscle,
Let's hustle and bustle!
While peace still holds steady
Make our foundries ready,
Weapons with speed
The army will need.

Ants, gather near,
We ask of you here
Bring metal, bring ore!
And dactyls so many
You smallest of any,
Do us all good,
Fetch us much wood!
Pile it up high,
High as the sky,
Of coals we need more!

PYGMY GENERALISSIMO:

With arrow and bow
March out to the foe!
Shoot me those herons
Down there by the marsh,
Clustering numberless,
Croaking so harsh,
Puffing and preening,

Their pride overweening!
Kill them, slay them,
All together,
So each of our helmets
Can boast its own feather!

GIANT ANTS AND DACTYLS:
Iron we bring them—
Ah, who is to save us!—
Which into harsh chains
They forge to enslave us.
The time's not yet come
To rise in defiance;
So bow to your tyrants
In lowly compliance.

THE CRANES OF IBYKUS:
Shrieks of murder, dying groans,
Wings that flutter in dismay,
Ah, what outcry and what moans
To us in flight here pierce their way!
They are all already dead,
The placid lake with blood is red.
Reckless passion for display
Raped the heron's plumes away.
Behold their helmets! See it wave
On each bowlegged paunchy knave!
You companions of our host,
Wedge-shaped wanderers of our coast,
Hear our cry, on you we call
For vengeance that affects us all.
Death, so we avenge their fate!
To this rabble deathless hate!

(They scatter, screeching, in the air.)

MEPHISTOPHELES: *(On the plain.)*
I've always known how to master Nordic witches;
it's these foreign types I just can't get the knack of.

Now, in the Blocksberg you know where you are,
it's quite convenient, really. I mean,
there's old Ilsa up on her rock keeping watch,
and Henry happy to be on his heights,
not to mention the Snorers snorting at Misery.
Things there stay put for eons on end;
you can count on it.
But here it's all a turmoil.
The earth blows up under you without a warning.
I mean, I'm walking along through a valley,
flat as a pancake, when all of sudden
a mountain pokes up in back of me—
well, maybe not a mountain, exactly,
but large enough to part me from my sphinxes.

Ah, but I see more fires
flickering there down the valley,
signaling the call to adventure.
The saucy little chorus is still there,
dancing, swaying, tempting and
enticing me with their coquetry.
Easy does it, now.
Too much noshing can spoil you.
Soon you can't forego an opportunity.

LAMIAE: *(Drawing MEPHISTOPHELES after them.)*
         Onward, still onward,
         Faster and faster!
         Then with a spiteful
         Coyness delaying,
         Prattling and playing,
         He'll think he's the winner.
         It's so delightful
         To see the old sinner
         Lured and seduced!
         Fretting and groaning,
         His clubfoot bemoaning,
         Hear, he comes grumbling,
         Stumbling and tumbling!

Do what he will,
While before him we fly,
Be it far, be it nigh,
He must follow us still!

MEPHISTOPHELES: *(At a standstill.)*
Blasted fate!
Stupid, idiotic man!
Deluded, duped, seduced since Adam's first day!
And age teaches us nothing! Nothing!
Ah! Men!
Eternal fools!

Rotten is what they are! Rotten!
Women! Worthless to the core!
Bodies tight-laced, faces painted,
bogs of depravity, touch them
and you touch decay!
We know it, feel it, see it at a glance,
but let them start piping,
we join their dance!

LAMIAE: *(Pausing.)*
Halt! He's hesitating, reflecting!
He's stopped!
Go toward him now,
so he doesn't escape.

MEPHISTOPHELES: *(Striding forward.)*
But once more unto the breach, as they say.
Just don't get all tangled up in doubt.
Face it, if there were no witches,
who the hell would want to be a Devil!

LAMIAE: *(Captivatingly.)*
Let's turn circles round this hero.
He's bound to find love in his
heart for one of us.

MEPHISTOPHELES:

> I must admit, in the twilight's glimmer
> you ladies really seem quite tempting.
> I can't complain about you, now can I?

EMPUSA: *(Barging her way among them.)*

> Nor about me!
> Let me join you, won't you?

LAMIAE:

> No, not her!
> She spoils our fun!

EMPUSA: *(To MEPHISTOPHELES.)*

> Greetings from Empusa, cousin!
> The sweetheart with the ass's foot?
> Though you have only a horse's hoof,
> I greet you all the same, don't you know.

MEPHISTOPHELES:

> I thought there'd be only strangers,
> but now there are relatives!
> Ah! The Devil's book's both old and huge:
> nothing but cousins from the Harz here to Hellas.

EMPUSA:

> I'm known not to dawdle
> but know in a flash
> what form of many forms to assume.
> In your honor, though,
> I've chosen this ass's head.

MEPHISTOPHELES:

> I note that these people are keen on kinship;
> and yet I make no bones about
> disclaiming this ass's head.

LAMIAE:

> Forget it! Forget that filthy old hag!

She frightens off all thoughts of
beauty and delight;
and where beauty and delight are,
let her appear and they've taken flight.

MEPHISTOPHELES:

These cousins so delicate and dainty
I find no less suspicious;
for behind their cheeks as red as roses
I expect a sudden metamorphosis.

LAMIAE:

Come on, give it a try, why don't you!
You've lots to choose from.
Take your pick. With a little bit of luck
you'll snatch the prize!
What's all this lascivious litany!
As a lover you're a washout,
strutting around like the cock of the walk!

Ah! You see? There!
That got him! He's mixing now,
joining the dance.
Slowly, now, one by one—
gently, gently, when your turn comes—
let your masks fall.
Show him the unvarnished truth.

MEPHISTOPHELES:

Here's the prettiest one of all!

(Embracing her.)

Ah! What's this!
A withered old broomstick!

(Seizing another.)

And this?

Disgusting sight!
Hideous!

LAMIAE:

Serves you right!
It's what you deserve!

MEPHISTOPHELES:

That clever little number
is one I'd like to snatch—
but as soon as I grab,
a lizard slithers from my hand,
her braid slick as a snake!

Ah! Then that one there,
tall and slender!
And what do I have but a bacchic wand
with a pinecone at its tip!
Where does this end?

Aha, this fat one, then,
for a bit of a revel,
but this the last! Here goes!
Ah, all squishy-squiggly!
Orientals, I've heard, pay in gold for this!
Oh, but the puffball bursts in two!
Phew!

LAMIAE:

Separate!
Flit round him,
this son of a witch!
Like lightning, like darkness,
swaying, hovering,
black bat wings pounding in
fearsome circles!
Let him not get off so lightly!

MEPHISTOPHELES: *(Shaking himself.)*
    Can't say I've learned too much from all this.
    It's as much a rat race here as in the North!
    Stupid!
    Ghosts, no matter where,
    are equally ridiculous, and poets
    not one jot less perverse than the people.
    The world, I'd say, is one great masquerade,
    a dance to titillate the senses.
    I grasped at ravishing masks,
    and in my grip found creatures
    that made me shudder.
    Ah, how I long to deceive myself,
    if only the deception lasted longer!

(Losing his way among the rocks.)

    Where have I come to?
    Where does this lead?
    I arrived on paths smooth and flat,
    and now this rubble of rocks and boulders.
    I clamber uphill,
    I clamber down,
    and never find my sphinxes!
    It's mad, it's insane,
    a mountain like this in a single night!
    I'd call that some lively witches' ride!
    They bring their Blocksberg with them!

OREAD: *(From a natural cliff.)*
    Come! Climb up!
    My mountains are old!
    Unchanged throughout antiquity!
    Show reverence for my rocky steeps!
    Come!
    The farthest spurs of the Pindus Range!
    I stood here unshaken as I stand here now
    when Pompey fled across me.
    These illusions you see around you

vanish with the first cock's crow.
Here one day, gone the next.

MEPHISTOPHELES:

I honor you, venerable head
crowned with dense and lofty oaks,
that not even the moon's bright glow
can pierce to its midnight depths!

But what's that faint light I see,
there, in the bushes?
Amazing how things work out!
It's Homunculus, to be sure!
Where have you been, little friend?

HOMUNCULUS:

Floating around from place to place.
Oh, I want so to find
the finest way of becoming,
and finally shatter in pieces this glass.
But what I've seen so far
isn't something I'd like to become a part of.
Promise not to tell,
but I'm on the trail of two philosophers.
I listened in on them,
and they never stopped talking about Nature:
"Nature, Nature!"
I'll want to stick close to them, for sure.
I think they must know the way of
living things, and can show me finally
the wisest course to follow.

MEPHISTOPHELES:

No, do it yourself,
forge your own path.
Where phantoms are, there are philosophers;
and in the bargain, to ingratiate themselves,
they'll invent a dozen phantoms of their own.
Make no mistakes and you'll never find wisdom!

If to become is your wish,
do it on your own!

HOMUNCULUS:
Good advice isn't to be scorned.

MEPHISTOPHELES:
Off you go, then! We'll see what happens.

(They separate.)

ANAXAGORAS: *(To THALES.)*
Will that stubborn mind of yours never bend?
What more will it take to convince you?

THALES:
The wave bends willingly to every breeze,
but stays away from rugged rocks like these.

ANAXAGORAS:
That cliff was made by fiery vapors.

THALES:
No, it's in water that life came to be.

HOMUNCULUS: *(Between them.)*
Please let me stay beside you.
I, too, want to come to be.

ANAXAGORAS:
Tell me, Thales,
have you ever in a single night
managed to make a mountain out of mud?

THALES:
Nature, and Nature's living flow,
has never been enslaved to hours and days.
Every form she fashions according to rules;
and no matter how huge the scale,
there's no place for violence.

ANAXAGORAS:

> But you saw it!
> That violence!
> Here! Now!
> Raging plutonic fire,
> monstrous bursts of Aeolian gases
> breaking through the ancient crust
> of the level earth, so that instantly
> a mountain came into being!

THALES:

> And what is that meant to prove?
> If it's here, it's here,
> and perhaps that's all to the good.
> Arguments like this are a waste of time;
> they lead people around by the nose,
> if they don't watch out.

ANAXAGORAS:

> Look there!
> Every rock and cleft is already aswarm
> with myrmidons searching out a home:
> ants and pygmies and tiny Tom Thumbs,
> and a host of other busy little bodies.

> *(To HOMUNCULUS.)*

> You've never aspired to great deeds,
> you've lived in quiet, hermitlike confinement—
> so if you can adapt yourself to governing,
> I'll see to it they crown you king of the mountain.

HOMUNCULUS:

> What does my Thales say?

THALES:

> He says don't do it.
> Little folk give rise to little deeds;
> but with the great,
> little folk can rise to greatness.

Look there!
That black cloud of cranes!
They threaten to attack the excited mob,
and they'd be no less a threat to the king
if they had one.
Look at them!
Jabbing down with beak and claw
on the little people! The flash of doom
is heavy in the air. It was criminal
killing those herons at their peaceful pond.
And now that murderous assault
takes a bloody vengeance, pygmy blood
for the brutally shed blood of the herons,
as next of kin rage against their enemies.
What use now are shield and helmet and spear?
What use those heron plumes to the dwarves?
Look, the poor dactyls and ants running for cover!
The army wavers, turns in flight, collapses.

ANAXAGORAS: *(After a pause, solemnly.)*
Till now I've always praised the gods below;
I turn now to those above.
Great goddess on high,
you who are eternal and unaging,
triple-named, triple-formed divinity,
Diana, Luna, Hekate,
I call on you to hear my people's distress!
You who swell the heart with inspiration,
goddess profoundly wise,
placid seeming, fiercely passionate,
open the fearsome chasm of your dark shadows,
and show us without magic your ancient powers!

(Pause.)

Is my prayer too quickly heard?
By its force
has the course
of Nature been disturbed and marred?

Greater, ever greater, looming nearer,
the goddess's encircling throne approaches!
Appalling, monstrous to behold!
Its flames grow dark,
they're turning red!
Gigantic round, come no closer!
You will destroy us all,
land, sea, and man!

It's true, then, what they say!
Thessalian witches once with wicked magic
chanted you down from your monthly round
and wrested from you the utmost in destruction!

Ah! Darkness now shrouds the luminous shield
that all at once explodes in flames,
showering sparks in every direction!
What a clattering! What a hissing!
The heavens thunder and hurricanes blow!
Goddess, humbly at the foot of your throne
I cast myself! Forgive!
It was I who called it down!

(He throws himself prostrate to the ground.)

THALES:
    The things this man hears and sees!
    I can't be sure exactly what
    happened to us, but I certainly didn't go through
    what he's been through.
    At least we'll agree these are very odd times.
    And yet, there's Luna
    rocking away up there
    just as she's always done.

HOMUNCULUS:
    Look! The pygmies' mountain!
    Up there!
    At first it was rounded,

now it's a peak!
What a tremendous crash that was!
A monstrous rock fell from the moon,
squashing, killing friend and foe alike
and no questions asked.
But how can I not admire the art, the skill,
that brought that mountain into being
from below and above—
in a single night!

THALES:
Settle down!
It was all a fantasy!
Good riddance to that nasty brood!
It's a good thing, though,
that you weren't their king.

But now we're off to the great sea festival!
They welcome and honor there
strange and wondrous guests.

(They withdraw.)

MEPHISTOPHELES: *(Climbing up the opposite side.)*
So here I am,
clambering up steep rocky ledges,
stumbling over roots of ancient oaks!
In my Harz mountains
there's a resinous mist in the air
with a soupçon of pitch in it—
a smell I dearly love, next after sulfur.
Among these Greeks one scarcely gets a whiff of it.
But I'm curious to know
what they use to stoke their Hellfires.

DRYAD:
Back home you may have had
native shrewdness,
but here you're at a loss.

Forget where you came from and
honor these sacred oaks.

MEPHISTOPHELES:

Forget what's left behind?
How do you do that?
What once you had is always Paradise.
But tell me.
What's that squatting in the dusk
of that cave down there?
Is it three of them I see?

DRYAD:

Ah! The Phorkyads! Yes!
Visit them if you dare—
if it doesn't turn your blood to ice.

MEPHISTOPHELES:

Why not?
What I see—what I see astonishes me!
I may be proud, but I must admit
I've never seen the like!
They're worse than mandrakes!
How will the most vile of sins
compare when faced with this triple monster?
Not the most horrendous of our Hells
could endure the sight of them at Hell Mouth.
But here they are,
in this land of beauty called classical.

They're stirring—
they seem to have sensed me—
twittering, whistling,
gibbering like vampire bats.

PHORKYAS:

Sisters, pass me the eye, to see
who's drawing near our sanctuary.

MEPHISTOPHELES:
> Most honored and reverend ladies!
> Permit me to draw near
> to receive your triple blessing.
> I approach you, a stranger, to be sure,
> but unless I'm mistaken,
> also a distant relative.
> I have laid eyes on ancient gods before;
> just yesterday I bowed my deepest
> to Ops and Rhea.
> The three Fates, sisters of Chaos,
> and yours as well, I saw yesterday—
> or was it the day before?
> But the likes of you I've never seen.
> So delighted am I,
> words fail me altogether.

PHORKYAS:
> He seems quite intelligent, this spirit.

MEPHISTOPHELES:
> What surprises me is no poet
> has sung your praises.
> Tell me, now, how is that possible?
> When have I ever seen statues of you,
> worthy ones? It's you, ladies,
> you that sculptors should sculpt.
> Not Juno, Pallas, Venus, and the like.

PHORKYAS:
> Sunk in the depths of solitude and stillest night,
> the thought has never crossed our mind.

MEPHISTOPHELES:
> No, and why should it?
> Withdrawn here from the world,
> seeing and seen by no one?
> You must live where splendor and art sit
> side by side on the same throne, where nimbly

and on the double a hero is freed daily
from a block of marble,
where—

PHORKYAS:
Enough of this! Don't tempt us!
What good would it do if we knew more?
Born in night, allied to nightly things,
unknown to the world,
we are scarcely known to ourselves.

MEPHISTOPHELES:
Yes, well, no problem there.
It's a matter of transferring oneself into another.
One eye, one tooth suffices the three of you,
so, mythologically speaking,
it should not be impossible
to condense the essence of three into two,
and lend me the shape
of the third for a short while.

ONE:
What do you think?
Could we manage it?

THE OTHERS:
Let's try!
Except for the eye and tooth!

MEPHISTOPHELES:
Well, but you're leaving out the best of all.
How is a perfect likeness to be achieved?

ONE:
By closing one eye, don't you see,
and projecting one of your tusks.
In a flash you'll be a spitting image of us.

MEPHISTOPHELES:
Well, then! So be it!

PHORKYAS:
>   So be it!

MEPHISTOPHELES: *(A PHORKYAD in profile.)*
>   And here I am!
>   Favorite son of Chaos!

PHORKYAS:
>   As we are his daughters,
>   without dispute.

MEPHISTOPHELES:
>   Ah! The shame of it!
>   They'll call me hermaphrodite!

PHORKYAS:
>   Ah! Sisters!
>   How lovely this lovely new trio!
>   Before we had one eye and one tooth,
>   now we have two!

MEPHISTOPHELES:
>   Now I'll have to hide from the sight of all,
>   then leap into Hell the devils to appall.

XLI ✒ ROCKBOUND BAYS OF THE AEGEAN SEA

The moon motionless at the zenith.
SIRENS recline here and there on the cliffs, fluting and singing.

SIRENS:
>   You whom once with magic's rite
>   Thessalian witches lured by night
>   Down into the impious dark,
>   Look down from your heavenly arc
>   And with silvery radiance lave
>   Every tremulous, rippling wave,
>   Shine your light on the grand commotion

Rising from the breast of ocean!
Lovely moon, your slaves are we,
Ready to serve you eternally!

NEREIDS and TRITONS: *(As marvels of the sea.)*
Sing louder, sing, with shriller sound!
Let the ocean's depths rebound,
With echo and summon all around!
Eager to escape the waves,
We took refuge in our caves,
Hiding from the wind and weather,
Yet your sweet song has drawn us hither.

Behold us in our raptures here
Decking ourselves with golden gear.
Brooch and clasp and diadem,
Rich with jewel and with gem.
These you gave us, all of these,
Treasure plucked from argosies,
Ships you wrecked, that rotting lie,
Lured to their destruction by
You, the spirits of our bay.

SIRENS:

Well we know that in the sea
Fish live well and merrily,
With no pain, no care, no wish!
Still, you throng so brisk and gay,
We would like to know today
If you're something more than fish.

NEREIDS and TRITONS:

We considered this before
We came here to your rocky shore.
Sisters, brothers, come! Let's go
The briefest journey just to show
Conclusively just who we are,
It won't take long, it isn't far.

(They depart.)

SIRENS:

> Swiftly on a breeze they race
> Off to sunny Samothrace.
> What can they expect to gain
> Where the high Cabiri reign?
> Gods of wondrous kind are they,
> Ever self-begetting,
> Ever self-forgetting,
>
> Hover on your height,
> Fair Luna, in the night!
> Keep day away,
> And let us stay!

THALES: *(On the shore, to HOMUNCULUS.)*
> I'd gladly take you to old Nereus,
> and, yes, we're not very far from his cave.
> He's stubborn, though, you see,
> the rascally curmudgeon,
> hard as nails. There's nothing
> the human race can do to please him.
> And yet, he does see into the future,
> and he's greatly respected for that, I must say,
> and people come to do him honor.
> Besides,
> he's been helpful to many a man.

HOMUNCULUS:
> Why don't we risk it?
> I dare say it won't cost me
> my glass and flame.

NEREUS:
> What's that I hear?
> Human voices?
> What a rage it puts me in

deep down to my heart's core!
Ridiculous creatures!
Wanting to be gods, they're doomed
to being just what they are!
I could have laid back eons ago
and lived like a god, except that
I felt the need to benefit the best of them.
Ah, but then I saw what they had done,
and it was as if I'd never advised them.

THALES:

True, Old Man of the Sea,
but we trust you all the same.
You're the sage, after all,
so don't send us packing.
See this flame?
Human enough, I admit,
but ready to follow your every advice
unconditionally.

NEREUS:

Advice! Ha!
What advice ever counted with men!
Wise words, deaf ears!
Always the same!
They do things,
condemn them afterwards,
and remain as headstrong as ever,
this tribe we call men!

What more could I have done for Paris
than give him a fatherly warning?
But lust had its way,
and so he ensnared the Spartan Helen.
He stood there boldly on the Grecian shore
as I told him the vision I foresaw:
air full of smoke, torrents of red,
roof beams blazing, death and murder
down below—

Troy's day of doom,
cast in epic rhythms,
as terrible now as it was millennia ago.
To that arrogant youth
mine were an old man's impotent words,
and off he went,
following his bliss,
and Troy fell—
a monster corpse,
stark after long torment,
a welcome feast for Pindus's eagles.

And Odysseus?
The same story.
I foretold him the wiles of Circe,
the horrors of the Cyclops,
his own hesitancy and his crew's frivolity,
and I don't know what all else!
What good did it do him?
Nothing.
Not till much tossed by the seas—
and late enough, too, may I say—
the waves decided to toss him
on a friendly shore.

THALES:
To the wise man such behavior is a torment;
and yet, if he's good,
he'll give it another try.
An ounce of thanks
will outweigh a ton of ingratitude.
But what we ask of you is no small matter.
This boy you see here wishes to come to be.

NEREUS:
Don't spoil my rarest of good humors.
I had other things in store today.
I've invited the Graces of the sea,
my daughters, the Dorids.

Neither Olympus, nor your dry earth
bears creatures of such dainty loveliness.
With utter grace
they leap from their sea dragons
to Neptune's horses,
and are so delicately one with the water's element
that even the foam seems to raise them up.

Venus's rainbow-colored seashell chariot
will bring Galatea to us,
loveliest of all,
she who, since Venus deserted us long ago,
inherits the temple city and the chariot throne,
and is honored now in Paphos as a goddess.

Off with you now!
A father's joy must not be spoiled
by hate in his heart nor sour words on his lips!
Away to Proteus!
Ask him, that man of miracles,
how one comes to be and
passes from form to form.

(He moves off toward the sea.)

THALES:
Our visit, I'm afraid,
hasn't borne much fruit.
Even if we do find Proteus,
he'll have dissolved and flowed away;
and even if he stays, his words
would only astonish and confuse.
Still, you need such advice,
so let's be off.

(Exeunt.)

SIRENS: *(On the rocks above.)*
What is this that we see riding

Toward us on the wide waves gliding?
As if by the wind's contriving
We behold white sails arriving!
Brightly they dance before our eyes,
These maidens of sea's paradise!
Let's climb down! Hear their voices!
Already my fond heart rejoices.

NEREIDS and TRITONS:

What we bring you here tonight
Will give pleasure and delight.
In Chelone's giant shell
Are austere gods, so praise them well.
Gods of radiant light we bring,
So let us all in glory sing!

SIRENS:

Small to the sight,
Potent in might,
They save sailors at sea
From ancient antiquity.

NEREIDS and TRITONS:

We bring you the Cabiri
To keep the revels cheery,
Where they hold sacred sway
Neptune smoothes the way.

SIRENS:

We yield to you, the stronger,
For when the sea's great anger
A mighty ship has wrecked,
You're there the crew to protect.

NEREIDS and TRITONS:

Here we've brought three,
The fourth wouldn't come.
He said he's the best,
And thinks for the rest.

SIRENS:

> One god, it seems, may mock another,
> Whether sister, son or brother.
> Better yet to honor all,
> Revere each one and never fall.

NEREIDS and TRITONS:

> Seven of them by rights there be.

SIRENS:

> Where, then, are the other three?

NEREIDS and TRITONS:

> To answer is no easy task.
> And yet you might Olympus ask.
> There the eighth you might well find,
> Who never yet has come to mind.
> Their grace we have and hope to get,
> But they are not complete as yet.
> These Incomparables aspire
> Ever upward, ever higher,
> Hungering for the unexplainable,
> For the ever unattainable.

SIRENS:

> We bow to every throne,
> Whatever its zone,
> Be it sun or in moon.
> It pays well and soon.

NEREIDS and TRITONS:

> How resplendent our fame must be
> To lead in triumph this jubilee!

SIRENS:

> The heroes of the ancient time
> Reached no glory so sublime,
> And however far their fame has run,
> They the Golden Fleece have won,
> But you have won the great Cabiri!

(Repeated in full chorus.)

> They the Golden Fleece have won,
> But we / you have won the great Cabiri!

(NEREIDS and TRITONS pass by.)

HOMUNCULUS:
> I see these misshapen creatures
> and they look like earthen pots.
> And yet wise men will break their heads
> trying to decipher them.

THALES:
> Yes, and it's what everyone wants.
> Its rust determines the coin's worth.

PROTEUS: *(Unnoticed.)*
> This tickles this old fabulator's heart!
> The odder it is, the greater its pedigree.

THALES:
> Proteus! Where are you?

PROTEUS: *(Ventriloquizing, now near, now far.)*
> Here! And here!

THALES:
> All right, I forgive you your tired old trick.
> Just don't waste words with a friend.
> I know you're speaking from where you're not.

PROTEUS: *(As if from a distance.)*
> Farewell!

THALES: *(Softly to HOMUNCULUS.)*
> He's quite near.
> Shine brightly now.
> He's curious as a fish;

and no matter what shape he's assumed,
he's lured by fiery flames.

HOMUNCULUS:
  I'll give you all I can,
  but in moderation so I don't break my glass.

PROTEUS: (*In the shape of a giant turtle.*)
  What is this that shines so pleasantly?

THALES: (*Concealing HOMUNCULUS.*)
  Good!
  Come closer for a better look, if you like.
  Let us see you on human legs.
  You can manage it, I'm sure.
  Whoever wants to see what we hide from view
  will do so with our will and favor.

PROTEUS: (*In a noble human form.*)
  Still up to your worldly arts, I see!

THALES:
  And you? Still the man of worldly parts!

  (*He has revealed HOMUNCULUS.*)

PROTEUS: (*Astonished.*)
  A luminous dwarf!
  Never before laid eyes on!

THALES:
  He wants advice on how to be born.
  By some very strange means, he tells me,
  he managed only to be half-born.
  For all of his considerable mental attributes,
  he's sorely lacking in corporeality.
  So far only this glass retort gives him weight;
  but now he longs to begin proper embodiment.

PROTEUS:

> A genuine virgin birth if there ever was one.
> Here you are before you're supposed to be.

THALES: *(Softly.)*

> Yes, well,
> there's another somewhat critical matter:
> he appears to be a hermaphrodite.

PROTEUS:

> All the better!
> Once incorporated,
> he'll adapt to the situation.

> *(To HOMUNCULUS.)*

> But of one thing there's not much doubt.
> It is in the vast ocean you must make your start!
> You will start there first on a small scale,
> happily consuming creatures smaller than you.
> Then gradually you will grow and,
> in growing,
> rise to higher forms and
> greater accomplishments.

HOMUNCULUS:

> How gentle the air is here!
> The soft, moist smell of growth.
> How good it feels.

PROTEUS:

> I believe you, darling boy!
> And farther along on this narrow sandy spit
> it will be even more pleasant,
> and the atmosphere still more ineffable.
> Out there we'll have a splendid view
> of the sea pageant as it floats into sight.
> Come with me.

THALES:

    I'll come, too.

HOMUNCULUS:

    What a remarkable trinity!
    God and man and spirit all in step!

    *(TELCHINES OF RHODES appear on hippocamps and sea dragons,
    brandishing NEPTUNE's trident.)*

CHORUS OF TELCHINES:

    We forged this trident for Neptune,
    and with it he rules the wildest of waves.
    When the Thunderer unleashes his pregnant clouds,
    Neptune answers the horrible rumble
    by rousing the sea to a violent response.
    As bolts of lightning plunge jaggedly downward,
    Neptune's waves dash upward to meet them,
    wave upon wave,
    mountain high.
    And whoever in ships is caught in between
    is tossed and blown till the sea overwhelms them,
    dragging them down to the sea's watery deeps.
    And so, he's lent us his scepter for the day,
    allowing us peace and joy in our play.

SIRENS:

            Welcome, devotees of Helios,
            Blessèd ones who honor light,
            Join us as we honor Luna,
            Glorious goddess of the night!

TELCHINES:

    Dearest of goddesses aloft in your orbit,
    with what delight you hear your brother praised,
    lending an ear to blessèd Rhodes,
    where a neverending hymn to him is raised.
    At the start and at the close of his daily round,
    he looks down upon us with his fiery gaze.

Our mountains, our cities,
our shores and sea
are pleasing to him, the god,
and are lovely and bright.
We have no fogs or mist, no sunless haze,
and should one steal upon us,
a beam of sun and a breeze
clears us of these,
and the island is once again bright.
From on high he sees himself,
your brother god,
in a hundred statues,
as a youth, a giant, now great, now gentle.
We were the first, you know, in all the world,
to cast the gods in the noble form of man.

PROTEUS: *(To HOMUNCULUS,)*
Let them sing, let them boast.
To the sacred life-giving rays of the sun
such lifeless things are nothing.
They go on sculpting, casting, endlessly,
and once they have it in bronze
they think they've really got something.
And what comes of all this pride in the end?
These godly statues stand there so grand—
and an earthquake destroys them.
They've been melted down long since.

What is this earthly life,
even at its best,
but a weariness of the flesh!
The sea is the proper element for life.
I'll be Proteus-Dolphin now,
and carry you into the eternal waters.

(He transforms himself.)

There, that's done.
Up on my back, now.

There's the proper place for you,
out there.
I'll marry you to the ocean.

THALES:
Yield to the splendid desire!
Begin your evolution at the beginning!
Be ready for action,
and never lose to doubt.
Progress by eternal norms through
many thousands of forms
till finally you are man.
But be prepared—
that will take time.

(HOMUNCULUS mounts the PROTEUS-DOLPHIN.)

PROTEUS:
Come, bright spirit,
let us plunge into the vast moisture
of creation, where no dimension or direction
will be denied you,
and you will range at will!
Take care, though,
and don't strive for higher orders.
Once you've attained the estate of man,
you've reached the end,
the rest is waste.

THALES:
Well, that depends.
It's not all that bad
being a worthy man
in your own time.

PROTEUS: (To THALES.)
Yes, well, if it's one of your sort.
They tend to last for awhile.
You, for example,

I've seen for hundreds of years now
bustling about among all those pallid ghosts.

SIRENS: *(On the rocks.)*

What clouds are those I see streaming
Round about the moon so bright?
They are doves, love-kindled, gleaming,
Their wings as white as purest light.
Paphos sent them to us, glowing
Harbingers of love and joy;
Our feast is perfect now, overflowing
Full with bliss without alloy!

NEREUS: *(Joining THALES.)*

Some night wanderer
might call that ring round the moon
a fanciful nocturnal illusion,
but we spirits see it quite differently,
and, indeed, in the only correct way.
They are doves
escorting my daughter's seashell ride.
A rare and wondrous flight it is, too,
taught them in days of old.

THALES:

What can be better
than a good man's simple faith,
nurtured in a gentle heart?
What else has a better reason to be right?

PSYLLI *and* MARSI: *(Mounted on sea bulls, sea calves, and sea rams.)*

In Cyprus's rude caverns,
not swamped by Neptune's waves,
unshattered by Seismos,
with eternal breezes blowing round,
we,
we guard the chariot of Venus,
guard it as in ancient times,
with peace and quiet contentment.

And here, in the folds of whispering night,
and through the delicate weave of the waters,
unseen by men of today,
we bring you the loveliest of Neptune's daughters.
We are quietly busy,
fearing no Eagle or Winged Lion,
no Cross, no Crescent,
while up above us they sit enthroned,
forever changing,
forever rampaging,
ever exiling,
ever reviling,
slaughtering, razing crops and cities.
But we,
we, as ever before,
bring our loveliest mistress once more.

SIRENS:

> Through the waters gently cleaving,
> Round about the car divine,
> Now like serpents interweaving,
> Row on row, and line on line,
> Come, you sturdy Nereids, gliding,
> Ocean's daughters, pleasing wild,
> And you graceful Dorids guiding
> Galatea, her mother's child.
> Grave she is, a godly face,
> As of an immortal race,
> And yet, like every human woman,
> Lovely with alluring grace.

DORIDS: *(Riding past NEREUS on dolphins, in chorus.)*

> Luna, lend us light and shade,
> Illuminate youth's flower here,
> Lovely lads with whom we've played,
> Now our bridegrooms, loving, dear.

(To NEREUS.)

> These are boys we saved from death
> In the tempest's wrack and ruin,
> We warmed them back to life and breath,
> Knowing each would be a true one.
> Now with kisses to delight us,
> They long to love us and to wed,
> And for the life we gave requite us.
> Father, on them your favor shed.

NEREUS:

> I praise the economy that wins a double treasure:
> To practice charity and yet have pleasure!

DORIDS:

> Since you praise our fond endeavor,
> Father, grant us our request:
> Let us hold them fast forever
> To our young immortal breast.

NEREUS:

> Enjoy your pretty catch while you can;
> make of each lad a splendid man.
> But never ask for immortality
> that only Zeus can give.
> The waves that rock you
> allow not even love a steady stance.
> So when your fancy's worn itself thin,
> and passion's on the wane,
> then shuttle them off once more to shore.

DORIDS:

> Sweet dear lads, fond lovely boys,
> We love you, we avow it.
> We wanted everlasting joys,
> But the gods will not allow it.

THE YOUTHS:

> Give us all you have to give,
> Kiss and caress this love-starved lad,
> We've never had such a life to live,
> It's the best time we've ever had!

(GALATEA approaches in her seashell chariot.)

NEREUS:

> Oh, my dear, it's you!

GALATEA:

> Oh, father! What joy to see you!
> Linger awhile, you dolphins!
> The sight of him enthralls me!

NEREUS:

> Past, gone past already,
> in the circling motion of dolphins!
> But what do they know of the heart's longing?
> If only I could sail with them!
> But a single look delights me the yearlong.

THALES:

> Hail! Hail!
> And hail again!
> How full my heart is with joy!
> How Beauty and Truth possess me!
> Water gave birth to all of life!
> All of life was cradled in water!
>
> Ocean,
> I pray you prevail forever!
> For if you had not send clouds,
> if you had not lavished on us brooks,
> if you had not sent streams twisting this way and that,
> and great rivers,
> winding, winding,
> if you did not—

if you did not—
where would mountains, the plains, the world,
where would they be?
You are the source of all freshness in life.

ALL: *(Echo of all groups in chorus.)*
You are the source of all freshness in life.

NEREUS:
They turn back in swaying motion,
but they do not come back to me.
In ever-expanding, circling chains
the countless numbers twist and turn
to show themselves in gay display.
But I see my Galatea's chariot
now and again like a star through the crowd.
What is loved shines bright and clear
amid the throng, however far,
yet ever near and true.

HOMUNCULUS:
In these waters bright,
Wherever I flash my light,
There is beauty fair.

PROTEUS:
Amid these waters bright,
Wherever you flash your light,
There is music rare.

NEREUS:
What new mystery in the multitude's midst
is about to reveal itself?
What are those flames surrounding the seashell?
The flames around Galatea's feet?
How mightily it flares,
then gently, sweetly,
pulsing as if with love and desire.

THALES:

It is Homunculus led on by Proteus!
These are the symptoms of imperious longing.
I hear his anguish,
the groan of his suffering.
He'll shatter himself against her radiant throne.
Look there! A flame! A flash!
And he's spilt in the sea!

SIRENS:

What radiant miracle transfigures our waters!
Wave breaks on wave in sparkles of light!
Everything lightening, flickering, brightening!
Each body aglow as it moves through the night!
All things radiant as fire flows round!
Let Eros reign here, who started it all!

Hail to the waves, to the sea unbounded
By the sacred fire surrounded!
Water, hail! Hail, fire, the splendid!
Hail, o Mystery here ended!

ALL AS ONE:

Hail bright airs that softly flow,
Hail mysterious vaults below!
Honored now forevermore
Be the Elemental Four!

ACT III

XLII ⤳ INNER COURTYARD OF FAUST'S CASTLE

Surrounded by fantastic medieval buildings.
HELEN. PANTHALIS as Chorus Leader.
CHORUS OF CAPTIVE TROJAN WOMEN.

PANTHALIS:
> Women!
> Ah! Headstrong, foolish females!
> Forever snatching at conclusions,
> playthings of every breeze!
> Good luck, bad luck,
> what's it to you?
> You don't know how to handle either!
> Always at each others' throats,
> it's only in joy or pain you
> laugh or wail as one!
>
> Quiet there now!
> Let's hear what our noble mistress
> decides for herself and us.

HELEN:
> Where are you, Pythoness?
> Whatever your name, come forth
> from within this somber castle's vaults.
> If you're off to find the wondrous hero prince and
> prepare a welcome for me, I thank you,
> and ask you to lead me to him with all dispatch.
> I'm weary of wandering.
> All I want now is rest.

PANTHALIS:
> There's no one to be seen anywhere, Queen Helen.
> The sorry creature's disappeared;
> stayed behind in the mist

that brought us here so suddenly, somehow,
without ever taking a step.
Or, confused perhaps, she wanders this maze
of many castles made into one,
looking for its master
to prepare you a princely welcome.

But there!
Look, up there!
I see a stir, a commotion,
crowds thronging galleries,
at windows, at every entrance!
Servants, many, scurrying every which way!
What else but a fitting reception
to honor Your Highness?

CHORUS:
Ah! How my heart leaps at the sight!
Look! Look at them!
How decorously they walk,
with such calm, unhurried step,
those dear, those lovely fair-skinned boys!
Down the stairs, so properly they come,
and in such order!
But how can it be?
Who can have ordered,
who can have trained
so wondrous a company of beautiful lads?
And in so little time!

What shall I admire most?
The grace of their walk,
the delicate curls adorning their radiant brows,
or their cheeks, ruddy as peaches,
and just as downy?
I'd bite them if I dared,
but of course I don't;
dreadful to tell, but once,
in a similar case, the mouth was
filled with ashes.

But here they come,
the little beauties,
and what are they carrying?
Steps to the throne,
carpet and seat,
curtain and canopy
richly embroidered,
wave upon wave,
like cloudy wreaths,
it flows on high
over the queenly head,
for already invited,
she has mounted the throne's
cushioned seat.

Come! Move forward!
Range yourselves
in rows on each step.
Worthy, worthy, oh three-times worthy
the dignity of so blest a reception!

*(Everything described by the CHORUS occurs in sequence. After the long
procession of PAGES and SQUIRES has descended, FAUST, dressed as
a medieval courtier, appears at the head of the stairs and comes down
with slow dignity.)*

PANTHALIS: *(Observing him attentively.)*
Unless the gods, as so often they do,
have lent this man for a short time only
his admirable figure,
his stately bearing,
and loving presence,
then he will succeed in all he undertakes,
whether battles of men or that lesser skirmish
with the loveliest women.
I have seen other men most highly esteemed,
but there can be no question that he takes preference.
I see the Prince approach her now,
solemnly, with slow reverent step.
Turn now, great Queen, and face him!

FAUST: *(Approaching, a man in chains at his side.)*
    In place of the solemn greeting that is your due,
    in place of reverential welcome,
    I bring you this man,
    fast-bound in chains,
    this servant who, failing at his duty,
    made me fail at mine.

    Kneel, Lynceus,
    before this most exalted of women
    and confess to your guilt!

    This, great Queen,
    is a man of rare and keen sight.
    I appointed him myself
    to observe from the lookout tower
    the full expanse of earth and sky,
    and to report any movement
    within the circle of our hills and valley,
    any approach on the fortress,
    whether of herds, which we protect,
    or armies, which we do not.

    But today, what a calamity!
    You arrive, and he fails to report!
    Making us derelict in our duty
    properly to honor a guest of such noble worth.
    His life is herewith forfeit,
    and he would already have paid with his own death,
    except that it is for you, and you alone,
    to punish or pardon, as you see fit.

HELEN:
    You honor me with the dignity of both
    judge and ruler—and even if it is only
    to test me, as I must assume,
    I will exercise the judge's high duty
    of hearing the accused.
    You may speak.

LYNCEUS THE WATCHMAN:
>O let me kneel,
>let me look at her,
>let me die,
>let me live—
>I give myself totally to this
>god-sent woman!
>As I looked eastward,
>awaiting the first rapture of morning,
>suddenly, miraculously,
>the sun arose in the south!
>I saw nothing else,
>neither heights nor depths,
>neither earth nor sky.
>My eyes,
>sharp as those of a lynx,
>were put to a test now,
>as if to fight free
>from a deep, dark dream.
>I could see nothing!
>Battlement, tower, gate!
>Nothing!
>But then,
>oh, then as the swirling mists vanished,
>she steps forth,
>this goddess we see here!
>
>My gaze, my heart turned toward her,
>and I drank in that gentle radiance.
>As her beauty now blinds us all,
>that same beauty,
>blinding me,
>made me forget my watchman's duty,
>forget to sound my watchman's horn.
>Threaten me with annihilation—
>but beauty silences all wrath.

HELEN:
>How can I punish an evil that I have caused?

Oh, what a relentless fate pursues me!
Why am I condemned to confound men's hearts
so that they spare nothing,
neither themselves nor anything of worth?
Abducting, seducing, fighting,
they dragged me this way and that,
demigods, heroes, gods, even demons,
led me astray, wandering, every which way.
Even as one I perplexed the world,
and twice again when I was double,
And now that I am three- and fourfold,
all I bring is calamity after calamity.

Set this good man free.
Folly caused by a god is no disgrace.

FAUST:

Your beauty, great Queen,
is a sure-shooting archer,
and there lies the victim, wounded.
But now those arrows,
arrow following arrow,
strike me, too, and I sense
their feathered flight from every side,
crisscrossing through castle and court.

What am I now?
In an instant
you turn my staunchest defenders to rebels,
making my very walls unsafe.
How can I not fear that my army will follow
the unvanquished vanquisher?
What choice have I
but to surrender to you myself
and all that in my delusion I once thought mine?
Freely and faithfully,
I confess myself here at your feet
your subject forever,
you who had only to appear
to assume my throne and my kingdom.

LYNCEUS: *(With a chest, followed by men carrying others.)*
You see me returned again, my Queen!
A rich man begging another glance.
To see you is to be prince and beggar at once.
What was I then?
What am I now?
What's there to want?
What's there to do?
What good is the keenest eye
if your radiant throne defeats it?

Out of the East we came,
and so it was all up with the West.
A multitude of nations so vast
the first knew nothing of the last.
When one man fell,
another stood tall,
and a third stood ready with lance in hand,
for each man there were a hundred more.
A thousand might fall,
and no one took notice.

We pushed onward,
onward we stormed,
conquering every place we came to.
Where today I issued lordly commands,
tomorrow another took my place,
plundering, robbing, looking in haste,
eyes peeled, no time to waste,
carrying off women, lovely creatures,
the fittest cattle and every last steed.

I spied out the rarest things.
What others held priceless was worthless to me.
It was treasure I hunted,
and my keen sight led me to it every time.
I saw into pockets,
and my eyes were the key to every chest.
Gold was mine in heaps and mounds,

and precious jewels.
But the emerald alone, great Queen,
is fit to grace and shed its green
on your fair breast.
An oval pearl from the ocean's depths
should dangle on your crimson cheek
where rubies would grow pale to compete.

And so,
accept these treasures I lay at your throne,
riches without comparison,
spoils of many a bloody battle.
All these I lay at your feet,
but there are more,
chests of iron,
and they will be yours.
Let me serve you, fair Queen, as your slave,
and I will fill your every vault with treasure,
for no sooner you mounted the throne
than all things bowed to you in obeisance—
Reason, Wealth, Power—
bent low to worship your perfect beauty.

All this I clung to,
it was mine,
but freed now it is yours.
I prized it once as the greatest worth,
but now see it was nothing.
All I owned has vanished
and is no more to me than withered grass.
But one glad glance from you
gives back its value!

FAUST:
Remove at once this burden you so boldly won.
You may have escaped censure,
but you'll have no reward.
Why offer this vision anything,
when everything we have is hers already?

Go, now.
Pile up treasure on treasure!
Create a display so exalted
it has never been seen!
Let our vaulted halls glisten
like skies new-fashioned!
Make paradises out of lifeless life!
Roll out soft flowered carpets for her to tread on.
Let her see splendor
that would dazzle all but the gods!

LYNCEUS:

Your orders, sir, are child's play to me.
Little sooner said than done.
This supreme beauty makes all things her servants.
Our army's already tamed,
every sword blunt and lamed,
and the sun itself is cold and dull
compared with her radiant beauty.
So grand a vision turns all things empty and base.

HELEN: *(To FAUST.)*

I wish to speak to you,
but come and sit beside me.
This empty seat calls for its master
who safeguards mine.

FAUST:

First let me kneel, noble lady,
and pledge you my heart!
Then kiss the hand that raises me to your side!
Confirm me now as coregent of your realm
that knows no bounds,
and allow me to be to you,
all in one,
admirer, servant, and guardian.

HELEN:

I've seen and heard so many wonders,

I'm astonished,
and should like to ask many questions.
Tell me why that good man's speech
sounds so strange,
strange but also pleasing.
One sound seems to fit so well with the next,
and no sooner is one word settled in the ear
than along comes another to caress it.

FAUST:

It's the way we speak.
But how much more our music will delight you.
It will move you to the very depths of your soul.
There's nothing better than practice to teach you how.
Shall we begin?

HELEN:

Tell me, then,
how I can speak so charmingly.

FAUST:

That's easily done.
You must simply speak from the heart.
And when the soul is touched with passion's flame,
we look around and ask—

HELEN:

—who burns the same?

FAUST:

Neither past nor future has power to bless;
the present moment—

HELEN:

—is our happiness.

FAUST:

It's treasure, wondrous gain, supreme command.
What gives it confirmation?

HELEN:
>   This—my hand.

CHORUS:
>   Who would reproach our mistress
>   for showing this castle's lord her loving favor?
>   We're captives, every one of us,
>   not once but many times
>   since the shameful fall of Troy
>   and the dreaded labyrinthine trials
>   of our endless journey.
>
>   Women, accustomed to lovers,
>   may be experts,
>   but they can't be choosers.
>   They take whatever opportunity offers,
>   giving their voluptuous limbs alike
>   to golden-haired shepherd boys and
>   bristly, black fauns.
>
>   Look, they're already drawing closer,
>   leaning together, shoulder to shoulder,
>   knee to knee, hand in hand as they
>   rock to and fro on the grandly cushioned throne,
>   unashamed of displaying their Majesty's secret affections
>   to the sight of their people.

HELEN:
>   I feel so far away, and yet so near;
>   What joy it is to say: I'm here, I'm here!

FAUST:
>   My breath is short, my words no longer free;
>   It's all a dream; time, place have ceased to be.

HELEN:
>   I seem to be long past, and yet so new;
>   Bound fast with you and to a stranger true.

FAUST:

> Never spoil our fate with brooding grief.
> Our duty is being, however long or brief.

(FAUST kisses HELEN.)

FAUST:

> With this we have both succeeded.
> Now let past be past.
> Know yourself, my love,
> sprung from the highest god,
> for you are meant only for the pristine world.
> It's not for me and these castle walls to confine you.
> I know a place not far where youth and peace
> are forever ours—
> Arcadia.
> Enticed to live upon this blessèd soil
> you flee now to embrace the happiest fate.
> Let our thrones be changed into leafy arbors,
> and our bliss be one of Arcadian freedom!

(The scene transforms completely.)

XLIII ~ ARCADIA

> *A series of rocky caverns with closed arbors in front of them.*
> *A shady grove extends as far as the high surrounding cliffs.*
> *FAUST and HELEN are not seen.*
> *The CHORUS lies scattered about the stage asleep.*

PHORKYAS:

> How long the girls have been asleep,
> I don't know.
> Nor do I know if in their dreams they saw,
> bright and clear, what I have seen
> with these very eyes.
> And so I'll wake them.

The young ones I'll surprise, and you
graybeards down there, too, sitting around
awaiting the solution to these
not impossible miracles.

All of you, up!
Up! Up! All of you!
Shake your locks!
Rub the sleep from your eyes!
Stop your blinking and listen to me now!

CHORUS:
Tell us, then, tell us!
Tell us of the marvels that have happened!
We'd most like to hear of things that are
quite unbelievable, for we're bored to death
of looking at these rocks.

PHORKYAS:
Bored to death, are you?
And your eyes scarcely wiped of sleep?
All right, then, listen.

Here in these caverns,
these grottoes,
behind these arbors,
our lord and lady have found protection and
security as in some lovers' idyll.

CHORUS:
What? In there?

PHORKYAS:
Isolated there,
apart from the world,
they called upon me, me only,
to serve them in silence.
Highly honored,
I took up my post quite near them;

and yet, knowing my place,
I kept my eyes averted,
looking here and there,
for this and that,
searching out roots, mosses and bark—
acquainted as I am with their virtues—
and so the loving pair were left to themselves.

CHORUS:
To hear you tell it,
there are whole worlds in there!
Woods, meadows, brooks, lakes!
Just listen to you!

PHORKYAS:
Yes!
And there are, you poor innocents!
Unexplored depths no man has ever fathomed!
Room upon room,
court upon endless court,
and I searched out every one with care.

All at once, then, a burst of laughter
echoes through the cavernous spaces.
And when I look, I see a boy
leaping from the lady's lap to the man's,
from father to mother.
And the cooing and caressing,
the shouts and shrieks of love's silly banter,
jesting and pleasure,
this side and that!
I was as good as deaf!

He's naked is what he is!
A wingless spirit!
Faunlike without animality!
Leaping on the ground,
the ground sends him skyward,
and on the second or third bound
he touches the vaulted roof!

His mother calls anxiously to him:
"Spring, spring to your heart's content,
but beware of flying!
It's not for you to fly!"
And his living father warned him as well:
"In the earth lies the force that will thrust you upward.
Touch it with only your toe,
you'll have the strength of that son of earth,
Antaeus."

And so he leaps, like a batted ball,
from one massive rock face to another,
bouncing freely every which way.
Then all at once he vanishes down a savage ravine
and seems lost to us forever.

Mother weeps; father comforts;
and I shrug my shoulders,
concerned and anxious.
Then suddenly he's there again!

Ah, what a sight!

Has he found treasures buried down there?
He's dressed now in flowered robes,
tassels dangling from his arms, ribbons
fluttering at his breast,
and like a miniature Apollo,
with golden lyre in hand,
cheerfully approaches the edge
of the precipice above us.

Wonderful!

His parents embrace in delight.
What glory is it shines about his head?
A halo?
It's hard to say.
A golden ornament?

Or the radiant glow
of an undaunted spirit's transcendence?

And so he moves, and every gesture,
as he stands there in his boyhood,
proclaims him the future master of Beauty,
through whose body eternal melodies will flow.

That is how you will hear him,
that is how you will see him,
with a wonder never before known.

CHORUS:
    Daughter of Crete,
    is this what you call a marvel?
    Have you never heeded
    the instructive words of poets?
    Never known Ionia's ancient tales,
    or Hellas's ancestral legends
    of gods and heroes?

    Today is a dreary echo of glories past.
    Your story pales to the lovely lies
    our forebears sang of Hermes,
    Maia's son,
    tales more persuasive than truth.

    No sooner born,
    he's bound in downy bands,
    and then again in sumptuous purple wrappings,
    by chattering nurses who know
    little what to expect.

    Slyly, then, the crafty little rogue works
    free his tender, limber limbs,
    leaving behind the wrappings,
    the purple shell that confined him,
    a butterfly slipping from the cell of its chrysalis,
    spreading its wings,
    flying freely in the radiant sunlight.

Nimblest of the nimble, Hermes then
proves himself the master of artful devices,
the patron god of thieves and rascals
and all self-seekers.

In a flash he's stolen the sea god's trident,
the sword from Ares's scabbard,
Apollo's bow and arrows,
Hephaestus's tongs, and would have stolen
Father Zeus's lightning
were he not in fear of the fire.
He wrestled and tripped up baby Eros,
and while she fondled him
filched the belt from Venus' waist.

*(Music of ravishing pure melody played on strings is heard from
the cavern. All listen, and soon are deeply moved. The music continues
with full orchestra until indicated.)*

PHORKYAS:
Listen!
Hear these ravishing sounds!
Free yourselves of the ancient fables,
cast off your gods,
they have no meaning now.
Now we make greater demands.
What moves the heart must
come from the heart.

(She withdraws toward the rocks.)

CHORUS:
If even you, dread being,
are moved by these pleasing sounds,
we who are newly restored to life
are moved to tears.
Let the sun lose its splendor
as long as there is light in the soul,
as long as in the heart's core
we find what all the world denies us.

(Enter HELEN, FAUST, and EUPHORION in the above-described costume.)

EUPHORION:

When children sing, your hearts sing with them;
when children dance, your hearts dance, too.

HELEN:

Love unites two, and there is delight;
but let it be three, and heaven is come.

FAUST:

When we have that, then we have all;
we stand as one: may it be so forever.

CHORUS:

How many happy years they have,
delighting in this boy's sweet glow.

EUPHORION:

Let me skip,
Let me leap!
Let me soar,
Let me circle!
Up into air,
Ever upward!
Passion drives me,
It's all my longing!

FAUST:

Gently, go gently!
Temper your daring!
To lose our dear son
Would cost us all joy!

EUPHORION:

I won't stay here,
Not here below!
Let go my hands,

Let go my hair,
Let go my clothes!
They're mine, mine!

HELEN:

Think, oh, think
Whose darling you are!
How it would hurt us
To lose what we've won!
Mine, yours, and his!
O what a pity!

CHORUS:

I fear this union
Will not be for long.

HELEN *and* FAUST:

Bridle this longing!
Think of your parents!
Think how they love you!
Bridle this mad,
Impetuous longing!
Stay with us here
In this quiet country!

EUPHORION:

I hold myself back
Only to please you.

(He weaves through the CHORUS, drawing them into a dance.)

Light as a feather
I float round these
Lovely girls.
Is this the melody?
Is this the right step?

HELEN:

Yes, and well done.

Lead these young lovelies
In a formal round.

FAUST:

I wish it were over.
These antics disturb me.

*(The CHORUS sings as it performs intricate dance patterns with
EUPHORION.)*

CHORUS:

When you raise your arms so fair,
Lifting them so charmingly,
When you shake your shining hair,
And shift your curls alarmingly,
When you with your foot so light
Brush the earth in hasty flight,
And your limbs with ours entwine,
First with hers and then with mine,
Then, sweet boy, you've reached your goal,
For you have won our very soul.

(Pause.)

EUPHORION:

Fleet-footed deer,
How many are here!
Come out and play
With me today!
I'll be the hunter
And you'll be my prey.

CHORUS:

Don't run too fast,
We're yours already.
First and last
We're willing and ready.
You sweet, you handsome,
You loveliest of boys!

EUPHORION:

> Off you go through
> Brake and bramble.
> Over hill and
> Dale go ramble.
> What's easily won
> Is quickly undone.

HELEN *and* FAUST:

> What is this madness! What is this daring!
> Where has moderation gone?
> Horns in wood and glen are blaring!
> What is this mischief! He calls this fun?

CHORUS: *(Running in quickly, one by one.)*

> Swift as an arrow he sped past us!
> Ignoring us, despising us!
> And then he seized the wildest of us!
> Here he comes dragging her in!

EUPHORION: *(Enters carrying a young girl.)*

> See what I've won!
> This sturdy quarry to fan my desire.
> For all her struggle,
> I'll hug her and kiss her
> to show her who's master here.

GIRL:

> Let go of me!
> Who do you think you are?
> I have mind and spirit
> to match yours any day!
> You think you've trapped me, do you?
> Just you wait! You'll see!
> Unhand me now, or just for fun
> get your fingers burnt!

> *(She bursts into flame and soars upward.)*

Follow me into airy regions!
Follow me down into dismal abysses!
Catch me, go on,
let's see you do it!

EUPHORION: *(Shaking off the last of the flames.)*
How cramped this press of rocks and tangled brush!
This is no place for youth and vigor!
I hear the rush of soaring winds and
the roaring crash of waves—
so far away—
if only I were there!

(He leaps higher and higher up the rocks.)

HELEN, FAUST, CHORUS:
Why must you outdo the mountain goat?
How dreadful if you fall.

EUPHORION:
I *must* mount higher,
I *must* see farther!
I know now where I am.
In the middle of an island,
Pelops' isle,
water one side, land the other.

CHORUS:
Come linger here in peace
in mountain and forest.
We'll seek out grapes,
whole hillsides of grapes,
fig trees and arbors with golden apples.
Stay gently here, gently,
in this gentle land.

EUPHORION:
Is it peace you're dreaming of?
Then dream away! War's the watchword!
War that leads on to victory!

CHORUS:

    If in peace you long for war,
    you've left behind all hope of happiness.

EUPHORION:

    You, oh you whom this land brought forth,
    leading you from danger to danger,
    men, free, boundless in courage,
    careless of the lives it cost you—
    lead, lead on with unquenchable spirit,
    an inspiration to all fighters.

CHORUS:

    Look! Look up there!
    How high he's climbed!
    And seems no smaller to us!
    Armor-clad and keen for conquest,
    in bronze and steel
    he gleams like the sun!

EUPHORION:

    No ramparts now,
    no walls to guard you,
    every man must know himself!
    A mighty fortress is man's stout heart!
    Is freedom your goal?
    Then charge light-armed onto the field!
    Let women be amazons,
    and every child a hero!

CHORUS:

    Sacred poetry, rise, oh, rise
    to the highest heaven,
    shine from on high though ever receding,
    the fairest of stars that reaches us always,
    no matter how far,
    eternal delight!

EUPHORION:

    Born a child, a child no longer,

behold me now,
a youth in arms.
Leagued with the strong, the bold, the free,
in spirit I have proved my worth.
Come! Let's be off!
The road stretches out to glory.

HELEN *and* FAUST:

Scarcely born to life,
scarcely known to light,
you strive to dizzy heights,
seeking scenes of strife and pain.
Are we nothing, nothing to you, then?
Was it a dream, our lovely union?

EUPHORION:

Do you hear the cannons thundering at sea?
Their echoes thundering from glen to glen?
Embattled armies clashing in dust and foam,
thrust upon thrust,
the pain, the torment?
What is there but to die?
The law is clear.

HELEN, FAUST, CHORUS:

Ah, the horror! Ah, the terror!
Why should death be a law for you?

EUPHORION:

Shall I look on from a distance?
No, I must share this pain.

HELEN, FAUST, CHORUS:

Rashness and danger!
A deadly fate!

EUPHORION:

And yet!
Oh, see, oh, behold my great wings unfold!

There! There!
Oh, let me fly!
I *must!* I *must!*

(*He hurls himself into the air, his clothes bear him up for a moment,
his head shines with a radiance, and a trail of light follows him.*)

CHORUS:
Icarus! Icarus!
O sorrowful sight!

(*A beautiful youth falls dead at his parents' feet; we appear to
recognize the face as that of a familiar figure; but the body vanishes
immediately, the radiance rises skyward like a comet, while his robe,
cloak, and lyre remain on the ground.*)

HELEN *and* FAUST:
How swiftly joy is
turned to pain.

EUPHORION'S VOICE:
Mother, don't leave me
alone in darkness!

(*Pause.*)

CHORUS: (*Threnody.*)
           Not alone! No matter where you
           Dwell we still will claim to know you;
           And even though from day you vanish,
           Our faithful hearts will not forego you.
           How ever can our hearts lament you,
           When we must envy you your fate?
           For your song in joy or sadness,
           Like your soul, was fair and great.

           Born to earthly fortune, rarely
           Gifted, blest with noble name,
           All too soon, alas! departed,

In your youthful bloom and fame!
With sharp eye you scanned the world,
To you the human heart was known,
Noble women's love regaled you,
Yours a music all your own!

And yet you ran in wild defiance
Straight into the fatal snare,
Daring law and staid convention,
Proving that you didn't care.
But at the last a higher yearning
Gave your mighty courage weight;
Glorious the goals you strove for,
Yet it was not to be your fate.

But whose fate *is* it? Dismal question,
At which Fate averts her eyes,
When on that day of greatest misery
A nation bleeds and dumbly cries.
So strike up new songs, bright and merry,
Renew your spirit, banish pain!
Earth has borne us songs forever,
And earth will bear us songs again!

(Complete pause. The music ceases.)

HELEN: *(To FAUST.)*
   An ancient proverb proves itself in me:
   that Beauty and Happiness can have no lasting union.
   The bond of life and the bond of love are snapped.
   Mourning both, my lord, I bid you a painful farewell,
   and give myself once more into your arms.
   Persephone, receive my boy and me!

*(She embraces FAUST. Her body vanishes; her dress and veil
remain in his arms.)*

PHORKYAS: *(To FAUST.)*
   Hold fast to what remains to you of Helen!

Never let loose of this dress!
Never!
Demons already are plucking away at its edges,
eager to drag it off to the underworld.
Hold fast to it, I say!
This may no longer be the goddess you've lost,
but it is divine.
Make the most of this favor beyond all price
and raise yourself up with it.
It will bear you swiftly above all things common
into vast spaces as long as you survive.

We'll meet again, we two,
far, very far from here.

(HELEN's clothes dissolve into clouds, surround FAUST, bear him aloft, and move off with him. PHORKYAS picks up EUPHORION's robe, cloak, and lyre and advances into the proscenium, holds them up, and speaks.)

PHORKYAS:
No mean find, these, no matter what.
The flame may have disappeared,
but it won't be the death of poetry,
you'll see. With these
I can always get things started, don't you know,
get the poetic juices flowing,
stir up a little jealousy among professionals.
And though I may not have talent to lend,
at least I have the costume to be lent.

(She sits down in the proscenium at the foot of a column.)

PANTHALIS:
Move along there, girls!
Quick, now!
We're rid at last of that witch's befuddling
Thessalian magic! No more jingle-jangle
of her tinkling tunes that so confuse the ears

and more the mind.
So down to Hades, now, ladies!
Our Queen has gone before with solemn tread;
it's for us, her loyal ones, to fill her footsteps!
We'll find her at the throne of the Inscrutable One.

CHORUS:
Queens, of course, are happy anywhere.
Even in Hades they're right at the top, rubbing
shoulders with the best, even Persephone.
As for us, we serve as the background,
buried in deep fields of asphodel,
companions to gangly poplars and fruitless willows.
And what are we to do?
Squeak and twitter like bats,
unpleasant, ghostly whispering sighs?

PANTHALIS:
They who have made no name nor sought great ends,
belong to the elements. So away with you all!
I have a grand longing to be with my Queen;
loyalty and merit preserve us as we are.

(Exit.)

FULL CHORUS:
Restored to the day's light,
we are beings no longer,
we feel it, we know it—
never to return to Hades,
never.
Eternal Nature, Nature undying,
claiming us, makes us one with her,
her spirits,
as we lay claim on her.

PART OF THE CHORUS:
Here amid these thousand branches,
swaying, trembling, rustling, whispering,

we Dryads, spirits of trees, lure lightly,
teasing, coaxing the springs of life
to rise from roots into trembling twigs.
Then we deck them out with leaves,
lavish them with lovely blossoms,
adorning our hair for prosperous growth.
And when the ripe fruit falls, they'll gather,
folks and flocks, to reap and nibble,
pressing on in eager masses,
everyone bowed down to earth,
as once they bowed to ancient gods.

A SECOND PART:

Mountain nymphs, Oreads are we,
who cling here, gently caressing, close to
smooth-polished rocks that reflect afar.
We will hearken, we will listen
for every sound, for songs of birds,
for fluting reeds, even for Great Pan's
fearsome shout: for every one
we have an answer always ready.
To a rustling wind we rustle back;
to the thunder's clap we clap, and again,
and again and again till we're all clapped out.

A THIRD PART:

Sisters, Naiads, water spirits,
we, more lively-minded than they,
will wander on with swiftly flowing
brooks that lure us to well-wooded hills.
Ever downward, ever deeper,
we will water now the meadows,
next the pastures, then, ah, then,
the lovely gardens that circle the houses.
We'll know the place by the slender line
of cypresses that tower above
the landscape, shore, and mirroring sea.

A FOURTH PART:

> The rest of you wander wherever you please;
> we'll be circling the close-planted hillsides
> where the well-staked vines grow green.
> There we will see the vintner's passion
> laboring every hour, daily,
> at his never-certain goal.
> With hoe, with spade, heaping, pruning,
> binding, he prays to all the gods,
> but to the sun god most of all.
>
> Soft-living Bacchus, caring little about
> his faithful servant's dedication,
> rests or lolls in caves or arbors,
> having his way with the youngest faun.
> All he needs for his half-drunken reveries
> is stored around him in skins and flagons,
> jars and vessels, right and left of him,
> forever on hand, forever preserved,
> in cool, shady grottoes for all eternity.
>
> But when all the gods together,
> and Helios sun god over all the rest,
> have aired and moistened, warmed and roasted,
> and piled the cornucopia high,
> then, where one sole vintner labored,
> there comes a rustling and bustling about,
> in every arbor, from vine to vine.
> Baskets creak, buckets clatter,
> shoulder hampers groan with their loads,
> all on their way to the mighty vat,
> on to the wine pressers' lusty dance.
> And so the sacred flesh of berries
> is rudely crushed, foaming, splashing,
> trampled to a repulsive mess.

The brazen clash of cymbals now
assaults the ear, and Dionysus,
emerging from his sacred Mysteries,
comes in view with his cleft-footed satyrs,
whirling about their cleft-footed females,
among them Silenus riding his long-eared
beast braying to split the heavens.
Nothing is spared! Nothing! Cleft hooves
trample decency into the dust,
senses whirl, ears are deafened,
drunkards grope their way to wine bowls,
heads are splitting, bellies bursting,
and anyone who calls for caution
only swells the raging tumult,
for to house the brave new wine
wineskins must be emptied fast.

*(The curtain falls. PHORKYAS, in the proscenium, rises up a gigantic
figure, then steps down from her cothurni, pushes back her mask and veil,
and reveals herself to be MEPHISTOPHELES—in order, as far as necessary, to comment on the piece in an epilogue.)*

ACT IV

XLIV ✒ HIGH MOUNTAINS

Jagged rocky peaks.
A cloud approaches, pauses as it touches a peak,
then settles onto a projecting rocky ledge, and divides.

FAUST: *(Emerging.)*
    Leaving behind my chariot of clouds,
    I step with caution onto this mountain crest
    and see below me the profoundest depths of solitude.
    I dismiss it now, that chariot once a robe,
    that vehicle that bore me gently
    through clear days over land and sea.
    Separating from me, it holds its shape,
    not scattering, but moves off eastward
    as a fleecy cumulus mass while
    I look on in wonder.
    For now I see it divide, shifting, changing in
    wavelike motions, as if seeking another shape.
    Yes, and there it has!
    There she lies! I see her!
    Gigantic! Reclining gloriously!
    A woman's form, but like a goddess—
    Juno, Leda, Helen!
    Majestic and lovely,
    it hovers before my sight.

    Ah,
    but now it begins to dissolve,
    disappear, shapeless, broad,
    a formless towering mound hanging in the east
    like distant icy peaks, mirroring
    the deep meaning of those fleeting days.

But, look, this wisp of cloud,
delicate, shining, lingering still
to cool and cheer my heart and brow—
gently caressing. It rises now,
lightly, higher, higher still,
massing itself together.

What!
Am I deceived?
Seeing things?
This rapturous image
so like my youth's first, long-lost,
highest good?
A wave of emotions from my earliest days
sweeps through me.
Aurora's love,
love's early dawn,
the soaring joy, soon felt, scarce understood,
which, if held fast to, would outshine
the most precious things of all!
Now, like the soul's beauty,
that gracious form grows ever more perfect,
holds,
then rising into the higher regions
takes with itself the best of me.

(A seven-league boot comes clomping in, immediately followed by the
second. MEPHISTOPHELES steps out of them. The boots hurry off.)

MEPHISTOPHELES:
Yes, well, that's what I call making tracks!
But tell me now,
what can you have been thinking? I mean,
to dismount in the midst of this horror,
these grizzly, yawning, gruesome crags!
Oh, I know them, all right,
just not exactly quite here.
Fact is,
this was once the bottom of Hell.

FAUST:

Ah, another one of your crazy tales.
You no sooner arrive than you're off and running.

MEPHISTOPHELES: *(Seriously.)*

When the Lord God—
and I know why, too—
cast us from the sky to the deepest of pits
(with central fire blazing eternally),
we found ourselves with something
too *much* illumination,
not to mention overcrowded accommodations.

We devils all began to huff and puff,
fore and aft,
to put out that great blaze,
while roundabout was an acid stink of sulfur
and a pressure of gas so monstrous
it burst through earth's flat crust,
thick as it was,
with a gigantic bang.

Yes, well, it's a different story now.
What was once Hell's bottom is now its top.
It's on this they base those theories required
to turn things topsy-turvy.
In any case,
we escaped that servile place of confinement
and came to gain free dominion of the air.
An open secret, well preserved,
revealed to the world only later.

FAUST:

Noble as they are,
these mountains say nothing to me,
nor do I ask why or where they came from.
When Nature created nature from herself,
she neatly rounded off the earth's vast sphere,
and rejoicing in peaks and chasms, arranged

rock upon rock and mountain following mountain,
then hills that gently slope down to valleys
where everything is green and full of growth.
Nature has enough to rejoice in
without your wild upheavals.

MEPHISTOPHELES:
That's what *you* say!
To you it's all so clear.
But one who was there knows differently.
And I was there.
I was there when the infernal abyss still seethed and
welled up into rivers shooting flames;
when Moloch, with his hammer,
welded rock to rock,
scattering mountain fragments far and wide.
The land is still littered with great masses of stone.
Who can explain the force that hurled them there?
Philosophers?
How, when they don't understand?
"Let them lie there," they say.
"We've made fools enough of ourselves
racking our brains."
It's only the common people in their simple dignity
who have understood, and their belief in
ancient wisdom is not to be shaken.
To them it's a miracle,
and Satan gets his credit!
This is the crutch of faith that lets them hobble
straight to Devil's Rock and Devil's Bridge.

FAUST:
I must admit,
a Devil's-eye view of Nature
is not uninteresting.

MEPHISTOPHELES:
I couldn't care less!
Let Nature do as Nature does!

This is a point of honor:
the Devil was *there!*
It's we, we're the one to achieve greatness—
tumult, violence, madness!
Look around you!
See the signs!

All right, let me speak plainly for once.
Was there nothing on this great vast earth
that satisfied you?
You have surveyed, in measureless expanse,
all the kingdoms of the earth and the glory of them.
Hard to please you may be—
downright fussy, I'd say—
but did you find nothing that tempted you?

FAUST:

Indeed I did.
One mighty plan possessed me.
Guess.

MEPHISTOPHELES:

My pleasure!
Yes, well now, let me see.

If I were you, I'd seek out some bustling capital,
with people scrabbling for food at its very heart,
twisted, narrow alleys, pointed roofs,
a vulgar, cramped little market with
cabbages, turnips, and onions,
and butchers' stalls beleaguered with flies
feasting off greasy joints.
No matter the time, day or night,
you'll find there all the activity and stink you can handle.

And then there's the open squares and broad avenues
where one plays the game of social pretension;
and finally the suburbs stretching out endlessly
with no city walls or gates to confine them.

There you'd see me riding in a carriage,
up and down, this way and that in the
noisy traffic, scrambling like scattered heaps
of swarming ants.
And whenever I drove or rode on horseback,
I'd be the center of attention for hundreds of thousands.

FAUST:

That could never satisfy me!
It's all very well that people multiply,
and in their way live comfortably,
learn how to read, get educated—
and yet, in the end,
what it teaches them is rebellion.

MEPHISTOPHELES:

Then I'd build myself a pleasure palace,
one grand and vast enough to match my worth,
with woods, hills, fields, meadows,
all converted to a splendid park.
Velvety lawns edged with wall-high hedges,
walks straight as a die, cleverly managed
shade, waterfalls leaping from rock to rock,
and fountains, fountains of every sort,
a grand jet of water over there,
and off to the sides a thousand piddling jets
hissing and pissing away.

Ah, and then, of course,
cozy little cottages
built for the loveliest of lovely ladies,
where I would spend endless hours in splendid solitude.
"Ladies," I say,
for I always think of them in the plural.

FAUST:

Mean but modern!
A latter day Sardanapalus!

MEPHISTOPHELES:

    Ah! I have it! Yes!
    What's fired you up so!
    Something exalted, I'm sure,
    not to say bold.
    With all your recent stratospheric travel,
    I suspect it's the moon you're after.

FAUST:

    No! Impossible!
    There's room still on earth for great deeds.
    Astonishing things will be achieved.
    I feel in me the power for this bold enterprise.

MEPHISTOPHELES:

    Ah, then it's fame you're after!
    That's what comes from consorting with heroines.

FAUST:

    No, not fame, fame is nothing.
    It's action I want.
    I want possessions, power!

MEPHISTOPHELES:

    There'll be poets aplenty
    to sing your praise to posterity,
    and in doing so endlessly perpetuate your folly.

FAUST:

    What do you know about human longing,
    human desire, human aspiration?
    You with your contrary nature, your
    hatred, your hostility! You know
    nothing of human need!

MEPHISTOPHELES:

    Well, then, by all means let's hear.
    Let's hear this latest craze.
    I'm all ears.

FAUST:
> I found my attention drawn to the open sea.
> I stood and watched as it swelled,
> mounting higher and higher,
> towering above itself, and then,
> relaxing,
> poured down in floods to storm the level shore.
> And that disturbed me—disturbed me
> as an honest mind that respects the rights of others
> must be disturbed when it sees arrogance
> exerting itself immoderately.
> I took it to be chance;
> then looked again more closely.
> The waves came to a standstill,
> then flowed back,
> receding from their proudly won conquest.
> The hour come round, it started all over again.

MEPHISTOPHELES: *(To the audience.)*
> Nothing new there for me to learn.
> I've known it for a hundred thousand years.

FAUST: *(Continuing with passionate excitement.)*
> Sterile itself, the water creeps up stealthily,
> flooding every inlet,
> spreading sterility everywhere.
> Swelling and swirling,
> rolling, running riot,
> it covers that ugly desolate expanse.
> Waves slash and pummel,
> and when they recede nothing has been achieved.
> Dismayed, I watch in despair
> this elemental energy uncontrolled!
> I dare myself now to rise to new heights.
> It's here my spirit will wage its war
> and prove itself victorious!

> And it is possible!
> The tide may rise and slip its way

past any hillock. Rage all it likes,
a modest height can proudly hold its own,
but a slight drop will powerfully draw it downward.
Knowing this,
plan upon plan invaded my mind.
I would bar the lordly ocean from our shore,
set limits to its domain,
and push it ever backward upon itself.
Ah, what satisfaction that would bring me!
I worked it out step by step.
This is my wish.
Dare now to help me achieve it!

(Distant drums and martial music are heard from the rear, to the right of the audience.)

MEPHISTOPHELES:
No problem.
Do you hear those distant drums?

FAUST:
Another war!
No man in his right senses
would welcome it!

MEPHISTOPHELES:
Oh, war or peace, what's the difference!
What's sensible is working it to your advantage.
You keep a sharp eye peeled,
take note of every favorable opportunity.
All right, then, the opportunity is
in your favor now, Faustus!
Seize it!

FAUST:
Enough of your nonsense!
Say it straight out for once!
What do you mean?

MEPHISTOPHELES:

    On my way here,
    I noticed our worthy Emperor
    has got himself into a mess.
    Well, you know what he's like.
    That time we entertained him and
    inundated him in paper money,
    you'd have thought the whole
    world was up for grabs.
    He came quite young to the throne—
    scarcely a beard to his chin—
    and arrived at the false though rather
    convenient conclusion that
    pleasure and imperial power were
    harmonious bedfellows.

FAUST:

    A grave mistake!
    A ruler must find his sole satisfaction in ruling.
    His heart must be filled with a high will and purpose,
    but no man should be able to divine its contents.
    Those secrets are alone for the ears of intimates;
    he has only to suggest,
    and it is done,
    and all the world stands amazed.
    In this way he will always reign supreme.
    Pleasure makes a man common.

MEPHISTOPHELES:

    He's not like that.
    While he took his pleasure
    the empire collapsed into anarchy.
    Great and small were at each other' throats,
    brother banished and murdered brother,
    castle warred with castle, town with town,
    guilds fought with gentry, bishops with
    chapter and parish. A wayward glance
    was enough to make an enemy.
    Your life wasn't safe even in a church.

And once beyond the city gates,
the merchant and wayfarer were as good as dead!
Audacity and daring were the orders of the day.
Life meant not lowering your guard for a second.
And so it went.

FAUST:

It went, it hobbled, fell and got up again,
then took a tumble and rolled into a great heap.

MEPHISTOPHELES:

And no one dared complain,
for everyone now had the right and the will
to be important, and they insisted on it.
Even a nonentity was considered a somebody.
At last the best and soundest among them
had had enough, and rose up in force
to declare that the man who could bring them peace
would rule as emperor.
"The Emperor," they said, "neither can nor wants to!
Let us elect us a new Emperor
who will breathe new life into the empire,
secure the rights of every man, and join
righteousness with peace in a new-made world!"

FAUST:

I hear a priestly ring in that!

MEPHISTOPHELES:

Ah, yes, indeed!
Priests!
Securing their well-stuffed bellies.
After all, they had more to lose than anyone.
The insurrection grew,
they blessed the rebels,
and our Emperor,
whom we so lately entertained,
comes here to fight—
perhaps his last battle.

FAUST:

    I pity him; he was an honest, good man.

MEPHISTOPHELES:

    Come, let's take a look.
    Where there's life, there's hope.
    Let's free him from this narrow valley.
    Save him this once,
    he'll have no further worries.
    Who knows how the dice will fall?
    And if luck is with him,
    he'll soon have a proper following.

(They cross the lower range of mountains and look down upon the deployment of the army in the valley. Drums and martial music rise from below.)

MEPHISTOPHELES:

    Their position is well chosen.
    Come, we'll join them.
    Their victory then is secure.

FAUST:

    What's the point of all this?
    Trickery! Deception! Illusion!

MEPHISTOPHELES:

    The point is to win battles—
    military cunning known as stratagems.
    Be secure in your great designs and
    keep an eye on your own purpose.
    If we manage to save this Emperor's throne and country,
    you will kneel as his feet to receive
    the boundless shoreline in fief.

FAUST:

    Since there isn't much you haven't done so far,
    let's see you win a battle.
    Show me how.

MEPHISTOPHELES:

>Me? No, you. This time
>you're the commander-in-chief.

FAUST:

>And wouldn't *that* be something!
>Ordering about in a language I don't even know!

MEPHISTOPHELES:

>Leave that to your General Staff
>and you're home free.

>Now,
>knowing the mess that war can be,
>I've anticipated and formed a war council
>out of mountain manpower as old as earth.
>He's a lucky man who can get them in harness.

FAUST:

>Who are those armed men there?
>Have you stirred up the mountain folk?

MEPHISTOPHELES:

>No, but, like Peter Quince,
>the very quintessence of the rabble.

>*(Enter THREE VIOLENT GIANTS.)*

MEPHISTOPHELES:

>Ah, here come my boys now!
>As you will note,
>they differ widely in age, clothing
>and the arms they wear.
>I think you'll find they'll serve you well.

>*(To the audience.)*

>Everyone these days delights seeing knights in armor;
>and since these brutes are allegorical,
>they'll just likely manage to please all the more.

BRAWLER: *(Young, lightly armed, brightly dressed.)*

> One crooked look at me
> You've got a fist in the kisser.
> Some yellow-belly flees,
> He gets it in the pisser.

GRABBER: *(Mature, well armed, richly dressed.)*

> Empty brawls, who needs 'em?
> Learn to put first things first:
> Siege, pillage, and plunder—
> When thirsty quench your thirst.

HOARDER: *(Old, heavily armed, scantily clothed.)*

> Not much profit there!
> You win first, then it's gone,
> Time's taken it in pawn.
> Down life's stream it flows,
> You watch it as it goes.
> To get is good, you bet!
> But to keep is better yet.
> Take an old man's word
> Anything else is absurd.

(They descend to the valley together.)

XLV ⤜ IN THE FOOTHILLS

Drums and martial music from below.
The EMPEROR's tent is being pitched.
EMPEROR.
COMMANDER-IN-CHIEF.
BODYGUARDS.

COMMANDER-IN-CHIEF:

> It was wise, I think,
> to withdraw the whole army into this valley.
> I'm confident we'll be successful.

EMPEROR:

    Yes, well, time will tell.

    Though I can't say I favor this semi-retreat.

COMMANDER-IN-CHIEF:

    Look there at our right flank, Sire.

    We couldn't ask for better fighting terrain.

    Slopes neither too steep nor too accessible,

    an advantage for us,

    a stumbling block for the enemy.

    Besides, we're half-hidden on a rolling plain;

    their cavalry won't even attempt it.

EMPEROR:

    I can only approve. Today we test

    our strength as well as loyalty.

COMMANDER-IN-CHIEF:

    Look at our phalanx.

    Do you see?

    On the flat central meadow?

    They couldn't be in better fighting spirit,

    their pikes flashing through the sunny morning mist.

    In that vast, dark, heaving square

    thousands of warriors are straining at the leash,

    aflame to do great deeds.

    You can feel their strength from here.

    I assure you, Majesty,

    they'll break the enemy's back.

EMPEROR:

    I've never seen a finer sight.

    Such an army is worth one twice its size.

COMMANDER-IN-CHIEF:

    The left flank speaks for itself.

    The rocky cliffs are well fortified with men;

    you can see their flashing arms from here.

    They'll cover the crucial pass into the valley.

It's there I see the enemy defeated
in a savage encounter.

EMPEROR:
And there they come,
treacherous, false kinsmen,
who called me uncle, cousin, brother,
taking one liberty after another,
robbing my throne of power and authority,
laying waste the empire with internal feuding,
and now, as rebels, they join to march against me.
Yes, and then the masses,
uncertain which way to turn,
follow wherever the current carries them.

COMMANDER-IN-CHIEF:
I've sent out as spies two men I trust.
Here comes the first.
I hope his news is good.

FIRST SCOUT.
Sire, we managed to get through and
work our way among them as ordered,
but the news, I'm afraid, isn't good.
Many of the princes swear loyalty to the crown,
but claim that rebellions in their own domains
force them to take no action.

EMPEROR:
Self-interest always wins out—
over gratitude, affection, duty, honor.
Do you never consider that when your neighbor's
house is burning yours may be the next?

COMMANDER-IN-CHIEF:
Here's the second.
How slowly he descends the hill,
every limb of him aching.

SECOND SCOUT:

> We were amused at first, Sire,
> at the wild confusion we discovered
> when suddenly a new Emperor appeared.
> Now, in order, behind false flags and
> following directions, the mob
> marches across the plain—
> like sheep!

EMPEROR:

> Gentlemen, I welcome this rival emperor,
> for I feel now for the first time
> that I'm the true one.
> I dressed in armor only as a soldier,
> but now I wear it with a higher purpose.
>
> At every court festival,
> no matter how brilliant,
> I always felt a deficiency.
> It was danger I lacked.
> Danger.
> When I tilted, I tilted at the ring,
> as you advised, though in my heart
> I longed to be truly jousting.
> You also counseled against war.
> Had I not listened,
> by now I would be a hero many times over.
>
> When I saw myself mirrored in that realm of fire,
> I felt myself stamped with the seal of independence.
> The fearful element pressed horribly in about me,
> but it was only illusion—
> a grand illusion!
> I've always dreamed vaguely of fame and conquest.
> I will make up now
> for what I so shamefully neglected.

*(HERALDS are dispatched to challenge the RIVAL EMPEROR.
Enter FAUST in armor, his visor half closed, along with the THREE
VIOLENT GIANTS, armed and dressed as earlier.)*

FAUST:

> We come here, Sire,
> hoping we're not unwelcome.
> Foresight can be a good thing,
> even when not needed.
>
> As you know,
> the mountain people are well versed
> in the lore of nature and rocks.
> The spirits who once lived on the low plains
> have left there now, more attracted
> than ever to mountain ranges.
> It's there they work quietly in cavernous labyrinths,
> surrounded by precious gases of metallic vapors,
> testing, separating, combining—
> with one only purpose:
> to discover the not-yet-discovered.
> With subtle power of mind
> they create transparent forms,
> and then in the ever-silent depths of the crystal
> they read of events in the upper world.

EMPEROR:

> Yes, so I've heard, and I believe you.
> But why, my good man,
> should it interest me now?

FAUST:

> I remind you, Sire, of the
> Sabine necromancer of Norcia,
> your ever-faithful and devoted servant.
> What a dreadful fate once threatened him!
> Twigs crackled, kindling,
> flames had begun licking upward,
> dry logs placed crosshatch around,
> mingled with pitch and sticks of sulfur—
> neither man, God, nor Devil could have saved him;
> except for Your Majesty who burst those chains of fire.

That was in Rome.
Since then, eternally indebted to you,
he thinks of your welfare alone,
never of himself, forever searching
the stars and the depths of earth for your benefit.
It is his urgent charge sends us here for support.
Great forces are at work in the mountains,
Nature works there unimpeded,
though the stupid priestly mind calls it sorcery.

EMPEROR:
On festive days when we welcome with
open arms pleasure-seeking guests who
crowd and jostle each other in their delight,
we are pleased to see our halls
inadequate to the multitude.
But this worthy man is supremely welcome.
He comes offering support
at the crucial hour of the morning
when our fate hangs in the balance.

And yet I ask you at this most auspicious hour
to withhold your hand from your willing sword,
for at this moment thousands are met
to join in battle for or against me.
A man must depend on himself alone,
he must fight his own battle.
A man who lays claim to crown and scepter
must be ready to prove in single combat
he's worthy of them.

Let this phantom, this rebel,
who rises up against us,
calling himself emperor,
master of my lands,
the army's commander,
my vassals' feudal lord—
let him be dispatched by this my fist
to the Fortress of Death that once held him!

FAUST:
>Majesty, to pledge your head,
>even in so noble an endeavor,
>is ill-advised, that head whose
>helmet is adorned with crest and plume,
>protecting it and firing your men with courage.
>Without that head, what of the limbs?
>When the head weakens, they all weaken.
>When the head is wounded, all are wounded.
>But restore it to health and all are restored.
>The arm quickly shields the skull,
>the sword parries and returns the blow,
>and the victor plants his foot on the slain man's neck.

EMPEROR:
>My wrath exactly. It's what I'll do.
>His proud head becomes my footstool.

HERALDS: *(Returning.)*
>They showed us little respect and no acceptance,
>scorning our noble challenge of single combat.
>"That emperor of yours," they cried,
>"is an echo fading away—
>a once upon a time . . ."

FAUST:
>This rebuff, Sire, cannot have been better.
>The wish of your staunch supporters is fulfilled.
>There comes the enemy.
>Your men are eager and straining for battle.
>Order the attack: the moment is right.

EMPEROR: *(To the COMMANDER-IN-CHIEF.)*
>I here resign all rights to the command.
>Prince, I call on you to do your duty.

COMMANDER-IN-CHIEF:
>Then let the right wing advance!
>The enemy's left is marching up the slope.

Our young and tested troops
will check their progress.

FAUST:

Then admit this vigorous hero into your ranks,
for once he's with you you'll see what he's capable of.

(He points to the one on his right.)

BRAWLER: *(Stepping forward.)*

        Who looks me in the face, he runs the hazard
        Of being well scored over cheek and mazard;
        Who turns his back to me—well, he may risk it,
        But down he'll topple, cleft from chin to brisket.
        And if your men will only then
        With sword and mace strike home like me,
        Your foes amain will strew the plain,
        Bathed in their blood as in a sea.

(Exit.)

COMMANDER-IN-CHIEF:

Center phalanx advance at full strength,
but with caution. Over there to the right
I see we've made good headway,
upsetting the enemy's plans.

FAUST: *(Pointing to the one in the middle.)*

This one, too, must join your command.
He'll sweep all before him.

GRABBER: *(Stepping forward.)*

        Add to the army's blood and thunder
        The all-essential lust to plunder;
        Let every man make his intent
        To pillage the rival emperor's tent!
        He hasn't long to flaunt his pride,
        As long as I the phalanx guide.

QUICKLOOT: *(A camp follower, sidling up to him.)*
    Although his wife I may not be,
    He's the dearest of men to me.
    What a harvest, what a catch!
    Women are regular fiends when they snatch!
    They plunder and rifle, they're ruthless, you'll see!
    All's fair in war! On to victory!

(Exeunt both.)

COMMANDER-IN-CHIEF:
  As expected,
  their right flank's attacking our left
  in full force.
  We must resist to the last man
  their desperate attempt
  to take the narrow pass.

FAUST: *(Pointing to the one at the left.)*
    If you please, sir, take this man, too.
    It never hurts to add to your strength.

HOARDER: *(Stepping forward.)*
    The left wing's safe, dismiss all care!
    No need for worry once I am there.
    The old one still has all his wits;
    What this hand grasps, no lightning splits.

(Exit.)

MEPHISTOPHELES: *(Descending from above.)*
  Look behind you there!
  You see?
  Men, hordes of them,
  thronging from every rocky gorge and ravine,
  overwhelming every narrow path in our rear,
  helmets, armor, shields, and swords
  forming a wall of strength not to be broken.
  Behold them straining to strike.

(Quietly to those in the know.)

Now, now,
not to ask where all this came from.
But one thing's certain,
I haven't been idle,
plundering old armories roundabout.
There they sat on horseback or standing,
believing themselves the lords of creation,
knights and kings and emperors and all,
and yet what are they but empty snail shells
for ghosts and devils to dress up in
and play the Middle Ages.

Well, whatever,
at least it's no shabby display.

(Aloud.)

Just listen to them!
Bumping and rattling about in their tin armor,
working up their fierceness in advance!
And there I see tattered flags fluttering,
longing impatiently for a fresh breeze.
Remember,
this is an ancient people you see here,
eager to join even a modern fight.

(A fearsome blare of trumpets from above; a noticeable wavering in the enemy ranks.)

FAUST:
　　The horizon has gone dark;
　　here and there an ominous red flash;
　　the bloody flare of weapons;
　　everything now joins in:
　　rocks, forest, air, even the heavens.

MEPHISTOPHELES:
    The right flank's holding up well;
    and there I see the giant Jack Brawler
    towering above all the rest,
    doing what he does best.

EMPEROR:
    First I saw only one arm raised in battle,
    now I see a dozen; it's not natural.

FAUST:
    Have you never heard of the streaks of mist
    that sweep the coast of Sicily?
    Shimmering in the bright light of day,
    they rise to the middle air and
    there present wondrous visions
    mirrored in their own peculiar haze.
    Cities are seen swaying this way and that,
    and gardens rising and falling,
    as image follows image,
    appearing, vanishing.

EMPEROR:
    Look there!
    How very strange!
    What's that light at the tips of my soldiers'
    lances? And flames dancing
    on the polished spears of our phalanx!
    I find it all very mysterious.

FAUST:
    By your leave, Sire,
    those are the traces of spirits now long vanished,
    the Dioskouroi, that sailors always swear by,
    summoning here the last of their strength.

EMPEROR:
    But why should Nature come to aid us
    with her most precious gifts?

Who's behind this?
Whom do we thank?

MEPHISTOPHELES:
Who else, Sire,
but that exalted Master,
the necromancer of Norcia,
who has your welfare at heart!
He's deeply disturbed
by the forces deployed against you.
In gratitude, he hopes to bring you victory
even if it costs him his life.

EMPEROR:
All Rome cheered as I
passed in pomp through the city.
I was someone, I said to myself,
and wanted to prove it,
and so, without plan,
I decided to rescue that
great white beard from the flames.
I spoiled those clerics their fun,
nor did they thank me for it.
And now after all these years
I reap the reward of that happy impulse.

FAUST:
Generous deeds bring generous rewards.
But look up there!
I dare say he'll send you a sign
whose meaning will soon be made clear.

EMPEROR:
I see an eagle hovering in midair,
and a griffin in hot pursuit.

FAUST:
Watch closely!
This appears a good omen.

Griffins are creatures of fable,
what presumption to take on a real eagle!

EMPEROR:
They're making wide circles around each other,
and now, at the same instant,
they turn to attack, each aiming
to tear at the other's heart and throat.

FAUST:
Look there!
That hateful griffin's had the worst of it!
Torn and badly mauled,
he lowers his lion's tail and,
sinking into the treetops,
disappears.

EMPEROR:
As you have read the omen, so be it!
I accept it, but not without amazement.

MEPHISTOPHELES: *(Toward the right.)*
A mighty series of assaults by us, Sire,
has forced the enemy back and to the right,
exposing and throwing its left into wild confusion.
Our phalanx has now swung in that direction
and with lightning speed
spearheaded that weakened position.
Both sides, equally matched,
go at it now like waves in a storm-tossed sea.
Magnificent!
What more can be said!
The victory is ours!

EMPEROR: *(On the left; to FAUST.)*
No! There! Over there!
There's something wrong.
Our position's in danger.
I see no stones flying;

the enemy's taken the lower ledges,
the upper ones abandoned.
I see them pressing forward now
in massing numbers, the narrow pass
may have been taken!
All the result of your unholy efforts!
Your arts have been in vain!

(Pause.)

MEPHISTOPHELES:
Here come my two ravens.
What news could they be bringing?
Things may be going badly for us.

EMPEROR:
What are these dreadful birds
sailing on great black wings from the
battle on the mountain?

MEPHISTOPHELES: *(To the ravens.)*
Come, sit close to my ear.
Your advice can always be trusted.
No one you protect is in danger.

FAUST: *(To the EMPEROR.)*
Surely you've heard of doves, Sire,
that fly back from distant lands
to their nests to brood and feed?
It's much the same here, but with a difference.
The dove brings messages of peace,
the raven of war.

MEPHISTOPHELES:
I've just had very grave news.
Look over there.
The edge of the cliff.
Our men are in great difficulty.
The enemy's taken the nearest adjoining heights,

and if they take the pass,
we're in real danger.

EMPEROR:
So I've been deceived after all.
You've lured me into your net.
I've been uneasy about it from the start.

MEPHISTOPHELES:
Don't lose heart, it isn't over yet.
Patience and a little cunning will do the trick.
It's always nastiest toward the end.
Besides,
I have messengers I can count on.
What say, Sire,
you let me take over the command?

COMMANDER-IN-CHIEF: *(Approaching the EMPEROR.)*
You allied yourself with these two, Majesty,
an alliance that has pained me from the start,
for trickery won't sustain you in the end.
There's nothing I can do at this point.
Let them finish it as they've begun.
I return to you my commander's baton.

EMPEROR:
Keep it for better times that
fortune perhaps may lend us.
This repulsive creature and his raven friends
make me shudder.

(To MEPHISTOPHELES.)

No, I can't give you the baton.
You're not the right man for it.
But issue what orders you need to and free us!
Do whatever it takes.

(He and the COMMANDER-IN-CHIEF retire to the tent.)

MEPHISTOPHELES:

So much for him and his precious stick!
Besides, it's useless to us,
what with that cross thing at one end!

FAUST:

What do we do now?

MEPHISTOPHELES:

Do? It's all but done!
Hurry, now, my black little cousins,
off to work at the mountain lake!
Greet the Undines, and tell them
we need to borrow some pretty water tricks.
They have an art we haven't,
they're female,
they know how to separate illusion from reality
so everyone thinks it's the real thing.

(Pause.)

FAUST:

Our ravens must have
flattered those ladies with a vengeance.
I see a trickle beginning over there.
And there a once dry rocky place
is flowing rapidly.
They can never win now.

MEPHISTOPHELES:

What a grand way to greet them!
Their boldest climbers are at a loss.

FAUST:

A single brook divides into many brooks
that then leap out of gulches twice their size.
And there, another, a river,
casts its arching back far out and down,

down onto rocky flats,
roaring and foaming every which way,
and step by step down into the valley.
What good is heroic resistance to such power?
I find even myself shuddering with dread.

MEPHISTOPHELES:
I see nothing of these watery lies.
Only human eyes can be deceived.
But it amuses me all the same.
Look at them,
masses of them out there, the fools,
thinking they're drowning, running,
paddling the air like swimmers,
when all the while they're standing on solid ground.
A madhouse of confusion!

(The ravens have returned.)

I'll see our exalted Master hears of your industry.
And yet, if you're so minded,
and want to prove masters yourselves,
hurry off to the glowing smithy
where the dwarf folk never tire at hammering
sparks from metal and stone.
Persuade them without fail to give you fire—
brilliant, flashing, sputtering, exploding—
fire such as sparkles in our Master's mind.
Heat lightning from afar,
or the fall of remotest stars,
are common sights on a summer's night.
But lightning playing in a confusion of shrubbery,
and stars hissing along the moistened earth
these are sights have power to amaze.
Don't put yourselves out too much, of course:
ask politely first, and then insist.

(The ravens fly off. The display described takes place.)

MEPHISTOPHELES:

> Thick darkness settles on the foe!
> Which way to turn, they do not know.
> Meteors crashing, blazing light,
> Dazzle and confound the sight!
> A marvelous view! But now, indeed,
> A shattering sound is all we need.

FAUST:

> The empty armor from ancient vaults
> Finds itself revived in air.
> Their rattling, banging, clattering there
> Creates a discord without faults.

MEPHISTOPHELES:

> Quite right! They're not to be held back!
> Fighting wildly, whack on whack,
> The same as in the good old days.
> With greaves and armlets, and cuisses, too,
> Guelphs and Ghibellines renew
> Full tilt their neverending frays.
> Firm in inherited rancor, they
> put implacable hate on display.
> Now far and wide the tumult brays!
> And so, at every devil's fête,
> Nothing succeeds like party hate,
> Down to the last convulsive throe.
> Wild sounds, that scatter fear and panic,
> Mingled with piercing yells Satanic,
> Ring down into the vale below.

(Tumultuous warlike music in the orchestra, finally giving way to cheerful military music.)

XLVI ↝ THE RIVAL EMPEROR'S TENT

A throne, rich surroundings.
GRABBER and QUICKLOOT.

QUICKLOOT:
> We got here first after all.

GRABBER:
> Faster than a raven's flight!

QUICKLOOT:
> Ah, and look at the treasure!
> Where do I start, where do I stop!

GRABBER:
> I never saw so much loot!
> What to grab first?

QUICKLOOT:
> That rug would suit me nicely!
> You should see the miserable beds I sleep on.

GRABBER:
> Ah! And here! A steel-spiked mace!
> A dream come true!

QUICKLOOT:
> Look here! A red cloak here with gold trim!
> I've wanted one of these for ever!

GRABBER: *(Taking the mace from the wall.)*
> One good stroke with this and the brain's a mush,
> then on to the next.
> Let's see what you've got there.
> Ah! Junk! Leave it.
> Take one of these chests.
> The army's pay. A bellyful of gold.

QUICKLOOT:

> It's murderous, the weight.
> Can't lift it, can't carry it.

GRABBER:

> Duck down, then.
> Stoop, I said!
> I'll heave it onto your back!

QUICKLOOT:

> Au! Ouch! Now you've done it!
> It's broke my back in two!

(The chest falls and bursts open.)

GRABBER:

> All that gold lying in a heap!
> Hurry, pick it up!

QUICKLOOT:

> Put it in my apron!
> There'll still be plenty.

GRABBER:

> There, that'll do!
> Hurry!

(She rises to her feet.)

> Oh, no! The apron's got a hole!
> Every step you take
> you waste more treasure!

IMPERIAL GUARDS: *(Of our Emperor.)*

> What's going on here!
> You've no right!
> Scrounging the Emperor's treasures!

GRABBER:

    We risked our lives,

    we'll take our share of the loot!

    That's war, this is the enemy's tent,

    and we're soldiers the same as you!

IMPERIAL GUARDS:

    Not in this army you're not!

    We're soldiers, not thieves.

    Only honest men serve our Emperor.

GRABBER:

    Yes, and we know your kind of honest.

    You call it "Contribution,"

    but it's more like "Hand it over!"

    You're all the same!

    (To QUICKLOOT.)

    Take what you've got and get out!

    I think we've worn out our welcome.

    (Exeunt GRABBER and QUICKLOOT.)

FIRST GUARD:

    You had the chance, why didn't you

    knock his teeth down his throat?

SECOND GUARD:

    I suddenly felt weak—

    the two of them looking so ghostly.

THIRD GUARD:

    I suddenly couldn't see straight, spots and all.

FOURTH GUARD:

    I don't quite know how to say it.

    All day was so close,

    so hot and muggy you could hardly breathe—

scary, too.
One man stayed standing, another fell.
You groped along blindly and struck, and for
every stoke an enemy went down.
It was like a veil covering your eyes,
and then humming and hissing and
buzzing in your ears.
And so it went,
and now we're here, and none of us
knows how it happened.

(Enter the EMPEROR with four PRINCES. The GUARDS withdraw.)

EMPEROR:
Magic or no, it is what it is!
We've won!
The fleeing enemy scattered across the plain.
Look here, the empty throne, the traitor's treasures.
I now await the arrival of foreign emissaries,
and news that the Empire is again at peace
and loyal to the crown.
There may have been trickery involved, but in the end
we fought our own battle and won it.
Accidents happen,
accidents that work in one's favor:
a meteor falls from the sky,
blood rains down on the foe,
and from mountain caverns blasts of miraculous sound
that rouse our spirits but utterly confound the enemy.
The loser fell, the object of scorn;
the victor rises, in triumph thanking his God!
But not he alone, a million throats
sing out in one voice:
Te deum laudamus.

But now I'll do what I've seldom done.
Look within. A young and lively prince may
squander his days, but time, in the end,
teaches him to value them.

Therefore, and with no hesitation,
I bind myself to you four worthy custodians
of my house, my court, and my empire.

(To the FIRST PRINCE.)

It was you, prince, who shrewdly organized the army
and struck out boldly when the moment was right.
Do so as well in peace, for with this sword
I invest you Lord Marshall.

LORD MARSHALL:
Majesty,
no sooner your borders are secured,
and your person and throne once more safe,
permit us with throngs of joyous friends
to serve you at table, to bear before
and hold beside you this radiant sword,
forever your Highness's escort.

EMPEROR: *(To the SECOND PRINCE.)*
On you, sir,
a man of courage and gentle demeanor,
I bestow the title of Lord Chamberlain.
Your task is no easy one.
Your jurisdiction is over the domestic staff,
where, it is not unknown to me,
there is no small discontent and inefficiency.
It is yours to serve as model of how one tends
one's liege, one's court, and one's fellows.

LORD CHAMBERLAIN:
To serve your noble person does me grace, Sire.
To help the good and not to harm the base,
to be open, honest, and calm without deceit
is all my desire. And if you see me, Highness,
for what I am, my joy could not be greater.
Already I look forward to the feast.
At table I will offer the golden bowl,

and hold your rings as you dip your fingers
and give me your sign of approval.

EMPEROR:
    I find it difficult just now
    to turn to festive thoughts.
    But no matter. A joyous beginning
    is always best.

(To the THIRD PRINCE.)

    You, sir, I appoint my Lord Steward.
    Yours is to oversee the hunt,
    the poultry yards and the farm.
    And then to prepare with skill and consummate care
    the choicest delicacies a season has to offer.

LORD STEWARD:
    I shall happily forego food, Majesty,
    till any given dish has met your approval.
    The kitchen staff and I will conspire together
    to procure the choicest viands from distant regions,
    and well before their seasons.
    And yet, Sire,
    such luxuries mean little to you
    who prefer the nourishing and simple.

EMPEROR: *(To the FOURTH PRINCE.)*
    Our unfailing topic being feasts and festivities,
    you, young hero, I appoint my Lord Cupbearer.
    It is your charge to see that our cellars
    are always well stocked with the finest.
    And be moderate, you hear?
    Don't let opportunity get the better of you.

LORD CUPBEARER:
    Give youth a chance, Majesty,
    and it will achieve maturity before you know it.
    I, too, see myself at that great feast,

where I will deck the imperial buffet
with sumptuous vessels of gold and silver.
For you, though, Majesty, there will be goblets
of gleaming Venetian glass
beckoning with delight.
In them the wine grows stronger but never intoxicates.
The goblet's virtue, of course, it too often invoked;
but Your Majesty's moderation will save you from that.

EMPEROR:

These honors as bestowed are sacred and valid;
and yet, for confirmation, we will put it to paper.
And here I see coming just the man to do that.

(Enter the CHANCELLOR-ARCHBISHOP.)

EMPEROR:

Once the arch entrusts itself to the
keystone, it is forever secure.
You see here four princes, my Lord Chancellor—
also our Archbishop—
with whom I have just discussed
the governance of my house and court.

Let us now consider the Empire as a whole,
for it is on you five that I now rest
its full weight and authority.

You will outshine all others in landed possessions,
and therefore I enlarge your present territories
from the holdings of those rebels who supported our enemy.
But not only are splendid estates
and domains now yours, yours is also
the right to extend them further by way of
succession, purchase, and exchange,
as opportunity affords.

In addition,
yours in perpetuity is the exercise
of those feudal privileges which accrue to you

as territorial princes.
The judgments you render are final
and may not be referred to a higher court.
Fees, too, levies, taxes,
rents and tolls, royalties on mines,
salt works, and mints, tributes, safe conduct, fiefs—
all are yours.

This I do to prove to you my gratitude:
you are raised today to a place quite close to Majesty.

CHANCELLOR-ARCHBISHOP:

Let me in the name of us all thank you, Majesty.
In strengthening us you strengthen yourself as well.

EMPEROR:

I have a yet higher privilege for the five of you.
Though I am still alive and long to live and
rule my realm ambitiously, I nonetheless
think back on my long ancestry and consider
the doom that awaits us all.
I, too, will one day part from my loved ones,
and so,
let it be your duty to name my successor and
solemnize his coronation.
May peace reign then,
and our stormy times be ended.

CHANCELLOR-ARCHBISHOP:

Proud in heart, humble in posture,
we princes, of all the earth the highest,
bow before you.
While blood flows through our veins,
consider us one body intent on your every wish.

EMPEROR:

To make an end, then, let all that we have concluded
be committed to writing and duly signed by us.
As lords of the realm,

you hold your possessions forever,
with the sole proviso that they are indivisible,
and however much they are aggrandized by you,
they will pass undiminished to your eldest son.

CHANCELLOR-ARCHBISHOP:
It will be done at once, Majesty,
for the good of ourselves and the Empire.
My office will see to the engrossment,
the seal affixed and readied for your august signature.

EMPEROR:
And so I dismiss you, that each man of you
may contemplate this day's great events.

(The SECULAR PRINCES go out, the SPIRITUAL PRINCE remains.)

CHANCELLOR-ARCHBISHOP: *(With pathos.)*
The Chancellor has withdrawn.
It is the Bishop remains.
Warned by an inner voice,
he wishes to speak as a father
with deep concern for his son.

EMPEROR:
But, Lord Bishop,
what could possibly distress you
on this happy occasion?
Speak freely.

CHANCELLOR-ARCHBISHOP:
It grieves me, grieves me deeply at this hour
to see your sacred head in league with Satan.
Admittedly you sit safely on your throne,
or so it seems,
but in truth it is a mockery to God
and the Holy Father, who, once informed,
will exercise to the full extent of his powers
the ban of excommunication on you

and your evil Empire.
Consider:
he has never forgotten your first act as Emperor,
when on your coronation day you freed
from the flames that nefarious sorcerer,
a deed done to the detriment of all Christendom.
It is now for you to beat your breast,
to be penitent and give to a holy cause
a modest mite of your ill-gotten fortune.
That expanse of hills where you pitched your tent,
where evil forces conspired with you for your safety,
where you turned your ear to the Prince of Lies—
give that land with its mountains and forests,
its high, green meadows for grazing,
its clear lakes well stocked with fish, and the waters
that wind and plunge to the valley,
and the valley itself
with its meadows, fields, and dales—
give this in piety as penance to the Church and
find yourself again in the state of grace.

EMPEROR:
My offence horrifies me so deeply,
I leave it to you to determine the boundaries.

CHANCELLOR-ARCHBISHOP:
But, first, to cleanse that place so defiled by sin,
it must at once be rededicated to the Most High.
In my mind's eye I see strong walls rising,
the early morning sun lighting the choir,
the transept next, the nave extending, rising
to the joy of all the faithful.
Already I see them thronging through the noble portals,
the first bell has just tolled over hill and dale,
booming from lofty towers that strive heavenward,
drawing the penitent to a life renewed.
On that day of consecration, Sire—
may it come soon!—
your presence will be its highest ornament.

EMPEROR:

> I pray the magnitude of this great enterprise
> will glorify God, but also bring me absolution.
> I already feel my spirit being lifted.

CHANCELLOR-ARCHBISHOP:

> As Chancellor I must now ask one final formality.

EMPEROR:

> A formal deed of transfer, yes—
> to the Church.
> Bring it and I'll gladly sign.

(The CHANCELLOR-ARCHBISHOP has taken his leave but turns back at the door.)

CHANCELLOR-ARCHBISHOP:

> You will, besides, assign to this work
> all of the revenues of said property,
> tithes, taxes, payments in kind—
> in perpetuity.
> Grand sums will be required for proper maintenance,
> not to mention administrative costs.
>
> What's more,
> given the desolation of the site,
> you will give us gold from your war booty.
> It will help to speed the progress.
> Ah, yes, and then timber—
> not to be overlooked—
> timber, lime, and slate and the like
> will need transport from distant areas.
> The workers, of course, will do that.
> The Church will promise blessings
> to those who offer use of carts in her service.

(Exit.)

EMPEROR:

What a dreadful sin I've brought upon myself.
That wretched tribe of sorcerers has cost me dearly.

*(The CHANCELLOR-ARCHBISHOP returns once more
and bows obsequiously.)*

CHANCELLOR-ARCHBISHOP:

Begging your pardon, Majesty!
I only now recall,
you granted a certain stretch of shore
to that most disreputable Faustus.
Unless in penitence you assign to Mother Church
all tithes, rents, gifts,
all revenue from there as well,
she will surely place a ban on *that* property.

EMPEROR: *(Irritably.)*

But the land doesn't yet exist!
It's under the tide!

CHANCELLOR-ARCHBISHOP:

The time will come for those with justice and patience.
Meanwhile, Sire, your word is your bond, as we know.

(Exit.)

EMPEROR: *(Alone.)*

I might as well sign away the whole Empire!

ACT V

XLVII ⤳ OPEN COUNTRY

WANDERER:
> There they are, the same dark, ancient lindens,
> strong and sturdy as ever.
> And to think I've found them again
> after all these years of wandering!
> The same old place,
> the same old cottage where they took me in
> and tended my needs when tossed ashore on those
> sandy dunes by stormy waves!
> How I long to thank that brave, dear couple
> that came to my aid.
> But they were old even then.
> I wonder if they're still here to welcome me now?
> What pious people they were!
>
> Shall I knock?
> Shall I call?
>
> Greetings to you in there if you're still here,
> still eager to find pleasure in doing good!

BAUCIS: *(A little, very old woman.)*
> Dear stranger! Gently! Gently!
> He's sleeping, my husband.
> Softly!
> Let him sleep.
> He needs long rest
> for the short time he's awake.

WANDERER:
> Is it really you, then, Mother?
> You, here, to receive my thanks,
> you and your ancient husband,
> who saved my young life so long ago?

Are you Baucis? The very same,
who when I was near to death
brought food to nourish me in my need?

(Enter PHILOMEN.)

And you—you're Philemon,
Philemon who rescued my treasure from the sea.
It was you who lit the beacon fire and
sounded the little silver bell;
you and Baucis
who rescued me from that catastrophe.

But now let me walk out onto the dunes,
and see again the endless, boundless sea.
Let me kneel and pray.
I'm deeply moved.

(He walks out onto the dune.)

PHILEMON: *(To BAUCIS.)*
Hurry, lay the table in the garden!
Where the flowers are nicest!
Let him have his look.
What a fright he'll take!
He won't believe his eyes!

(Coming up beside the WANDERER.)

The place that treated you so fiercely,
mountains of wild and foaming waves,
is a garden now,
a paradise.

I was no stripling then,
not able to help as I could have once,
no strength in me even then,
but I watched,
watched and saw the water pushed

farther and farther back, my strength
disappearing along with the waters.

Clever masters they were,
masters whose bold servants
dug ditches and damned high the waters,
only to rule themselves where the water once ruled.

Look there,
meadow after green meadow,
gardens, villages, forests.

But come eat something now.
The sun will soon be down.

Out there! You see?
Sails making for home tonight!
Like birds, they know where safety lies.
The harbor's over there now.

Ah, it's so far off,
a thin blue strip on the horizon—
the sea.
Right and left, as far as you can look,
all this new land is thickly populated.

(The THREE at table in the garden.)

BAUCIS:
    Why so silent? And nothing
    to quench your thirst?

PHILEMON:
    I think he wants to hear about the miracle.
    You like talking. You tell him.

BAUCIS:
    Yes! Well!
    And it *was* a miracle, too!

I think of it even today.
Something wrong there, I'd say.
Something not right.

PHILEMON:
Can the Emperor have sinned
in giving him the seashore?
Didn't a herald proclaim it
throughout the land?

Well,
the first foothold
was planted not far from our dunes.
Tents and huts!
And before we knew it there was a palace
in the midst of green meadows and trees.

BAUCIS:
All day long workers toiled and slaved,
pick and shovel forever hacking away,
and all for nothing. But at night
we saw little flames swarming everywhere,
and the next day—
there stood the dam.

Men were sacrificed,
you could hear them at night
howling in their torment.
Floods of flame flowed seaward,
and at morning light we beheld a canal.

He's a godless man.
He covets our cottage and our grove of lindens.
He boasts of being neighborly,
but expects us to be his slaves.

PHILEMON:
Yet he offered us a nice property
on the new-made land.

BAUCIS:
>I'll never trust the ocean bottom.
>We'll stand fast here on our headland.

PHILEMON:
>Let's go to the chapel now
>and watch the sunset.
>We'll ring the bell, kneel down,
>and pray to the God of old.

XLVIII ☞ PALACE

>*Extensive formal garden.*
>*A wide, straight canal.*
>*FAUST in extreme old age pacing thoughtfully.*
>*LYNCEUS, the tower watchman, speaks through a megaphone.*

LYNCEUS:
>Setting sun and the last ships making for port, sir.
>I see a great vessel entering the canal
>preparing to dock;
>pennants flying, sails ready to furl
>on motionless masts.
>Her sailors sing your praises, sir, and
>Fortune smiles upon you at your crowning moment!

>*(The little bell rings out on the dunes.)*

FAUST: *(With a violent start.)*
>Damn that infernal clattering!
>It wounds me like a stab in the dark!
>Spread out before me, my realm is endless;
>but from behind I'm taunted by what I lack,
>reminded by teasing, envious sounds
>that my vast holdings are not unblemished.
>Not the linden grove,
>the brown cottage,
>the crumbling chapel—

not one are mine, not one!
And if I wished to rest there I could not
for all the ghostly shadows to unseat my soul!
It is a thorn,
a thorn in the eye, the foot, the mind!
Oh, if only I were away from here!

LYNCEUS: *(As above.)*
Look how it sails serenely in the evening breeze!
Its cargo, bales and boxes,
towers higher as it approaches!

(A splendid vessel docks, laden with rich and colorful products from foreign ports. Enter MEPHISTOPHELES and the THREE VIOLENT GIANTS.)

THE THREE VIOLENT GIANTS: *(In chorus.)*
          Back already!
          Almost ashore!
          Hail our Master!
          Hail our Patron!

(They disembark. The cargo is unloaded.)

MEPHISTOPHELES:
So here we are, back again,
and well done, too, if the master approves.
We sailed from port with two ships,
we bring back twenty to scrape at the wharf.
If need be, measure our success by our cargo.

As the saying goes:
Who needs scruples on the open sea?
A fast firm hand is all that counts.
You catch a fish, you catch a ship,
and once you've grappled three,
there's a fourth and a fifth.
Well, as they say,
you've got the Might you've got the Right.

And don't ask How, ask What.
If I've learned one thing at sea,
it's the sailor's Holy Trinity.
War, Trade, and Piracy,
a three-in-one, a one-in-three.

THE THREE VIOLENT GIANTS:
What's this, no thanks, no greetings?
You'd think, looking at him,
we brought back garbage.
Look at him, screwing his face!
He thinks it stinks?

MEPHISTOPHELES:
You've had your share!
You won't be getting more!

THE THREE VIOLENT GIANTS:
But that was only to pass the time.
We demand our equal share.

MEPHISTOPHELES:
First, then, you'll have to arrange it room by room,
treasure upon treasure—spare nothing.
Once he's dazzled by the wealth of it all,
he'll see reason,
he'll calculate it piece by piece,
and give the fleet a whole daisy chain of parties,
you'll see. Besides,
the chippies arrive tomorrow.
Rest easy, you'll all be well provided.

(The cargo is removed.)

MEPHISTOPHELES: *(To FAUST.)*
Why is it when I speak of your great good fortune
you meet it with gloom and despair?
What more can you ask?
Your wise plan has triumphed!

Sea and shore are at peace. The sea
welcomes your rapid ships from shore,
and standing here at your palace
you can say with pride that all the world
is encompassed by your arms' embrace.

And where else did it start but here?
The first rude hut,
a tiny scratch of a ditch to the sea,
where today your oars splash lustily in the waves.
Your noble purpose and the industry of your men
have won the rewards of earth and sea.
Standing here—

FAUST:
Yes, and it's that *here,*
that *here* that so oppresses me!
I confess it to you, you who are so wise
in the ways of the world,
it cuts me to the very heart,
to my heart's core,
making it impossible to bear!
And how it shames me to say it!
They, up there, the old couple,
they'll have to go. I want those lindens,
want them for myself, to sit under.
Those trees, those few trees,
those trees that are not my trees,
destroy it all,
my worldwide possessions.
In those trees I want to build platforms,
great platforms from branch to branch,
a place to stand and see the totality
of all that I have accomplished, to survey
at one glance this masterpiece
of the human mind that raises from the sea
new land for humans to live on.

This is the bitterest torment of all,
to suffer for the little one doesn't own.

The ringing bell,
the scent of the lindens,
oppresses me with the feeling of church or the tomb.
The freedom of my will is laid waste in that sand.
How do I free my soul of this weight?
The bell tolls, while I go mad.

MEPHISTOPHELES:

Yes, well, what can one expect?
Life is always soured by something or other.
That infernal jingle-jangle would distress anyone,
clouding the evening sky,
blighting everything between baptism and burial,
as if between a ding and a dong
life were no more than an idle dream.

FAUST:

That couple's perverse obstinacy
mars all my glorious profit. To my pain
I grow weary of being just.

MEPHISTOPHELES:

Then why all these scruples?
Shouldn't you have relocated them long ago?

FAUST:

All right, then, get them out of my sight!
You know the pleasant little property
I'd set aside for them.

MEPHISTOPHELES:

First we pick them up,
then set them down.
And before you know it,
they're on their feet again.
Once they've seen the lovely little place,
they won't mind the violence it cost them.

(He whistles shrilly. Enter the THREE VIOLENT GIANTS.)

MEPHISTOPHELES:
>   You heard the Master! Get to work!
>   Tomorrow there's a seamen's festival!

THE THREE VIOLENT GIANTS:
>   The old man welcomed us like animals.
>   A he-man's fest might set it right.

MEPHISTOPHELES: *(To the audience.)*
>   So here we have it once again;
>   it was Naboth's vineyard then.

XLIX ∽ DEEP NIGHT

LYNCEUS: *(On the watchtower, singing.)*
>   Begotten to see,
>   To watch day and night,
>   Sworn to my tower,
>   The world's my delight.
>
>   I scan the far distance,
>   I note what is near,
>   The moon and the stars,
>   The forests, the deer.
>
>   Thus beauty eternal
>   I see all around,
>   I'm glad to be praising
>   The joy I have found.
>
>   O fortunate eyes,
>   Whatever you've seen,
>   Whatever its outcome,
>   How lovely it's been.

(Pause. Speaks.)

It's not alone for enjoyment I'm posted here.

What horror threatens me
from the world grown dark!
I see flashes of sparks
exploding among the dark lindens;
fire raging, fanned by the whipping breeze;
the moss-covered cottage burning inside!
I see no help in sight, no rescue!

Ah, that dear old couple,
always so careful with fire,
victims now of the smoky blaze.
What a disaster!
The house's mossy frame stands
black against the crimson flames.
Oh, if only they've escaped,
those dear, good people,
from that raging inferno.
Tongues of flame lick upward
through leaves and boughs,
dry branches catch fire and as they burn
break off and crash to earth.

Why,
why must I have eyes to see this?
Why so farsighted?

There, the chapel,
collapsing under falling branches!
Great swirls of pointed flames rage in the treetops,
and down to their roots the hollow trunks glow crimson.

(Long pause. Sings.)

> What was once so dear a sight
> Now is swallowed up in night.

FAUST: *(On the balcony, facing the dunes.)*
    What is that wailing dirge I hear?
    Too late, too late.

My watchman grieves,
and my inmost soul is
vexed by this impatient deed.
But no matter.
The linden grove may be reduced to
dismal half-charred trunks,
but a lookout can soon be built,
affording me a view into infinity.
And I see, too, the old couple
settled in their new surroundings,
that ancient pair who,
grateful for the mercy shown them,
will there live out their final days.

MEPHISTOPHELES *and* THE THREE: *(Appear below.)*
Here we are back, sir, on the double.
Excuse us if it didn't go quite as planned.
We rapped, we knocked at the door,
no one answered.
We rattled it then and started banging,
and the rotted old door caved in.
We yelled at them, threatened,
and got no answer. They didn't hear,
didn't want to hear.
But that's the way these things happen.
We wasted no time and
got them out any way we could.

They didn't suffer much, the old couple.
They died of shock.
A stranger who'd taken cover there
wanted to fight us, but we soon finished him off.
In the brief course of our wild struggle
coals got scattered and fired some straw.
It's all a big blaze now,
a funeral pyre for those three.

FAUST:
Were you deaf to my words?

I wanted exchange, not robbery!
I curse this wild, this heedless deed!
Share it among you!

THE THREE VIOLENT GIANTS: *(In chorus.)*
                    The ancient warning still makes sense:
                    "Bow willingly to violence!"
                    But if you're brave and make resistance,
                    Risk house and home and—your existence.

FAUST: *(On the balcony.)*
    The stars hide their light.
    The fire's dying,
    except for a chill breeze that fans it,
    bringing the smoke and stench to me.
    Too quickly ordered, too quickly done!

    What are these shadowy shapes approaching?

XLX ✒ MIDNIGHT

Enter FOUR GRAY WOMEN.

FIRST WOMAN:
    My name is Want.

SECOND WOMAN:
    My name is Debt.

THIRD WOMAN:
    My name is Care.

FOURTH WOMAN:
    My name is Need.

WANT, DEBT, NEED: *(Together.)*
    The door is locked,
    we can't get in.

A rich man lives here,
and we don't want to.

WANT:

This makes me a shadow.

DEBT:

This makes me a nothing.

NEED:

They pay me no heed;
there's nothing they need.

CARE:

Sisters, you cannot and may not enter.
But here, through this keyhole,
Care will creep in.

(CARE disappears.)

WANT:

Come, gray sisters, away from here!

DEBT:

I'm with you, sister, close at your side.

NEED:

And I at your heels, near as breath.

WANT, DEBT, NEED: *(Together.)*
Clouds scurry by,
stars disappear,
and there, over there!
From afar, from afar!
Our brother is come!
He's here!
Brother Death!

(Exeunt.)

FAUST: *(In the palace.)*
Four of them came, three have left.
I made no sense of what they said.
Some echoing word like "breath,"
and then a rhyme sounding like "death."
A dismal word.
Hollow, muffled, a sigh so ghostly.

Ah,
why have I not won my way to freedom?
Why?
Into the open?
To Nature?
Why?
Not stripped myself of magic,
unlearned all incantations?
Forever!
And stand before you, Nature—
a man —

only a man!

Then, ah, then
it would be worthwhile to be human.

I was that once,
before I plumbed the depths of darkness,
damning the world and myself with evil blasphemies,
the world that is now so thronged with phantoms and
specters that there is no escape.

Daylight may be sweet,
hours of sun and sanity;
and then night comes and trammels us
in a net of dreams.
Home we wend from a happy springtime
romp in the fields,
and a bird croaks.
And what does it croak?

Some evil thing.
Superstitions hem us day and night,
always something ominous,
a hint, a foreboding, a warning.
And so, we stand there, terrified,
alone.
The door creaks, and no one enters.

(*Profoundly shaken.*)

Is someone there?

CARE:
The question demands a yes.

FAUST:
And you, who are you?

CARE:
It's enough that I'm here.

FAUST:
Leave this place!

CARE:
It's where I belong.

FAUST: (*Angry at first, then calmer; to himself.*)
Be on your guard, Faustus,
no more magic.

CARE:
Refuse to listen, Faustus,
and you'll hear me resound like
thunder in your heart.
I take many forms,
and my power is great.
A fierce companion by land or sea,
never looked for, always found,

cursed in one breath, flattered in the next.
Dare to say, Faustus, you've never known me.

FAUST:

I've spent my life chasing through the world,
grabbing at will by the hair all I longed for;
what didn't please, I let go its way,
what eluded me, I let escape.
My life was desire and satisfaction,
and then again desire—
and with power and might in my grip
I stormed through life;
great and mighty at first,
but now more wisely,
now more prudently.

I know this world well, and I know, too,
that the view into the world beyond is blocked;
and only a fool turns his sheep's eyes heavenward,
imagining men like himself above the clouds!

Why go floating off into eternity?
Let him stand on firm earth,
let him look around him:
earth has much to offer the man of worth.
What his mind can grasp, that can be his.
When he walks, let him walk with his feet on the ground.
And if spirits haunt him, ignore them,
keep walking, walking, expecting in his path
both pain and pleasure,
never once in all his earthly progress
to know satisfaction.

CARE:

Once in my grip,
the world to a man becomes nothing.
A drear cloud settles,
the sun neither rises nor sets,
a darkness fills his soul, and all his

treasure gives him no pleasure.
Sadness, gladness are a whim,
he starves amidst his plenty,
and pain and rapture are both postponed,
for only the future has his interest,
and nothing is ever accomplished.

FAUST:
　　Stop!
　　You'll never get to me that way!
　　I won't hear such nonsense!
　　Leave here!
　　This litany of yours
　　might deceive the wisest of men!
　　It won't deceive me!

CARE:
　　Shall he go? Shall he come?
　　He simply can't make up his mind.
　　Midway in the beaten path
　　he gropes and staggers, step at a time,
　　growing ever more confused,
　　sees the world about him whirling,
　　a burden to himself and others,
　　who, breathing, takes a breath and smothers;
　　no, not smothers, not quite dead yet.
　　Never yielding nor despairing,
　　he rolls on down his endless incline,
　　resigning everything delightful,
　　doing what he deathly hates,
　　sleeping badly, badly waking,
　　pinned to the spot that makes him ready
　　to suffer eternal hellish perdition.

FAUST:
　　Cursed specters!
　　This is how you've treated the human race
　　time out of mind! Even indifferent days
　　you turn into tangles of ensnaring torment!

How well I know that demons are hard to be rid of,
that the spirit bond cannot to be broken!
And yet, oh, Care,
I will not acknowledge your power,
your insidious power!

CARE:

Then feel it now in my parting curse!
Mankind is blind from birth;
you, Faustus, are blind now at your last!

(She breathes on him. Exit.)

FAUST: *(Blinded.)*

Night closes in now, deeper, darker,
yet in my heart's core a light shines clearly.
I must hurry,
must complete what I have planned!
Only the Master's word has any weight here.

Up! Up from your beds!
Servants, workers!
Every man!
Give final form now to my boldest thoughts!
Take up your shovels, your spades, your picks!
What is only planned must now be realized!
The work staked out must be completed with speed.
Strict order and swift diligence
will bear the fairest rewards.
To realize so vast a design
one mind is worth a thousand hands.

XLXI ⚘ GREAT FORECOURT OF THE PALACE

Torches.
MEPHISTOPHELES as overseer leading a gang of LEMURS.

MEPHISTOPHELES:

Hurry! This way! This way! Come on!

Come on, you shambling gaggle of
misbegotten, half-alive lemurs!

LEMURS: *(In chorus.)*

> Here we are at your command;
> We've half heard why we came. It
> Is all about a stretch of land,
> And we are here to claim it.
>
> Stakes sharp pointed we have here,
> Long chains to measure sections.
> But why you called us, sir, we fear,
> Has fled our recollections.

MEPHISTOPHELES:
This job will need no artist.
Use yourselves as measuring rods.
The tallest of you stretch out on the grass,
the rest mark out his shape, then
dig a hole,
long and deep,
the same as was done for our forebears.
From palace to narrow abode;
it always arrives at the same stupid ending.

LEMURS: *(Digging away with mocking gestures.)*

> In youth when I did live, did love,
> I thought it very sweet;
> Where mirth was free, and jollity,
> That place for me was meet.
>
> But old Age with his stealing steps
> Clawed me with his crutch.
> I stumbled, tumbled in the grave
> Why must they open such?

(Enter FAUST from the palace, groping along the doorposts.)

FAUST:

    Ah, how this clattering of spades delights me!
    These gangs of men laboring for me here;
    reconciling earth with earth,
    setting boundaries to the waves,
    confining the sea's vast power!

MEPHISTOPHELES: *(Aside, to the audience.)*

    And yet, who else have you toiled for but *us,*
    with your dams and dikes, preparing a grand feast
    for sea devil Neptune's pleasure?
    Mankind hasn't a chance, do what it will.
    It's with us the elements are in league.
    Annihilation is the law of Nature.

FAUST:

    Overseer!

MEPHISTOPHELES:

    Here!

FAUST:

    Use every means,
    great gangs of men are needed,
    do anything, persuade them,
    pay them, treat them well,
    drive them, use force, anything,
    but I want daily a full report
    on the progress of the ditch I've begun.

MEPHISTOPHELES: *(In an undertone.)*

    According to my report,
    it's a grave has been ordered.

FAUST:

    There is a marsh skirting the foot of those mountains
    that poisons with its pestilence all I've accomplished.
    If I could drain that pool, my final deed
    would also be my greatest, for I would then

be opening land for millions to inhabit.
Not in total security, of course,
but safe enough, a life of free activity.

I see endless fields, vast and fruitful,
where man and beast alike will flock to live,
contented and at peace on the new-made land,
protected by the massive sheltering barrier
raised by the labor of a bold and fearless people.
Life in this interior will be a paradise,
while outside the sea may rage to the crest
of the mighty dam. And when the waters gnaw
and threaten to rush in through the masons' work,
the people as one will rise to close the breach.

Yes!
To this philosophy I am wholly given,
wisdom can reach no further: He alone
is worthy of life and freedom who has to win them
by conquest every day. And so, ringed round
with danger, young and old will live a life
dedicated to vigorous activity.

Such a lusty throng I long to see,
and stand on free ground with a people free!
If this were so, I might say to the passing moment:
"Linger awhile, you are so fair!"
The traces of my days on earth can never—
no, not in eons—pass away.
In expectation of that highest bliss,
I now enjoy my greatest moment—this!

(FAUST sinks back, the LEMURS seize him and lay him on the
ground.)

MEPHISTOPHELES:
Pleasure never satisfied this man,
no bliss contented him,
and so he went on whoring after shifting forms.

And it was to this,
this final, miserable, meaningless moment,
this pathetic creature chose to cling to.
This man who stood against and opposed me so mightily
is conquered now by time.
There he lies—the old man.
The clock stands still.

LEMURS: *(In chorus.)*
Stands still!
Like midnight—
silent—still.
The hand drops down.

MEPHISTOPHELES:
Drops down.
It is fulfilled.

LEMURS:
It is past.

MEPHISTOPHELES:
Past! A stupid word! Why past?
Past and sheer nothingness —
one and the same!
What use is endless creation,
only to be dragged back into nothingness?
"It is past!"
What does it mean?
No more than if it had never been.
And yet it makes its rounds as if it were something.
Eternal Emptiness is all my longing.

XLXII ✒ INTERMENT

LEMUR: *(Solo.)*

> Who has built this house so vilely,
> With shovel, pick, and spade?

LEMUR CHORUS:

> For you, dull guest, in hempen vest,
> This house was too well made.

LEMUR: *(Solo.)*

> Who was it decked the hall so badly?
> Chairs, tables, are there any?

LEMUR CHORUS:

> It was loaned, not to be owned;
> The creditors are many.

MEPHISTOPHELES:

> There lies the corpse.
> If it tries to flee I'll simply whip out
> the blood-signed document.
> Ah, but you never know.
> There are many ways of outwitting the Devil.
> They'd steal a soul right from under my nose.
> Our old ways are passé,
> the new ones haven't caught on yet;
> besides,
> in the old days I'd have done this solo,
> today I need accomplices.
>
> This isn't the best of times for devils.
> Tradition, custom, ancient privileges,
> gone with the wind!
> What can you trust these days?
> Time was, when a man breathed his last,
> swoosh!
> out slipped the soul like a mouse on the run,
> and I like any old self-respecting feline

would snatch it up in my claws.
These days, though, it tends to hang around—
the soul—
takes its time, malingering in that
dismal, gloomy carcass.
But out it comes in time,
forced by the battling elements
into ignominious retreat.

While I wait, I plague myself with
when, how, and *where* it will appear.
Death, it seems, has grown a bit weary.
Sometimes it's actually a question of
will it or won't it?
Many a time I've looked down greedily
at limbs grown rigid with rigor mortis;
and what a farce that was!
for the thing began to twitch and stir and rise.

(He executes fantastic gestures of conjuration.)

Hear me, devils!
Up! Come! Up!
On the double!
You of the straight and
you of the crooked horns!
Devils of ancient stock, tried and true!
Up! Come up!
And with you bring the gaping maw of Hell Mouth!
Hell-of-many-jaws devours its victims
in proper rank and order!
But let's not stand on precedent,
not even in this final game of parting.

(A grotesque Hell Mouth opens on the left.)

Already tusks appear, tusks are bared,
the vaulted gullet yawns, spews flames,
a raging sea of fury! And there

in the dismal murk of the awful cavern
I see the Infernal City in eternal glow!
The red surf surges forward to the teeth,
the souls of the damned swim frantically to reach it,
desperate for escape,
only to be mauled by colossal hyena jaws,
and begin again their scalding backward plunge.

Much more there is to see in nooks and crannies,
so much unequalled terror in so small space.
You do well to frighten the hearts of sinners;
and yet—
to them it's all a dream, a lie, a fake.

(To the fat DEVILS with short, straight horns.)

All right, you paunchy rascals with cheeks of fire,
so filled with sulfurous fumes you fairly glow,
you stumplike, no-necked clods,
keep a sharp lookout here on this body
for glint of phosphorous!
That will be winged Psyche,
his petty soul.
Beware, don't pluck her wings,
she turns a hideous worm!
Once I have her I'll stamp her with my own seal,
and off with her to the firestorm!

Your duty, my bloat-bellied friends,
is to mount a guard at his nether regions.
Where the soul takes her stand isn't certain.
The navel perhaps,
though it might be where he farts,
a favored orifice. So keep a sharp eye,
don't let it slip out.

(To the skinny DEVILS with long, crooked horns.)

And you, you flailing, gangly buffoons,
keep your arms astir over the body,
so if it escapes you'll catch it in your claws.
I suspect it's growing tired of its old quarters,
and spirits always seek the upward path.

(A glory is lowered from above right in a burst of light.)

THE HEAVENLY HOST:

Kin to the blest above,
Envoys of heavenly love,
Follow in flight:
Sinners forgiving
Bounteous giving
To all things living,
A trace of delight!

MEPHISTOPHELES:

Ah!
These jarring, jangling discords!
Sounds, terrible, falling from the sky,
unwelcome, ah!
unwelcome as that hated light!
Androgynous bungling!
Boyish-girlish pranks that
only the godly can abide!
You know how in the depths of black depravity
we planned the annihilation of the human race?
Well, in creating the gravest of all sins,
we found that they were *welcome* in *their* worship.

Hypocrites! Mincing milksops!
They rob our prey using our own weapons!
Devils, they're devils, too, the same as us!
Ah, but disguised!
If they get the better of you,
you never live it down!
Stand fast at the grave!
Hold it against all odds!

CHORUS OF ANGELS: *(Strewing roses.)*

> Roses, you glowing ones,
> Balsam-bestowing ones,
> Fluttering, quivering,
> Sweetness delivering,
> Blossom half-opening,
> Branching unblightedly,
> Budding delightedly,
> Scatter around you Spring,
> Purple and green.
> Take him to Paradise,
> This sleeper serene!

MEPHISTOPHELES: *(To the SATANS.)*

> What's all this?
> This dodging and ducking?
> Is that what they taught you in Hell?
> Stand fast,
> let them strew till they're blue in the face!
> To your posts, you idiots!
> They're trying to snow-in flaming-hot devils
> with their fluttery flurry of flowers,
> but you have only to breathe
> and it melts and shrivels!
> Blow now, you blowhards!
> Puffers and snorters, blow!
>
> Stop! Enough! Enough!
> Your foul breath is blighting the whole swarm!
> Not so hard!
> Muzzle your mouths, harness your noses!
> You've overblown those roses.
> Show moderation!
> They've not just wilted,
> they've browned, they've dried,
> they're *burning!*
> Pelting us now, they are,
> with shining, poisonous flames!

Protect yourselves!
Huddle close!
Stand fast!

Ah! Ah!
They've lost it, their valor!
Where's courage gone?
My devils scent a strange, voluptuous glow.

CHORUS OF ANGELS:
                    Flowers so beautiful,
                    Flames burning bright,
                    On hearts that are dutiful
                    Shed pure delight,
                    Love every way.
                    Words with pure truth that ring,
                    Clear as heavens opening,
                    To hosts immortal bring
                    Everywhere day.

MEPHISTOPHELES:
    Ah, the fools! The dolts!
    My Satans standing on their heads,
    the fat ones turning cartwheels head over heels and
    tumbling ass-first into Hell!
    Oh, and I hope it agrees with you!
    But I'm standing by my post, no matter what.

(Beating off the roses floating down around him.)

    Will-o'-the-wisps, away!
    Ah, you shine so brightly till I've caught you,
    and then you're a sticky mess
    Away, I say! Now!
    Ah, there's something like pitch and sulfur
    nipping at my neck!

CHORUS OF ANGELS:

> What is not meant for you,
> You must abjure it;
> What harms the heart of you,
> You must not endure it!
> And if it force its way,
> Fight it we must and may,
> Only the one who loves
> Will lead to Heaven's day.

MEPHISTOPHELES:

My head, my heart, my liver are afire!
Ah!
Crueler, crueler, worse than Hellfire,
this Love,
this Love,
this super-devilish element!
So this is why lovers moan when scorned by Love,
and crack their necks for one glimpse of the loved one!

As I, too, now!
Aiiiii!
As I do now!

What draws my head in that direction?
My mortal enemy!
Whose sight I abominated!
What is it, what, has pierced me through and through?
How lovely they appear to me now,
those lovely boys!
Why can't I curse them?
Ah!
It sticks in my craw!
Ah, once myself a fool for love,
who can ever be a fool again?
And yet I hate them, hate them—
but love them, too, those loveliest,
those tenderest of love-sweet boys!

Beautiful, ravishing children, tell me, please,
aren't you, too, kin to Great Lucifer?
You prettiest of the prettiest,
how I long to kiss you!
I think you're going to suit me very well!
How at ease I am, so natural around you,
as if I'd seen you a thousand times over.
The more I look, the lovelier you become,
and I more like a common rutting alley cat!
Come to me, come!
Come, just one look at you!
Only one!

THE ANGELS:
We're coming! You see?
Why shrink away so?
Closer, closer.
Stay if you can stand it.

(The ANGELS hovering about take up the entire stage.)

MEPHISTOPHELES: *(Pushed forward into the proscenium.)*
You call us spirits of the damned,
but what about you?
You're the real witch masters,
seducing men and women both!

Ah, what a blasted affair!
Love? Can this be it?
The stuff of love?
My body's so on fire, I almost feel no
burning pain in my neck!

You sway, you sashay, this way, that way.
Come down, why don't you,
come, and move those
lovely limbs a bit more profanely!
Oh, I know, I know,
this serious air becomes you,

but try, won't you,
a smile, just one, one smile,
one I'll never forget!
A lover's look, don't you know,
a little, very little twist of the mouth.

Oh, you long-legged beauty you,
it's you I like best! Except that clerical look;
it doesn't suit you.
Try something a soupçon more lascivious.
And you all could show a bit more flesh;
those long pleated robes, ah! are much too moral.

They're turning!
Ah, the rascals!
Ah!
A view from the rear!
From behind, ah,
they're far, far too delectable!

CHORUS OF ANGELS:

> Flames of love, hasten,
> Grow ever clearer;
> To the self-damned
> Bring holiness nearer,
> So that from evil
> They may be free,
> And in the Great Unity
> Transformed may be.

MEPHISTOPHELES: *(Pulling himself together.)*
What's happened to me?
All over me, boils,
boils head to foot, like Job!
I shudder at the sight!
And yet—
and yet I triumph, seeing through it all,
and put trust in myself and my family tree!
This Devil's noble parts are still intact.

That weird attack of sex ends in a rash,
those blasted flames are now burned out,
and so, as well I should,
I curse you each and every one!

CHORUS OF ANGELS:
> He whom the Light of
> Creation embraces
> Finds in salvation
> All of the graces.
> Singing great praises,
> Rise up to your goal;
> The air now is purified,
> Breathe now, blest soul!

(They rise into the air, bearing FAUST's immortal part.)

MEPHISTOPHELES: *(Looking about.)*
What's this, what's this?
Where have they moved off to?
That gang of juveniles caught me off my guard!
And off they fly to heaven with their booty!
That's it, yes, now I know,
that's why they kept nibbling away at the grave!
I've been robbed!
A great, a unique treasure, the noble soul
that pledged itself to me, has been
cunningly filched from under my very nose!

Where to lodge an appeal?
Where to find an ear to bend?
Restore to me what's rightly mine?

Ah, you old goat,
bested in your old age!
And you deserved it, too!
A fine pickle you've got yourself in, you have!
Mismanaged disgracefully!
All that waste of energy!

Shameless!
All gone!
All!
And all because of some vulgar, absurd little itch—
Love!—
that got the goat of this
case-hardened old sot of a Devil!

Here I stand,
this shrewd old all-knowing fiend,
confessing entrapment by some childish nonsense!

Well—
at least it was no small thing brought him to his knees!

XLXIII ⚮ MOUNTAIN GORGES

Forest, rocks, wilderness.
HOLY ANCHORITES have settled in clefts up and down the
mountainside.

CHORUS *and* ECHO:
> Swaying forests,
> beetling boulders,
> tree-roots clutching,
> tree trunks crowding,
> leaping brooks,
> wave upon wave,
> our caves give shelter;
> lions slip silently,
> honoring the hallowed ground,
> love's blessèd home.

PATER ECSTATICUS: *(Floating up and down.)*
> Bliss of immortal fire,
> radiant bond of love,
> seething heart's anguish,

love divine rising!
Arrows, come, pierce my flesh,
lances, come, master me,
bludgeons, come, batter me,
lightning, come, shatter me,
till all that is vanity
is purged away,
leaving the star to shine,
kernel of Love divine.

PATER PROFUNDUS: *(In the lower region.)*
Abyss rests on abyss at my feet;
a thousand rills join the great fall
to plunge below into foaming depths;
of its own urge the towering tree
rises high into pure air:
just as all-powerful Love
shapes and shields all things.

What a roaring tumult about me,
as if all Nature surged like the sea!
And yet it is only the wealth of waters
tumbling in love to the valley below;
the lightning blast has cleared the air
of poison and evil mist:
and all this done in love—

proclaiming the Creative Spirit
that ever wraps us round in glory!
May it light a holy flame
to stir my cold mind,
my dulled senses,
lost in anguish,
bound in chains of
doubt and torment!
God!
Bless me with your light!

PATER SERAPHICUS: *(In the middle region.)*
What is that wisp of
cloud in the pine trees?
Do I guess aright?
A host of infant souls?

CHOIR OF BLESSÈD BOYS:
Tell us, Father, where we're drifting,
good one, tell us who we are.
We're happy here.
Being is gentle.

PATER SERAPHICUS:

Innocents,
babes born at midnight,
mind and senses
barely roused,
lost at once to
grieving parents,
delightful gain to
angelic hosts!
You sense a loving soul here present.
Come, draw near,
obey your feeling,
you fortunate few to whom Earth's harshness
is spared, who bear no earthly traces.
Come, descend,
come into me,
enter my eyes and see the world,
use them as your own.
Do come.

(He takes them into himself.)

Those are trees.
And these are rocks.
And there a mighty stream flows downward,
shortening its steep descent.

THE BLESSÈD BOYS: *(From inside him.)*
> The sight is great,
> but earth's too gloomy,
> it moves us with dread,
> we tremble in fear.
> Good father,
> let us free from here.

PATER SERAPHICUS:
> Mount, rise up, to higher circles,
> grow invisibly as God's
> presence makes you ever stronger
> with eternal purity.
> This it is that feeds the spirit,
> this that fills ethereal space,
> love's eternal revelation,
> love that leads to pure salvation.

CHORUS OF BLESSÈD BOYS: *(Circling around the highest peaks.)*
> Join hands and sing!
> Join hands in a ring!
> Dance and sing your deepest feelings!
> Divinely schooled,
> be certain to see,
> Him that you love in eternity!

ANGELS: *(Hovering in the upper atmosphere, bearing FAUST's immortal part.)*
> Saved now, saved from Satan's power,
> this great soul rejoices.
> Who strives, and never ceases striving,
> is worthy of redemption.
> And if the love that reigns on high
> has shown him gracious favor,
> then angel hosts will sing his praise,
> and give him joyous welcome.

THE YOUNGER ANGELS:

Roses from the hands of women,
love-devoted penitents,
rosebuds of their love to scatter,
helped us gain this radiant gift,
brought our Great Work to fulfillment,
brought to us this noble prize.
Devils, evil, fled before us,
struck not with the pains of Hell,
but love's searing fire from Heaven,
accosted by the pangs of love.
Even Satan, Hell's great master,
felt the ravishing stings of love.
Praise the hallowed!
Hell is harrowed!

THE MORE PERFECT ANGELS:

To bear on high
this remnant of earth
is no small task.
Burned to ashes
it would not be pure.
When power of spirit
unites elementally,
no angel force can
wrest them asunder,
the two from the one.
Love, only love
eternal can part them.

THE YOUNGER ANGELS:

I see a mist,
a trailing cloud,
there at the peak,
and sense a spirit life
hovering near.
The cloud now brightens
and I see there before me
a circling host of

blessèd boys.
Joyously freed of
earth's heavy load,
they revel now
in the springtime beauty
of this loftier sphere.
Let us join him
with their company
to begin his growth
with them to perfection.

THE BLESSÈD BOYS:

Gladly we take up this
chrysalid entity,
for we achieve with this
angel identity.
Loosen the earthly flakes
clinging around him!
See, for he now awakes,
Heaven has crowned him!

DOCTOR MARIANUS: *(In the highest, purest cell.)*
The outlook here is free,
spirit raised high.
Women pass by me,
climbing the sky,
and in their midst,
serene,
star-crowned,
resplendent,
behold!
I see Heaven's Queen,
transcendent in glory!

(In ecstasy.)

Supreme Mistress of sky,
Mother of earth below,
in your bright azure vaulted,

show me, show, oh, show,
your mystery exalted!
Bless all that in man's heart
has fired emotions,
gentler, dearer,
and, with sacred love inspired,
draws it to you,
ever nearer!

Since your wish inspires our will,
what could daunt or curb it?
Bid us only to be still,
nothing could disturb it.
Virgin, pure from spot or taint,
Mother, holy, tender,
Queen, elect of us, and saint,
throned with God in splendor!

Light clouds entwine
about her face—
penitent women,
hovering in space,
kneeling to render
lowly contrition,
entreating remission
of sins from her grace.

Spotless maiden,
undisturbed
in your matchless glory,
these penitent women,
led astray,
may bring to you
their story.

Those whom frailty has bound
are hard to save, or never;
what soul can break the bonds of sin
by only his endeavor?

How swiftly then the foot that slips
slides to its destruction.
Fervent glances, flattering lips,
lead to heart's seduction.

(The MATER GLORIOSA soars into view.)

CHORUS OF PENITENT WOMEN:
You who rise soaring
to regions eternal,
hear our imploring,
great vision supernal,
you without rival,
give us your grace!

MAGNA PECCATRIX:

By my love that
bent in weeping
over your son,
divinely born,
wetting His feet with
tears of balsam
despite all Pharisaic scorn;
by that jar that
poured in reverence
precious ointment
so profusely,
by my hair that
dried those sacred
limbs, that fell
around them loosely—

MULIER SAMARITANA:

By that well,
that ancient station
where Father Abram's
flocks were led;
by the pail that
wet the parched lips

of the Holy Savior dread;
by the full, clear
source that ever
lends itself,
forever spending,
outward flowing to
all the nations,
watering all
realms unending—

MARIA AEGYPTIACA:

By that holy
garden where they
lay the Blessèd
Lord Immortal;
by the arm that
barred my way
through the holy
church's portal;
by my forty
years' repentance
in a searing
desert land;
by my blest and
parting sentence
written on the
burning sand—

ALL THREE:

You who never
turn your face
from any sinner
however great,
who raise us up in
our repentance
and lead us in through
Heaven's gate,
have mercy on this
one who only

once forgot
herself in pleasure,
grant her all your
graces, Lady,
give her pardon
in her measure.

ONE OF THE PENITENTS: *(Formerly named Gretchen; nestling close.)*
Incline, incline,
your face divine,
sweet Mother, and shine
benignly on me!
My early lover,
his troubles over,
returns to me,
is mine!

THE BLESSÈD BOYS: *(Approaching in circular formation.)*
Already above us
he towers in might;
us for our tendance
he will require.
We soon were withdrawn
from life's busy choir;
he will instruct us who
lived through life's fire.

THE SINGLE PENITENT: *(Formerly named Gretchen.)*
By these noble
choirs surrounded
this soul newborn here
barely knows,
scarcely senses his
life newfounded,
and how like us
he quickly grows.
Behold him shed his
earthly leaven,
see him cast his

hull at length,
clad in the airy
garb of Heaven,
and show himself
in youthful strength.
Kind Lady, allow me
to instruct him,
blinded still
by the dawning day.

MATER GLORIOSA:

Then soar to higher spheres! Conduct him!
Sensing you, he'll know the way.

DOCTOR MARIANUS: *(Prostrate in adoration.)*

Penitents, look up and see
Her fair redeeming face,
Regenerating you and me
With her kind saving grace!
Let every noble mind be seen
Serving you alone,
Virgin, Mother, Heaven's Queen,
Goddess on your throne!

CHORUS MYSTICUS:

All things destructible
Are but a parable;
All things ineluctable,
The undeclarable,
Here they are seen,
Here they are action;
The Eternal-Feminine
Leads to perfection.

❦

GLOSSARY OF
CLASSICAL REFERENCES

ACHILLES: son of the sea goddess Thetis and the mortal Peleus; greatest of the Greek heroes of the Trojan War; central figure in Homer's *Iliad;* in one version of his myth he becomes the lover of Helen of Troy following their death.

AESCULAPIUS: semi-divine son of Apollo by a mortal woman; placed in the charge of the centaur Chiron for his education; worshipped as the founder of medicine and the god of healing.

ANAXAGORAS: Ionian philosopher of the fifth century B.C.E.; Goethe appoints to him the theory that fire is the formative principle of the material world.

ANTAEUS: son of Poseidon and the earth goddess Gaia, from whom he derives his strength; only by holding him from touching the ground could Hercules defeat him.

APHRODITE: goddess of sexual love and desire; Greek equivalent of the Roman Venus; in later mythology the mother of Eros.

APOLLO: son of Zeus and the earth goddess Leto; the second in importance among the Olympian gods after Zeus; associated with order, beauty, prophecy, medicine, archery, music, art; his central place is Delphi where his seat of prophecy is situated.

ARCADIA: mountainous region in the central Peloponnese; associated with Hermes and Pan; became the ideal literary setting for pastoral poetry.

ARES: Greek god of war.

ARGONAUTS: legendary Greek heroes sailed to Colchis in the ship Argo to rescue the Golden Fleece.

ATHENA: daughter of Zeus who was born fully armed from his head; legendary protector of Athens; associated with wisdom and warfare.

ATLAS: one of the Titans, a race that warred against Zeus; when defeated his punishment was to support the globe of the world on his shoulders.

BACCHUS: see Dionysus.

BAUCIS: a poor peasant who, along with her husband Philemon, offered hospitality to Zeus and Hermes traveling incognito; a legendary icon of selfless hospitality.

BOREADS: winged sons of Boreas, the god of the north wind.

CABIRI: ancient pre-Hellenic deities; subject of a little-known mystery cult; portrayed as not fully developed young boys desirous of total development; protectors of sailors from stormy seas.

CHAOS: the cosmic void that preceded all; sometimes said to be the progenitor of the first gods.

CHIRON: divine son of Zeus in the form of a horse and the sea goddess Philyra; the original centaur, half man, half horse; wise, kind, and the educator of Apollo in medicine, prophecy, and the arts; tutor of Achilles, Aesculapius, Jason, among many others.

CIRCE: daughter of the sun god; an evil enchantress who lured men to her island and turned them into animals; only Odysseus/Ulysses defeated her.

CYCLOPES: race of giants with a large single eye in the forehead; also known as the forgers of Zeus's thunderbolts and the builders of the fortifying walls of ancient cities.

DELOS: small Aegean island said to be the birthplace of Apollo and his sister Artemis, the children of Zeus and the earth goddess Leto; it rose from the sea to allow for the birth of the twin gods when all other places refused them at the order of Zeus's jealous wife Hera.

DIANA: Roman name of Artemis, the daughter of Zeus and Leto; goddess of the hunt, but also of the moon in the form of Luna.

DIONYSUS: son of Zeus and the Theban mortal Semele; associated with a primitive Greek (or perhaps non-Greek) mystery cult; god of wine, inebriation, and sexual ecstasy; leader of promiscuous fauns, satyrs, bacchants, who, in the orgiastic celebration of the god, tear and devour the raw flesh of the goat, an animal sacred to Dionysus; also known as the Roman Bacchus.

DORIDS: daughters of the sea god Nereus; sisters of the Nereids.

DRYAD: a nymph living in a tree; wood nymph.

ELEUSIS: town on the western coast of Greece, northwest of Athens; site of a religious mystery cult.

EMPUSA: monster with donkey's feet; capable of changing shapes; lascivious.

ENDYMION: young beloved of Luna the moon goddess.

ERICHTHO: Thessalian sorceress; blood-sucking monster; prophetess; raiser of the dead.

EROS: originally one of the first gods to emerge from the original Chaos; the original life force; later the personification of sexual desire.

EUPHORION: in Greek mythology the son of Achilles and Helen after their union in death; represents fertility of his native soil.

FATES: goddesses of destiny; three wizened women who spin the thread of life; the Norns of Nordic mythology.

FAUNS: see Satyrs.

GALATEA: sea nymph; favorite daughter of sea god Nereus.

GRACES: goddesses of beauty and charm.

GRIFFIN: monster with the body of a lion and the head and wings of an eagle; guarders of gold.

HADES: god of the underworld; brother of Zeus and Poseidon; abducted and married Persephone; also known as Pluto.

HEBE: daughter of Zeus; goddess of eternal youth; marries Hercules upon his arrival on Olympus.

HELEN: daughter of Zeus and the mortal Leda; Zeus in the form of a swan impregnated Leda who laid the egg from which Helen was born; the most beautiful of women; wife of Menelaus; abducted by Paris; her abduction the cause of the Trojan War.

HELIOS: sun-god; also known in later legend as Apollo.

HERCULES: son of Zeus and the mortal woman Alcmena; most famous of the Greek heroes; legendary for his strength; performed twelve famous labors inflicted by a jealous Hera; finally worshipped as a god on Olympus.

HERMAPHRODITE: son of Hermes and Aphrodite; body becomes joined with that of a nymph; having the physical characteristics of both sexes.

HERMES: son of Zeus and the goddess Maia; served as messenger of the gods and as guide of the dead to the underworld; associated with merchants, thieves; known for cleverness and trickster exploits.

HOURS: goddesses who represented the seasons and other fixed periods of the cycle of nature.

ICARUS: son of the legendary craftsman Daedalus; flew on wings of feather and wax made by his father. Flying too close to the sun, which melted the wax, he fell into the sea.

JASON: one of the Argonauts; with others of the Argonauts rescues the Golden Fleece; husband of Medea who, when he marries the daughter of Creon of Corinth, murders his children in revenge.

JUNO: wife of Jupiter; the Roman equivalent of Hera.

JUPITER: the Roman equivalent of Zeus.

LAMIAE: female monsters who ate human flesh and blood; assumed seductive shape to lure their victims.

LEDA: see Helen.

LEMURS: restless ghosts of the dead.

LERNAEAN HYDRA: monstrous water serpent with many heads, which when cut off multiplied; killed in the swamp at Lerna by Hercules.

LETHE: one of the rivers of the underworld; when drunk by the dead it extinguishes the memory of earthly life.

LETO: goddess loved by Zeus; the mother with Zeus of Apollo and Artemis/Diana.

LUNA: moon goddess; loved a beautiful youth named Endymion and descended to him as he slept in a cave.

LYNCEUS: a hero of the Argonaut expedition; known for keen sight; name derived from Greek word for lynx.

MAIA: goddess daughter of Atlas; mother of Hermes with Zeus.

MANTO: a prophetess or sibyl; daughter in Greek mythology of the blind prophet Teiresias; transformed by Goethe into the daughter of Aesculapius, the god of healing.

MARSI: see Psylli.

MENELAUS: brother of Agamemnon; husband of Helen who was abducted by the Trojan Paris and became the cause of the Trojan War.

MUSES: goddesses who serve as the inspiration of music, poetry, and other intellectual pursuits.

NEPTUNE: god of the sea; brother of Zeus and Hades; controller of elemental forces such as earthquakes and storms at sea; Roman equivalent of the Greek Poseidon.

NEREIDS: sea nymphs; daughters of Nereus.

NEREUS: ancient sea god; possibly older than Poseidon in the role; prophetic and warned Paris of the disaster of abducting Helen.

ODYSSEUS: hero of Homer's *Odyssey;* also appears in the *Iliad;* victim of the Sirens who stops his ears with wax and has himself tied to the ship mast in order not to be lured to his death by their song.

OEDIPUS: son of Laius and Jocasta; exposed as an infant on a mountainside by his parents because of a prophecy that predicted he would kill his father and marry his mother; raised by foster parents the king and queen of Corinth; returns, unknown, as a young man to Thebes and is rewarded with the kingship for having rid the city of the plague of the Sphinx; in the course of his journey to Thebes, he unwittingly kills his father and later is wed to his mother upon becoming king of Thebes.

OLYMPUS: the highest mountain in Greece; seat of the Olympian gods.

OPS: see Rhea.

OREAD: mountain nymph.

ORPHEUS: legendary inventor of poetry; possibly one of the Argonauts; his song was capable of moving animals, trees, and rocks; descends into Hades to rescue his wife, Eurydice, is given permission if he leads her without looking back at her until reaching the surface of earth; he fails the test and she returns to Hades.

PAN: god of woodlands, forests, and pastures; symbol for the fertility of herds and flocks; face, torso, and arms of a man, with the legs, horns, and ears of a goat; symbol of the wild phallic potency of life and nature; lusty pursuer of nymphs; inspirer of sudden "panic" fear.

PAPHOS: site on Cyprus at which Aphrodite, born of the sea, first came to land.

PARIS: son of Priam and Hecuba, king and queen of Troy; prophecy said he would bring about the destruction and end of Troy; exposed as baby on mountain to be devoured by animals; survives, judges the beauty contest between Aphrodite, Hera, and Athena and receives Helen as his reward for judging Aphrodite the winner; abductor of Helen from Sparta and cause of the Trojan War.

PARNASSUS: vast mountain that towers over Delphi, the site of Apollo's oracle; also, in winter months, the dwelling place of Dionysus.

PELION: two gigantic mountains southeast of Olympus.

PELOPS: descendent of Zeus who came to rule the southern peninsula of Greece known as the Peloponnese.

PENEIOS: the main river of Thessaly in northeastern Greece; eventually empties into the Aegean.

PERSEPHONE: daughter of the earth goddess Demeter; abducted by Pluto to the underworld where she was made queen; allowed to return to the earth for a certain term each year.

PERSEUS: slayer of the Gorgon Medusa.

PHERAE: city in Thessaly ruled by Admetus whose wife Alcestis sacrificed her life for her husband's.

PHILEMON: See Baucis.

PHILYRA: ocean nymph and mother of Chiron

PHOEBUS: alternate name for Apollo that means bright, shining.

PLUTO: see Hades.

PLUTUS: god of wealth.

POSEIDON: see Neptune.

PROTEUS: a minor sea god endowed by Neptune with prophecy; capable of transforming into many shapes.

PSYCHE: personification of the human soul; represented with a human body and butterfly wings.

PSYLLI: along with Marsi, ancient peoples from Libya and central Italy respectively; changed by Goethe to be from Cyprus and be guardians of the goddess Galatea.

RHEA: sister and wife of Cronus and mother by him of Zeus and the other Olympian gods.

RHODES: island in the southeastern Aegean specially favored by Apollo as sun god.

SAMOTHRACE: island in the northern Aegean associated by the mystery cult of the Cabiri.

SATYRS: reveling followers of Dionysus; part human, part animal; symbols of the wild and uninhibited life of nature; known to the Romans as fauns.

SEISMOS: personification by Goethe of earthquake and volcanic forces.

SIBYL: name for ancient world prophetesses.

SILENUS: forest god and nature spirit who, like Pan, is both animal and human; represented as an old man usually drunk but always wise.

SIRENS: female demons whose singing lures seafarers to destruction; half women, half birds.

SPARTA: city in the southern Peloponnese ruled, when Helen was abducted, by her husband Menelaus; became an important military state and the archenemy of Athens.

SPHINX: monster of Egyptian mythology; a winged lion with the head of a woman.

STYMPHALIDS: monstrous birds from the forest surrounding the Arcadian Lake Strymphalus; their destruction was one of Hercules' twelve labors.

TELCHINES: legendary inhabitants of Rhodes; possessed of magical powers; skilled metal workers.

THALES: traditionally the first of the Greek philosophers; taught that all things are modifications of one substance, which he believed to be water.

THERSITES: in Homer's *Iliad* a repulsive, low-born Greek who with his cynicism abuses the Greek heroes of the Trojan War.

THESSALY: in myth the area overrun with sorcerers and witches who could predict the future and lure the moon down to earth from its course.

THETIS: sea nymph daughter of the sea god Nereus; married Peleus, a mortal; mother with him of Achilles.

TITANS: original generation of gods; offspring of Sky (Uranus) and Earth (Gaia); Cronus, the youngest, overthrew and castrated Uranus, married his sister Rhea, with whom he generated Zeus and his siblings, who in turn overthrew him and became the Olympian gods.

TRITONS: Sons of sea god Poseidon; human above, fish below.

TROY: ancient city in northwest Asia Minor; also known as Ilium.

TWINS: Castor and Pollux; twin sons of Leda by Zeus in the form of a swan; known also as the astrological Gemini.

VENUS: see Aphrodite.

ZEUS: supreme god of the Olympian pantheon; son of Cronus and Rhea; brother and husband of Rhea; brother of Poseidon and Hades.

ZOILUS: fourth-century philosopher and rhetorician of the Cynic school of thought; known for his bitter attacks on men of genius, even Homer; combined by Goethe with Thersites (Zoïlo-Thersites) as a disguise for the frequently cynical Mephistopheles.

SELECTED BIBLIOGRAPHY

Atkins, Stuart. *Goethe's Faust: A Literary Analysis.* Cambridge, Mass., 1958.

Butler, E. M. *The Myth of the Magus.* Cambridge, 1948.

———. *The Fortunes of Faust.* Cambridge, 1952.

Dieckmann, Liselotte. *Goethe's Faust: A Critical Reading.* Landmarks in Literature. Englewood Cliffs, N.J., 1972.

Fairley, Barker. *Goethe's Faust: Six Essays.* Oxford, 1953; reprinted 1965.

Gillies, Alexander. *Goethe's Faust: an Interpretation.* Oxford, 1957.

Gray, Ronald. *Goethe the Alchemist.* Cambridge, 1952.

Jantz, Harold. *Goethe's Faust as a Renaissance Man.* Princeton, 1951.

———. *The Mothers in Faust: The Myth of Time and Creativity.* Baltimore, 1969.

Mann, Thomas. *Essays of Three Decades.* London, 1947.

Mason, Eudo. *Goethe's Faust: Its Genesis and Purport.* Berkeley, 1967.

Salm, Peter. *The Poem as Plant: A Biological View of Goethe's Faust.* Cleveland, 1971.

Santayana, George. *Three Philosophical Poets: Lucretius, Dante and Goethe.* Cambridge, Mass., 1910.

Williams, John R. *Goethe's Faust.* London, 1987.

CARL R. MUELLER has since 1967 been a professor in the Department of Theater at the University of California, Los Angeles where he has taught theater history, criticism, dramatic literature, and playwriting, as well as directing. He was educated at Northwestern University, where he received a B.S. in English. After graduate work in English at the University of California, Berkeley, he received his M.A. in playwriting at UCLA, where he also completed his Ph.D. in theater history and criticism. In 1960 to 1961, he was a Fulbright Scholar in Berlin. A translator for more than forty years, he has translated and published works by Büchner, Brecht, Wedekind, Hauptmann, Hofmannsthal, and Hebbel, to name a few. His published translation of von Horváth's *Tales from the Vienna Woods* was given its London West End premiere in July 1999. For Smith and Kraus, he has translated individual volumes of plays by Schnitzler, Strindberg, Pirandello, Kleist, and Wedekind, and he has also cotranslated the complete plays of Sophokles. His two-volume translation for Smithand Kraus of *Aeschylus: TheComplete Plays* appeared in 2002, and his four-volume translation of *Euripides: The Complete Plays* will appear in 2004. His translations have been performed in every English-speaking country and have appeared on BBC TV.